INSPIRE / PLAN / DISCOVER / EXPERIENCE

VIETNAM

VIETNAM

CONTENTS

DISCOVER VIETNAM 6

EXPERIENCE VIETNAM 52

NEED TO KNOW 238

Vietnam

Angkor

Left: Typical street with yellow-painted
buildings in Hoi An's Old Town
Previous page: Rice fields in Northern Vietnam

DISCOVER

Ho Chi Minh City skyline at sunset

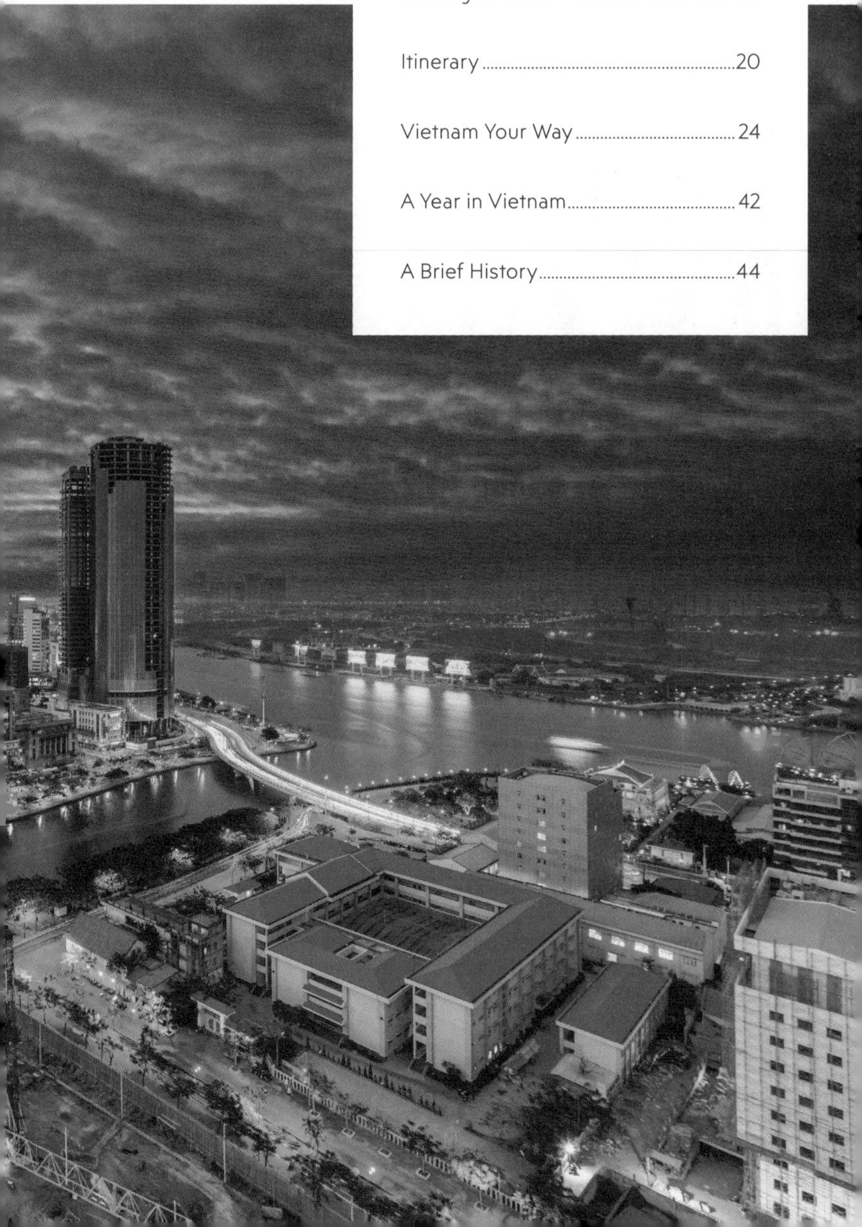

WELCOME TO VIETNAM

With its golden beaches, lush green mountains, jungles, fertile river deltas, ancient pagodas and temples, and delicious cuisine, Vietnam is a fascinating country of diverse landscapes and peoples. Whatever your dream trip to Vietnam entails, this DK Eyewitness Travel Guide will prove the perfect traveling companion.

① Thac Ban Gioc, Cao Bang, Vietnam's largest waterfall.

② Vendor of tropical fruit in Hoi An Old Town.

③ The dramatic Cau Vang "Golden Bridge", held up by giant concrete hands, Ba Na Hills near Danang.

As well as the famous picture-perfect Halong Bay, Vietnam has a wealth of other natural beauty to savor. Enjoy spectacular vistas from the north's dramatic mountains at Sapa, laze on long stretches of pristine, palm-fringed sands by an azure sea on the east coast, and inland, trek through the rugged jungle of the cool central highlands. Meanwhile, in the south, watch the rich birdlife and bucolic rural landscape of the Mekong Delta from a river boat, or chill out offshore on the remote and beautiful Con Dao Islands. The human landscape is no less varied. Explore the ancient temples and pagodas dotting the capital Hanoi, try a steaming bowl of *pho* noodles at a bustling night market, or stroll the moped-clogged streets of Ho Chi Minh City with its imposing French-Colonial architecture. Between the two main cities lie the country's most spellbinding historic sites that include the grand ancient capital of Hue, reminders of the Vietnam War in the Demiliatrized Zone, the weathered ancient Cham temples rising from the jungle at My Son, and pretty, pastel-colored French and Chinese buildings in Hoi An.

We've picked out themes and planned itineraries to whet your appetite, broken the country down into easily navigable chapters, and created colorful, comprehensive maps to help you plan the perfect visit. Whether you're staying for a week, a month, or longer, this Eyewitness guide will ensure that you see the very best the country has to offer. Enjoy the book, and enjoy Vietnam.

REASONS TO LOVE
VIETNAM

With its rich history, diverse cultures, dynamic and charming cities, and stunning landscapes, Vietnam offers a wealth of sights and experiences. Superb food and welcoming people add to the many reasons to visit.

1 NATURE AND WILDLIFE

In Vietnam's stunning national parks you can explore the coastline, mountains, rivers, and jungles, and the world's biggest cave. Look out for birds, elephants, monkeys, deer, dolphins, and other wildlife.

2 STREET FOOD IN HANOI

Try a steaming bowl of *pho* noodles at one of the many street food spots in Hanoi. *Goi cuon* (spring rolls), *banh thom* (shrimp patties) and *banh cuon* (steamed rice rolls) are other delicious, healthy staples.

CRUISE IN HALONG BAY 3

Take a boat trip around the steep, jungle-covered limestone outcrops jutting out of an azure sea in one of the most beautiful bays in Southeast Asia *(p200)*.

RIVER BOAT TRIP THROUGH PADDY FIELDS 4

Chug gently up the Mekong River on a boat from Nam Binh to Tam Coc, traversing verdant rice paddies with a backdrop of dramatic karst mountains.

COLONIAL ARCHITECTURE IN HO CHI MINH CITY 5

Stroll along the grand streets of Vietnam's capital, where France's legacy of imposing colonial buildings is stamped on a varied and vibrant cityscape.

HOI AN 6

Wander or cycle through the narrow streets of the beautiful, laid-back historic town of Hoi An *(p132)* past well-preserved traditional Chinese and French architecture.

MY SON ANCIENT TEMPLE RUINS 7

Don't miss the fascinating, vegetation-cloaked ancient temples and towers – known as Vietnam's Ankor Wat – that rise up through the jungle at My Son *(p138)*.

NHA TRANG BEACHES 8

Vietnam's most popular beach destination, Nha Trang *(p116)* is replete with beautiful stretches of sand and excellent accommodations, with some great dive spots just a boat ride away.

9 WATER PUPPET THEATER

The most Vietnamese of art forms was originally performed in rice paddies and village ponds. See a show at Hanoi's highly acclaimed Thang Long Water Puppet Theatre *(p172)*.

10 HISTORIC HUE

The faded but atmospheric Citadel, palaces, pagodas, and tombs at Hue *(p142)* reflect the glories of imperial Vietnam under the Nguyen Empire. Take a stroll by the Perfume River at sunset.

CON DAO ARCHIPELAGO 11

Relax on the golden beaches and enjoy the fresh air and remarkable nature on the remote string of Con Dao islands *(p98)*, most of which form a national park.

TRADITIONAL MARKETS 12

Colorful, noisy, and vibrant, a traditional market is the best place to get an authentic feel for local life and the art of haggling.

EXPLORE
VIETNAM

This guide is divided into six color-coded sightseeing areas, as shown on this map: Ho Chi Minh City; Mekong Delta and Southern Vietnam; South Central Vietnam; Central Vietnam; Hanoi; and Northern Vietnam. There is also an excursion to Angkor in Cambodia. Find out about each region on the following pages.

Lao Cai

Red River

Da River

Muang Khoua

Dien Bien Phu

Son La

Luang Prabang

Tuong Duong

LAOS

Vientiane

Udon Thani

MYANMAR

Thaton

Tak

Phitsanulok

Khon Kaen

Roi Et

Mawlamyine

Nakhon Sawan

THAILAND

Thanbyuzayat

Nakhon Ratchasima

Lop Buri

Tavoy

Sa Kaeo

Siem Reap

EXCURSION TO ANGKOR
p216

Palaw

Bangkok

Chon Buri

Battambang

Andaman Sea

Pattaya

Chanthaburi

Myeik

Tanitharyi

Prachuap Khiri Khan

Gulf of Thailand

Chumphon

Sihanoukville

Ha Tien

Kawthoung

Phu Quoc Island

Surat Thani

Ha Giang

Cao Bang

CHINA

Nanning

Bac Kan

Lang Son

Yen Bai

Thai Nguyen

HANOI
p164

Halong

Haiphong

**NORTHERN
VIETNAM**
p190

Nam Dinh

Nam Binh

Ca River

Thanh Hoa

*Gulf of
Tonkin*

Vinh

Ha Tinh

Thakhek

Dong Hoi

**CENTRAL
VIETNAM**
p128

Dong Ha

Khanthabouli

Hue

Danang

Hoi An

Tam Ky

LAOS

Quang Ngai

Ubon
Ratchathani

Pakxe

Plei Kan

Kontum

Sa Huynh

Pleiku

Quy Nhon

CAMBODIA

**SOUTH CENTRAL
VIETNAM**
p112

Tuy Hoa

Buon
Ma Thuot

Mekong River

Kampong
Cham

Gia Nghia

Dalat

Nha Trang

Phnom
Penh

**HO CHI
MINH CITY**
p54

Di Linh

Phan Rang-Thap Cham

Chau Doc

Phan Thiet

Ho Chi Minh City

*Phu Quy
Island*

Rach
Gia

My Tho

Vung Tau

South China

Can Tho

Sea

**MEKONG DELTA AND
SOUTHERN VIETNAM**
p86

Ca Mau

*Con Dao
Islands*

SOUTHEAST ASIA

CHINA

BHUTAN

NEPAL

INDIA

MYANMAR

BANGLADESH

LAOS

VIETNAM

PHILIPPINES

THAILAND

*South
China
Sea*

CAMBODIA

*Bay of
Bengal*

SRI
LANKA

BRUNEI

MALAYSIA

SINGAPORE

INDONESIA

Indian Ocean

0 kilometers   150

0 miles   150

N

GETTING TO KNOW
VIETNAM

From lush, rugged mountains, shimmering paddy fields, and beautiful beaches to river deltas and remote tropical islands, Vietnam has stunning natural landscapes, as well as vibrant cities both ancient and modern. Its geographical diversity is reflected in its varied peoples and regional cultures.

HO CHI MINH CITY

PAGE 54

Hot and frenetic, the moped-filled streets of Vietnam's largest city and commercial capital are the most dynamic and cosmopolitan in the country. More famously known as Saigon, the former French capital city offers a wealth of grand colonial buildings and a wide range of sights. From brightly colored pagodas to humble mosques and ornate Hindu temples, fascinating museums, busy markets, street food stalls, cafés, bars and restaurants, there is a buzzing atmosphere both day and night.

Best for
Colonial architecture and a vibrant culture

Home to
Jade Emperor Pagoda; Cao Dai Holy See

Experience
Riding a moped around the city, as the locals do

MEKONG DELTA AND SOUTHERN VIETNAM

You are never far from water in this region, the rice bowl of the country. Here you can get a glimpse of authentic rural life. Experience one of the famous floating markets or simply cruise down the river past brilliant-green rice paddies and villages of floating or stilt houses. Relax on the golden sands of the rugged tropical islands that lie off the coast, or spot some birdlife in the wetlands.

Best for
Discovering rural Vietnam

Home to
Can Tho; Con Dao Islands

Experience
A boat tour along the canals around Vinh Long

SOUTH CENTRAL VIETNAM

Famous for its white sand and azure sea, the coastline of South Central Vietnam has a string of beach resorts where there are ample opportunities for watersports and diving. Further north are deserted stretches of unspoiled sand. The cooler uplands of the interior house tiny villages sprinkled over the rugged landscape, populated by many indigenous minorities. The region also has beautiful lakes, coffee plantations, and Yok Don, Vietnam's largest national park, home to a huge number of flora and fauna.

Best for
Lazing on the beach and diving

Home to
Nha Trang; Dalat

Experience
Sampling the excellent Highlands coffee; visiting the hill tribe villages of Tur and Ako Dong

→

PAGE 128

CENTRAL VIETNAM

Some of Vietnam's most famous archaeological sites and best-preserved historic towns can be seen in this region, which is steeped in history. Here you can enjoy some of the best vegetarian cooking in the country and the sophisticated imperial cuisine of the former royal capital Hue. Head into the Central Highlands to visit some of the most significant battle sites of the Vietnam War, along the Ho Chi Minh Trail. With the oldest karst mountains in Asia and numerous cave systems and underground rivers, Phong Nha-Ke Bang National Park is truely awe-inspiring.

Best for
Learning about Vietnam's history and culture

Home to
Hoi An; Hue

Experience
Visiting some of the major battle sites of the Vietnam War

PAGE 164

HANOI

A melting pot of cultures, the oldest capital in Southeast Asia is a sprawling city with an ancient center and a French colonial quarter surrounded by sleek skyscrapers and interspersed with parks and tranquil lakes. The cultural heart of Vietnam, Hanoi is the birthplace of the nation's most delightful theatrical format, water puppetry. Discover Vietnam's history and culture at a range of superb museums, concert venues, and theaters. Every backstreet is full of small kitchens where you can pull up a plastic chair and indulge in authentic, delicious street food among the locals.

Best for
Museums; shopping for silk; lacquerware and handicrafts; water puppet theater

Home to
The Temple of Literature

Experience
Wandering the atmospheric streets of the Old Quarter

NORTHERN VIETNAM

Karst outcrops form a dramatic seascape in Halong and Bai Tu Long bays and Cat Ba Island, and stretch inland to Ba Be and Dong Van, while the stunningly beautiful coastal landscape has golden beaches and coral reefs. The Red River Delta is lined with ancient temples and pagodas, while to the south are the tropical forests of Cuc Phuong National Park. The real joy of visiting this region, however, is the chance to venture into the remote hills in the north and northwest and encounter the diverse hill-tribe peoples and dramatic upland scenery.

Best for
Stunning karst landscapes at sea and on land

Home to
Halong Bay; the Perfume Pagoda

Experience
A homestay with hill people at a stilt house in the Mai Chau Valley

←

1 Street vendor in Hanoi's Old Quarter.

2 Tourist boats cruising Halong Bay.

3 *Bun bo* (beef noodles), a dish associated with the cooking style of the former royal court in Hue.

4 Dragon Bridge in Danang.

Perhaps the most popular route for touring Vietnam, this itinerary takes you from the north to the south via some of the most important historical sights and idyllic beaches.

2 WEEKS
from Hanoi to HCMC

Day 1: Hanoi

Stroll around the narrow streets of Hanoi's Old Quarter *(p188)*, with its heady cocktail of colorful shop displays, exotic aromas, and loud calls from street vendors. Pop into the Memorial House Museum and the Bach Ma Temple, then check out the streets specializing in particular crafts, most famously Hang Gai, or Silk Street or Hang Ma Street, or Votive Paper Street. After a classic Vietnamese lunch at Red Bean (94 Ma May Street), wander south to the pretty Hoan Kiem Lake *(p174)*, then delve into the leafy boulevards of the French Quarter. Visit the Opera House *(p177)* and the National Museum of Vietnamese History *(p178)*, both of which testify to the city's colonial past. Dine at Namaste (46 Tho Nhuom Street) on superb Indian cuisine.

Days 2 and 3: Halong Bay

Join a tour from Hanoi to Halong Bay *(p200)* and spend a night in the magnificent landscape of limestone pinnacles rising dramatically from the emerald green waters. Take a cruise around the bay, paddle a kayak, explore illuminated caves, and make use of the many photo opportunities. Dine on succulent seafood at 1958 restaurant on Tuan Chau Island, overlooking the bay, or on the water itself at one of the many floating restaurants.

Days 4 and 5: Hue

Devote a day to exploring the Imperial City *(p142)* in the heart of the Hue Citadel, the nation's capital from 1805 to 1945. Don't miss the Thai Hoa Palace with its splendidly decorated throne hall and the beautifully restored The Mieu temple. End the day with a sumptuous multi-course dinner of imperial cuisine. The next day, take a boat trip along the Perfume River *(p152)*, stopping off to visit a few of the Royal Tombs *(p150)*, all of which have lavish ornamentation and are set in delightful gardens. For a taste of the famous local street food, head to Le Hanh *(p148)*.

Day 6: Danang

In the morning travel by taxi or hire a driver to take you to the Marble Mountains just south of Danang *(p156)*. Enjoy the views along the coast and stop off to explore atmospheric shrines sheltered in huge caves. Then return to the city to visit the Museum of Cham Sculpture *(p155)*, which contains exquisite stone carvings created by this ancient civilization. In the evening, take a stroll by the Han River, whose banks are lined with restaurants, and admire the dramatic Dragon Bridge, which literally breathes fire after 9pm every evening.

→

Day 7: Hoi An

Take a walk around Hoi An's atmospheric Old Quarter (p132), the highlight of a trip to Vietnam for many visitors. Admire its ornate Chinese pagodas, ancient tea houses, and long, narrow tube houses. Be sure to try the local gastronomic delights served at its famous restaurants, such as Morning Glory Original (p135).

Day 8: My Son

Spend the day exploring My Son (p138), the most important religious center of Cham culture. Although damaged during the Vietnam War, the ruins here are still impressive and are reminiscent of Angkor Wat in Cambodia. Many of the brick towers are overgrown, lending the site an irresistible mystique, but restoration work is ongoing. The nearest place to stay is Quang Ngai (p127), where the best eating options overlook the river.

Day 9: Quy Nhon

A large port town with a broad swathe of beach, Quy Nhon (p126) will give you an authentic experience of Vietnam without being hassled by hawkers. Visit the twin Cham towers of Thap Doi Cham, sample delicious seafood, and take a motorbike ride along the coast road south of town, stopping off at picture-postcard beaches lapped by azure waters.

Days 10 and 11: Nha Trang

Vietnam's premier beach resort, Nha Trang (p116), has a few interesting historical sights that can be visited in a morning. Begin at the Gothic-style Nha Trang Cathedral, before heading for the ornate hilltop Long Son Pagoda. From here, visit the well-preserved Po Nagar Cham Towers (p117), one of the most important Cham sites in Vietnam. Spend the afternoon lounging on the beach,

1 A lantern-filled street in Hoi An.

2 Cham ruins at My Son.

3 Nha Trang Beach.

4 Sand dunes at Mui Ne.

5 L'Usine, a clothes shop and café in Dong Khoi, Ho Chi Minh City.

before heading out for a seafood dinner at Lanterns (p117). The next day, take a boat trip to the islands, which lie just offshore, for a day of snorkeling and sunbathing. Round off the day at a floating bar.

Days 12 and 13: Mui Ne

The long stretch of beach at Mui Ne (p124) is a great place to spend the morning windsurfing or kitesurfing; there are several places along the 12-mile- (20-km-) beach that offer instruction for beginners. Afterward, take off for the enormous red and white sand dunes on the fringes of the resort. Rent a plastic sled for some sand-sledding, a great and fun way to experience these geological wonders. Devote the rest of the day to snoozing on the beach, relishing fresh seafood, or pampering yourself at a spa.

Day 14: Ho Chi Minh City

Begin at Independence Palace (p68), a symbol of Vietnam's political history, and learn about the last days of the Vietnam War. From here, head to Dong Khoi, the city's main street, to see the Notre Dame Cathedral (p67) and Central Post Office (p68), which serve as reminders of the city's French colonial past. Walk down Dong Khoi toward the Saigon River, stopping briefly to look at the elegant People's Committee Building (p65). Relax over a leisurely lunch in one of the many elegant restaurants along here. In the afternoon pick up a few distinctive souvenirs in the shops on Dong Khoi before visiting the 49th floor of the Bitexco Financial Tower (p66) for a bird's-eye view of the city center. End the day experiencing the vibrant nightlife – try the street food around Ben Thanh Market (p70) followed by a drink at one of Dong Khoi's many clubs and bars.

River Deltas

From the mountains of Tibet, the mighty Mekong River flows 4,500 km (2,800 miles) to reach the sea south of Ho Chi Minh City. Here it becomes a maze of ecologically rich and incredibly picturesque tributaries. Small islands in the Mekong Delta offer idyllic accommodations, ideal for experiencing local life and visiting floating markets, or just for listening to the birds sing while relaxing in a hammock. At the other end of Vietnam, the Red River Delta is smaller in size, but culturally more significant, since it is the cradle of the ancient Vietnamese civilization and culture. Its rich mangrove forests are full of many species of plants and animals. Hundreds of tranquil pagodas are dotted around the countryside, and there are many bustling craft villages.

Irridescent green paddy fields in the Red River Delta

Did You Know?

May-Oct is rainy season. It remains relatively dry Nov-Feb, while the hot season is Feb-April.

VIETNAM FOR
NATURAL
WONDERS

The abundance of Vietnam's natural wonders can leave visitors spoiled for choice. Relax on pristine beaches, savor verdant tropical forests, explore immense caves, splash in pools at cooling waterfalls, or trek through hilly terrain sculpted by rice terraces – there's truly something for everyone.

Coastline and Islands

Vietnam offers a plethora of seaside delights. From the southern tropical paradise of Phu Quoc Island *(p108)* to the northern limestone islands and grottos of Halong Bay *(p200)*, there is an amazing variety of coastal environments. Whether sunbathing, wind-surfing, riding the waves, boat trips to offshore islets, or the freshest of seafood is your preference, all are easy to find.

Secluded beach in Ninh Van Bay, near Tha Trang

TOP 5 NATIONAL PARKS

Phong Nha-Ke Bang
Home to the world's largest cave and popular for kayaking (p163).

Yok Don
Superb jungle trekking, wildlife, and minority villages (p126).

Cat Tien
A bird-watcher's paradise (p81).

Bai Tu Long
Equally beautiful but less busy than Halong Bay (p206).

Cuc Phuong
Great for hiking, spelunking, and bird-watching (p205).

Central Highlands

Cool and misty, and home to diverse wildlife, thundering waterfalls, and peaceful lakes, this region of Vietnam, bordering on Laos and Cambodia, is one of the least visited. Bach Ma and Phong Nha-Ke Bang's dense forests are home to an incredible variety of flora and fauna.

→

Dray Sap Waterfall in Buon Ma Thuot, Central Highlands

Northern Mountains

Northwest of Hanoi, a spec-moutain range rises from the Red River valley, populated by two-thirds of Vietnam's indigenous peoples. Vietnam's highest mountain, Mount Fansipan, is accessible by cable car. For the hardier, treks through these mountains are a fantastic experience.

→

Red Dao of Sapa, who maintain a traditional way of life in the mountains

25

Pagodas and Temples

Both pagodas and temples usually consist of several structures containing statues of the deities to which the faithful pay their respects, as well as open-sided pavilions for the worshippers to rest and chat outside the reverential and subdued atmosphere within the main buildings. Some honor Buddhist as well as other faiths' deities.

One Pillar pagoda in Hanoi, nominally Buddhist, but full of Taoist imagery

VIETNAM'S STUNNING
ARCHITECTURE

Influences from China, India, the ancient Khmer Empire, and more recently France and other Western countries have blended with indigenous styles, forming an amazing variety of architectural delights in Vietnam. Traditional pagodas and temples stand side by side with secular French colonial buildings.

DIFFERENCES BETWEEN TEMPLES AND PAGODAS

A pagoda (chua) refers to a Buddhist or Taoist place of worship sometimes both at one site), whereas a temple (den) is a place where offerings are made to actual historical beings, such as kings and queens, or mandarins, whose eminence gives them a semi-divine status. An example of a pagoda is the Jade Emperor Pagoda in Ho Chi Minh City, where primarily Taoist, but also Buddhist deities are worshipped, whereas the Temple of Literature in Hanoi venerates the historical personage of Confucius.

Cham Sites

The Hindu Champa empire, which ruled parts of Vietnam, Laos, and Cambodia from the 4th to the 14th centuries, had its most holy site at My Son (p138) near Hoi An. Although heavily damaged by American bombers in the 1960s, some magnificent examples of Cham architecture remain.

Traditional Tube Houses

Varying from traditional to modern in style, the concept of these tall, narrow multi-story urban family dwellings dates back to the 15th-18th centuries. They can be as little as 6.5 ft (2 m) wide, up to 262 ft (80 m) deep, and five stories or more in height. Each family chooses a color scheme, resulting in a multi-hued palette of habitats. There are many in Hanoi and Ho Chi Minh City, but some of the best preserved are in Hoi An.

→

Brightly painted tube house in Hanoi's Old Quarter

French Colonial Architecture

Splendid neoclassical, modernist, and Art Deco buildings, often with orientalist embellishments, are the most enduring legacy of French Colonial rule in Vietnam (1880-1954). The best surviving examples are in Ho Chi Minh City and Hanoi.

←

Notre Dame cathedral, Ho Chi Minh City, built by French colonists in 1863-1880

Royal Citadel

The gem of Vietnamese citadels lies in Hue *(p142)*, the capital of Vietnam's final dynasty the Nguyen. Built on the banks of Perfume River and modeled after Beijing's Forbidden City, this 19th-century complex of palaces, pavilions, and gardens has been carefully restored and presents a superb overview of Vietnam's imperial history.

←

Remains of Champa towers at My Son, a world heritage site

→

Gate leading to The Mieu and Hung Mieu temples in the Imperial City, Hue Citadel

Theater

The musical element, particularly singing, which characterizes traditional Vietnamese theatrical performance, is due to Chinese influence, and results in opera-like shows. *Hat Cheo*, or popular theater, explores local legends, and often has a satirical note, while *Hat Tuong*, which was once performed only for royalty in Hue in the 19th century, is highly stylized and deals with more elevated themes.

Cheo, a form of popular theater with pantomime, music, and dance

VIETNAM'S TRADITIONAL
MUSIC AND THEATER

With a heritage dating back to the Bronze Age drums and flutes of the Dong Son culture of the Red River Valley, it's not surprising that the musical and theatrical arts of Vietnam have a huge repertoire. Chinese and European influences have been added to these performing arts, which flourish today.

Music

Vietnamese traditional music comprises several genres, including court, religious, ceremonial, chamber, folk, and theater music. Recognized by UNESCO as an intangible cultural heritage, *Cat Tru* is an enchantingly melodic form of chamber music. It features female singers, who play wooden percussion instruments *(phach)* and are accompanied by a lute player. *Hat Chau Van*, which originated in the 16th century as an incantation during religious rituals, is a form of rhythmic singing and dancing. Dating to the 13th century, *Quan Ho* are folk singing contests that form an important part of spring festivals to this day.

→

Musicians performing traditional music at the Tomb of Tu Duc, near Hue

Water Puppetry

Dating back over 1,000 years, this uniquely Vietnamese performance art originated in flooded rice paddies. Brightly painted wooden puppets are manipulated from behind a screen by skilled puppeteers. Performances center on themes of village life and legends, enlivened by music and special effects. Enjoy a show at Hanoi's Thang Long Water Puppet Theatre.

Water puppet show and detail of colorful wooden puppets *(inset)* ↑

TOP 5 TRADITIONAL MUSICAL INSTRUMENTS

Dan Trung
Originating in the Central Highlands, this bamboo xylophone is now used in much of Vietnam's traditional music.

Broh
Also from the Central Highlands, this two-stringed bamboo lute has been used by Western musicians, such as Stevie Wonder

Dan ty ba
This pear-shaped, four-stringed guitar is plucked and played upright.

Cong chien
Bronze alloy gongs are used in musical performances and religious ceremonies.

Trong
Vietnam's many types of drum *(trong)* include the venerable bronze drums of the Dong Son.

Street Food

Some of the best food in Vietnam can be found at street-side stalls. Popular dishes include *pho banh mi* (a baguette stuffed with paté, sausage, and condiments that include fish sauce and mayonnaise); and *banh xeo* (crispy rice crepes filled with pork, shrimp, and vegetables) – tear off a piece, wrap it in the lettuce provided, add some herbs, and dip in one of the savory sauces.

People eating lunch at a bustling street market in Bac Ha

VIETNAM FOR
FOOD LOVERS

Vietnamese cuisine is characterized by a subtle range of flavors, complemented by fresh herbs such as mint, basil, and lemongrass. Balance is the Vietnamese cook's goal – in flavors, colors, and textures – creating delicious, healthy dishes. The Vietnamese eat with chopsticks, but if you're not comfortable with them, ask for a fork *(nia)* and spoon *(muong)*.

INSIDER TIP
Beer

Bars serving refreshing *bia hoi* (fresh draft beer) are usually simple, hole-in-the-wall places, visited mostly by local men. Foreign visitors are welcome as long as they don't mind squatting on tiny stools. The beer is light in taste and alcohol, and is accompanied by snacks. For craft beer, head to Ho Chi Minh City – rich brews there use local herbs, fruits, and spices, such as lemongrass and passion fruit.

Northern Vietnam

The regional specialties of Northern Vietnam closely resemble those of neighboring China. Hanoi is where the iconic noodle dish *pho* (flat rice noodles served in a broth of beef or chicken bones, topped with pieces of meat) originated. Other famous dishes here include crab spring rolls *(nem cua be)* and rice noodles with grilled marinated pork *(bun cha)*. Try the latter at Bun Cha Huong Lien (24 Le Van Huu, Hanoi).

Traditional *pho* rice noodles, the "national dish" of Vietnam

↑ *Banh khoai*, a potato pancake dish typical of Central Vietnam

Central Vietnam

With an Indic Cham influence, dishes in Central Vietnam can be spicy, such as *bun bo* (fried noodles with beef, garlic, cucumber, chili peppers, and tomato paste). The most famous dish here is *banh khoai*, a potato pancake stuffed with shrimp and pork belly. Restaurants in Hue still offer the banquet meals that were served to royalty during the 19th century. Farther south, Nha Trang is famed for its seafood.

COFFEE CULTURE

The coffee grown in the Central Highlands is of excellent quality and is both exported and consumed locally in large quantities. It can be drunk in a variety of ways, both hot and cold. Here are some of the most popular types:

Ca phe den: standard black coffee brewed into the cup through a metal filter called a *phin*.

Ca phe sua: black coffee served with condensed sweetened milk, served with ice.

Sua chua ca phe: yoghurt coffee, always served cold.

Ca phe trung: black coffee with cream of egg yolk and condensed milk.

Sinh to ca phe: a fruit smoothie to which black coffee is added.

Southern Vietnam

The warm climate and rich soil of the south result in an abundance of tropical fruits and vegetables. Sweet flavors abound – coconut milk is part of the mix in mild curries and coconut pancakes. *Nuoc mam*, Vietnam's famous fish sauce, produced by fermenting anchovies for several months, originated here. A signature dish of the Mekong Delta is *canh chua ca* – sweet and sour catfish soup with vegetables and herbs.

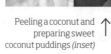

Peeling a coconut and ↑ preparing sweet coconut puddings *(inset)*

Hoi An

From Hoi An it's an easy 3-mile (4-km) bicycle ride (or a quick taxi trip) to the coast. The first beach you reach is Cua Dai, great for a cocktail at sunset. For a larger beach, venture a bit further north to An Bang with its relatively unspoiled white sand. Both beaches offer excellent seafood restaurants and views of the Cham Islands.

People relaxing on Cua Dai Beach, near Hoi An, at sunset

VIETNAM FOR
BEACH LOVERS

With its entire east coast of over 2,000 miles (3,000 km) facing the South China Sea, Vietnam is a beach lover's paradise. From the tropical palm-fringed beaches of the south to the limestone karst islets of Halong Bay, each beach has its own ambience and is suitable for different aquatic pursuits. Dive in!

TOP 5 BEACHES FOR DIVING

Phu Quoc
The best sites are on the southeast coast.

Hon Ko
A small island south of Phu Quoc, home to a breathtaking coral reef.

Nha Trang
This offers good scuba diving courses and many dive sites.

Cham Islands
Off the coast of Hoi An, these islands teem with coral and tropical fish.

Con Dao Archipelago
These islands off the southern coast have pristine waters.

Nha Trang

The coastline near Nha Trang in South Central Vietnam has dozens of fine beaches. Many are good for surfing November to March. For a more special experience, head to secluded Hon Ong (Whale) Island, which lies in a sheltered bay, and where you can sometimes spot humpbacks. As well as diving, it offers good swimming, windsurfing and kayaking.

Halong Bay

Of the innumerable islands in Halong Bay, the tiny islet of Ti Top is famous for the incredible panoramic views from its summit. It's a climb of 400 steps, but well worth it, and afterwards you can take a dip or just relax on the island's small beach. If you still have energy to burn, go kayaking among the famous limestone karst formations.

→

Ti Top Beach in Halong Bay, overlooking the karst formations

South of Ho Chi Minh City

Between Phu Quoc and Ho Chi Minh City there are many excellent beaches, but their proximity to the city has led to overdevelopment. A wonderful exception is the isolated beach of Ho Coc, where golden sand dunes reach inland from a long beach studded with boulders. It's perfect for long walks and swimming, and is especially quiet on weekdays.

←

Beautiful Ho Coc, one of Vietnam's most pristine beaches

Phu Quoc Island

Lying in the Gulf of Thailand, Phu Quoc island has some of the most placid and clear waters of coastal Vietnam, as well as many alluring white sand beaches, making it ideal for snorkeling, scuba diving, and kayaking. Lovely beaches abound – one of the best is Star Beach (Bai Sao) near the southern tip of the island on the sheltered east coast. The water is unbelievably clear and the curved beach stretches for miles.

←

Nha Trang Municipal Beach, fringed by palm and casuarina trees

→

White sands and crystal-clear waters of Star Beach, Phu Quoc Island

Bai Tu Long Bay

Only 37 miles (60 km) east of the world-famous Halong Bay, Bai Tu Long Bay offers equally spectacular karst formations, numerous uninhabited islets, and a tranquil atmosphere away from tourist hordes that its acclaimed neighbor often lacks. Quan Lan island has a spectacular crescent-shaped beach, Minh Chau. Even more pristine is Tra Ban island, with its dramatic karst formations and a jungled interior that is home to many flora and fauna.

↑ Limestone gate leading to Vung Vieng floating village, Bai Tu Long Bay.

VIETNAM OFF THE
BEATEN PATH

They may take a little more effort to reach than more famous tourist spots, but Vietnam's hidden corners, though lacking in facilities, offer beautiful unspoiled landscapes and traditional ways of life.

Con Dao Islands

This archipelago of 16 mostly uninhabited islands lies 80 miles (135 km) off the southern coast of Vietnam. It is a pristine environment ideal for lounging on the beach, snorkeling, scuba diving, or exploring the jungles in the interior. Parts of the archipelago and the surrounding coral reefs are a national park and home to many unique species of flora and fauna. The main island of Con Son offers a range of accommodations and good restaurants.

Clear waters and white sands of the Cao Dao Islands, an unspoiled paradise

Pu Luong Nature Reserve

Away from most tourists' radar, Pu Luong Nature Reserve is an area of spectacular beauty 30 miles (50 km) from Mai Chau Valley in Northern Vietnam. This very fertile region of rich forests and rice terraces has diverse landscapes, flora, and fauna. Trek the mountainous paths, swim in the rivers, visit traditional markets of the White Thai and Muong, or just relax in the peace and quiet in this idyllic spot.

↓ Terraced rice field in the lush Pu Luong Nature Reserve

Ben Tre

Ben Tre's quiet, pretty riverside promenade is great for strolling or cycling and is perfect for a glimpse of traditional life, away from the hustle-and-bustle of other nearby towns in the Mekong Delta. You can also explore the surrounding picturesque countryside with its coconut plantations and villages by small boat or by bicycle.

←
Woman paddling a traditional small boat in the Mekong delta at Ben Tre

→
Wooden stilt house in the Mai Chau Valley, surrounded by green rice fields

 HIDDEN GEM
Dong Van Karst Plateau Geopark

Designated a geopark by UNESCO due to its unique geography, this remote area is Vietnam's northern-most point, on the border with China. Minority villages, an amazing Sunday market, and spectacular mountain scenery are the attractions here. A travel permit is required but easy to get, and it's heaven for motorcyclists *(p214)*.

Homestay on Stilts in Mai Chau Valley

Southwest of Hanoi, the beautiful, unspoiled Mai Chau Valley is surrounded by rolling green hills with terraced rice paddies. It's home to the White Thai ethnic minority, relatives of the people of Thailand and Laos. The friendly villagers offer homestays in traditional stilt houses in the villages of Lac and Pom Coong, a great way to experience traditional rustic life.

Clothing

Vietnam is renowned for its lustrous silk clothing, though cotton and hemp are also used. The traditional *ao dai* can be found off the rack, but local tailors can also custom-make these. Known as the tailoring capital of the world, Hoi An has a multitude of excellent tailors, but Hanoi and Ho Chi Minh City are also good places to shop for bespoke tailoring.

←

Elegant silk *ao dai* – a tunic split at the sides worn with loose trousers

VIETNAM FOR
SHOPPERS

Prized as being among the best in Asia, the handicrafts and jewelry made by ethnic minorities in Vietnam are exquisite. Local markets and Hanoi and Ho Chi Minh City are good places to shop. However, Hoi An, with its amazing array of lacquerware, clothing, and crafts, is the ultimate shopper's paradise.

TOP 5 MARKETS IN VIETNAM

Traditional markets in Vietnam not only provide a great selection of goods at the best prices, but also open a window into the lives of the locals. Here are some of the best markets:

Cai Be Floating Market near Vinh Long *(p103)*

Hoi An Central Market *(p136)*

Dong Ba Market, Hue *(p146)*.

Dong Xuan Market, Hanoi *(p172)*.

Bac Ha Market, northern hills *(p213)*.

Ceramics and Lacquerware

Using the famous white clay deposits found near Hanoi, Vietnam's potters produce lovely ceramic vases and tea sets using traditional glazes with intricate hand-painted designs. The best place to find these is Hanoi. Beautiful lacquerware items, often inlaid with mother-of-pearl, are ubiquitous.

INSIDER TIP
Haggling

Smilingly offer half of the asking price. If the counter-offer is too high, politely decline and walk away. It's likely that a further drop in price will be offered.

Hand Embroidery and Woven Handicrafts

The minority groups of Vietnam's Highlands excel in these traditional art forms. The designs and complex appliqué textiles traditionally used in tribes' clothing are also applied to pillowcases, scarves, handbags, and other souvenir accessories.

→

Hmong woman using a traditional weaving loom

Jewelry

Silver is a traditional symbol of wealth among many hill peoples. Ornate silver belts, earrings, and bracelets, all handworked, are commonly available in shops in major towns and villages. Lowland Vietnamese specialize in 23 or 24 karat gold jewelry, burnished in color. It is sold by weight in gold shops in most cities.

←

Traditional silver bracelets, carved with birds and flowers

Paintings

The fine art scene thrives in Hanoi, and while famous Vietnamese artists command high fees, many lesser-known names do excellent work at reasonable prices. Any art lover should visit a gallery or two while in Hanoi, such as Thang Long (41 Hang Gai), which showcases new and established artists.

→

↑ Decorative Vietnamese ceramic pieces with attractive designs

Artist painting scenes of rural Vietnamese life in a gallery in Hanoi

◁ Trekking

Sapa in Northern Vietnam is the epicenter for trekking, offering not only spectacular views but fascinating hill peoples' villages. For hiking in remote parts and visiting local mountain tribes, book a trekking trip through Topas Adventure (www.topas travel.vn). Most of the treks are steep and challenging, including the two-day hike up Mount Fansipan, Vietnam's highest peak. Other great destinations for trekking are Cat Ba and Bach Ma national parks with their stunning waterfalls and lakes.

VIETNAM
OUTDOORS

From diving and snorkeling among spectacular coral reefs to hiking vertiginous mountain trails, you're sure to find something to enjoy outdoors in Vietnam. While some pursuits require special training and high fitness levels, others, such as bird-watching or a short nature walk, are open to all.

◁ Surfing, Kitesurfing, and Windsurfing

Mui Ne is world-renowned for wind- and kitesurfing due to its nearly constant breezes. Training is available from the shops, such as Jibe's Beach Club (www. windsurf-vietnam.com), who rent the gear. Conversely, wind is not the friend of surfing, which relies on ocean swells – these are best at Danang and Nha Trang. Unless you're a very experienced surfer, start with a small and light boogie board before attempting a stand-up surfboard.

Bird-Watching ▷

With over 800 bird species indigenous to the country, and many butterflies, the national parks, particularly Cuc Phoung and Bach Ma, are the best places for birders. Vietnam Birding (www.vietnam birding. com) is the leading local specialist for birding tours.

◁ Snorkeling, Diving, and Swimming

Exploring the aquatic life of the South China Sea can be as easy as donning a mask and snorkel. Phu Quoc and Con Dao islands are the best destinations for snorkeling. To reach greater depths, scuba diving is popular around Nha Trang and the Cham Islands. Trips are organized by Rainbow Divers (www.dive vietnam.com), which has branches in all the best offshore dive spots. The best beaches for swimming are around Mui Ne and Nha Trang, as well as Hoi An, Danang, and south of Quy Nhon.

 INSIDER TIP
Safety Advice

Research tour companies carefully, and check that your travel insurance does not exclude claims for any activities you are pursuing. Keep a sharp eye on the weather – storms approach quickly. Don't have your first experience on a motorcycle here as the traffic is chaotic and drivers often don't adhere to rules. Don't stray from established paths when hiking – Vietnam still contains unexploded ordnance.

△ Kayaking

Placid waters, innumerable grottos, and spectacular scenery make Halong Bay the best place for kayaking. Overnight trips, with camping on an island, can be booked via Asia Outdoors (www.asiaoutdoors.com.vn). Other key destinations include the Con Dao Islands, Cat Ba Island, Dalat, and around Hoi An.

Cycling and Motorbiking ▷

From a two-week cycling tour from Hanoi to Ho Chi Minh City to an afternoon pedal to the beach in Hoi An, a bicycle is a great way to explore Vietnam. The route from Dalat to Mui Ne is largely downhill, while the Mekong Delta offers level terrain through rice paddies. Spice Roads (www.spiceroads.com) offers tours that include homestays with locals. Motorbiking, especially popular in the North, is great for sightseeing if you have the requisite skills *(p245)*. Alternatively, you can hire a driver via Easy Riders (www.easy-riders.net).

◁ Buon Ma Thuot

The last major battle of the war took place in March 1975 at Buon Ma Thuot in the South Central Highlands. North Vietnam used tanks and heavy artillery to rout the South Vietnamese forces, which fled in disarray. Today there is a memorial to the battle in the center of the town.

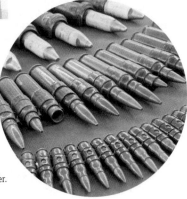

Ap Bac ▷

South of Ho Chi Minh City, in the Mekong Delta, Ap Bac *(p100)* is the site of the first major victory of Viet Cong against the US-backed South Vietnamese army in January 1963. The Viet Cong forces were able to inflict heavy casualties on the enemy, and then disappear into the local population, a classic technique of guerrilla warfare. Today there is a memorial and museum at the site of the fiercest fighting, displaying a downed American helicopter, ammunition, and an armored personnel carrier.

ON THE TRAIL OF THE
VIETNAM WAR

Vietnam has suffered many wars throughout its long history. Traces of the most serious conflict in recent times – the Vietnam War (known locally as the American War) – merit a visit as a vital way of understanding Vietnam's history and people.

◁ Ho Chi Minh Trail

Begun in 1959, this vast network of trails and paths, also known as Duong Truong Son, extended from Vinh in North Vietnam to the South, often crossing into Laos and Cambodia *(p163)*. An amazing logistical and engineering feat, the tunnels were used by Ho Chi Minh's Communist forces to transport men and equipment in the North to the battlefronts fighting the Americans in the South. The tunnel network included warehouses, field hospitals, and even a fuel line. Today, you can travel the trail by motorbike – Easy Riders offer tours *(p39)*.

△ Demilitarized Zone

Created as a buffer zone between North and South Vietnam by the 1954 Geneva Accords, this narrow band of terrain saw heavy fighting during the war. The most interesting site is the Vinh Moc Tunnels *(p161),* where villagers sheltered from American bombing. Other sites include Camp Carroll, a former American artillery base, and Hamburger Hill battle site. All can be visited on a guided day tour from Hue.

◁ My Lai Massacre Memorial

On March 16, 1968, US infantry systematically massacred around 500 Vietnamese civilians in My Lai village in Quang Ngai Province, an atrocity which shook the world. Today, the Son My Memorial *(p127)* documents this war crime with a display of harrowing photographs and a stone sculpture of a woman with a dead child, raising her fist in defiance. It's a testament to the Vietnamese desire to move beyond the war that the museum also honors the GIs who tried to stop the massacre and those who exposed the story to journalists. A visit here is incredibly disturbing, but moving.

MUSEUMS ON THE VIETNAM WAR

The Vietnam Military History Museum in Hanoi (28 Dien Ben Phu St; (024) 6253 1367) displays weaponry and military equipment, including a B-52 bomber. Not for the faint of heart, the War Remnants Museum in Ho Chi Minh City *(p73)* documents the horrors of the war in graphic fashion. Photographs of torture and napalm victims and the fetuses of babies deformed by defoliants used by US forces are included. Mention is also made of Americans who opposed the war.

△ Hidden Tunnels

Just north of Ho Chi Minh City, the Cu Chi Tunnels *(p76)* once served as hideouts and ammunition dumps for Vietcong guerrillas, from which they could stage dramatic attacks on the capital and disappear underground. The tunnels, made very narrow to deter invaders, have now been enlarged, but are still found to be claustrophobic by some visitors as they are so low that you have to crouch. Unlike the Cu Chi Tunnels, those at Vinh Moc were built for long-term habitation, and some of the network is high enough to walk through standing up. Sections have been kept in good condition and are easy to visit.

A YEAR IN
VIETNAM

JANUARY

△ **Tet Nguyen Dan** (late Jan–early Feb).
Vietnam's main festival marks the onset of the
lunar New Year, a time of rebirth and renewal.
Celebrations last for at least three days, and
families gather for meals and to exchange gifts.

FEBRUARY

△ **Founding of the Vietnamese Communist
Party** (Feb 3). Commemorates the day Ho Chi Minh
established the party in 1930.
Lim Festival (Feb). Locals in traditional dress sing
folk songs and play games at Lim village.
Perfume Pagoda Festival (mid-Feb). Thousands of
pilgrims descend upon this famous Buddhist site.

MAY

International Workers' Day (May 1). Parades
of workers march through the streets to show
solidarity with working people worldwide.
△ **The Buddha's Birthday** (mid–late May).
Lanterns are hung outside temples and homes
to mark the Buddha's birth, life, and death.

JUNE

△ **Tet Doan Ngo** (early Jun). Signaling the summer
solstice, offerings are made to the God of Death
at Taoist temples around the country.
Chem Temple Festival (mid-Jun). Held in
Thuy Phuong village in Hanoi, dragon boat
races take place in honor of the 3rd-century
warrior Ly Ong Trong.

SEPTEMBER

△ **National Day** (Sep 2). This public holiday
celebrates the declaration of independence
made by Ho Chi Minh in 1945 following the
defeat of the Axis powers.
Trung Thu/Mid-Autumn Festival (mid-Sep).
The harvest festival is when children receive
new toys and eat moon cakes, with lantern
processions and lion dances in the streets.

OCTOBER

Kate Festival (Oct). The main Cham festival takes
place at the three Champa towers in the southern
Ninh Thuan Province. Droves of devotees in
colorful processions make their way to the towers
to pay homage to the Cham deities.
△ **Confucius' Birthday** (late Oct–early Nov).
Ceremonies are held and offerings made at
Confucian temples around the country.

APRIL

△ **Hung Kings' Temple Festival** *(early–mid-Apr)*. Four-day national festival commemorating the Hung Kings that includes cultural events and parades around temples. The second day is a public holiday.

Liberation Day *(Apr 30)*. Public holiday to mark the capture of Saigon and the end of the Vietnam War in 1975, featuring parades around the country.

Hue Festival *(Apr, May, or Jun)*. This popular week-long celebration of Nguyen traditions and culture is held on even years in Hue city.

MARCH

Hai Ba Trung Festival *(early Mar)*. The statues of the famous Trung Sisters are taken from the Hai Ba Trung Temple in Hanoi for a ritual bath in the river.

△ **Thay Pagoda Festival** *(late Mar–early Apr)*. A celebration of the life of renowned polymath and Buddhist monk Tu Dao Hanh, who invented water puppet theater. Several puppet shows are staged to mark the occasion.

AUGUST

△ **Trung Nguyen/Vu Lan** *(mid-Aug–early Sep)*. Celebrated by both Taoists and Buddhists, the ghost festival involves the burning of paper money and other items to placate the wandering spirits.

Le Van Duyet Temple Festival *(late Aug–early Sep)*. Traditional opera and dance are performed to mark the anniversary of the statesman's death.

JULY

Mui Ne Street Food Festival *(Jan, Apr & Jul)*. Thrice-yearly, week-long festival celebrating Vietnamese and international street food.

△ **Hanoi Pride** *(Jul, Aug, or Sep)*. Week-long, colorful gay pride festival featuring a march, bike rally, parties, film-screenings, and talks.

DECEMBER

△ **Dalat Flower Festival** *(Dec)*. Expect an explosion of floral colors at this celebration of Dalat's locally grown flowers, vegetables, and ornamental plants.

Christmas *(Dec 25)*. With many churches and cathedrals, both Hanoi and Ho Chi Minh City are good places to celebrate Christmas.

NOVEMBER

△ **Oc Om Boc Festival and Ngo Boat Races** *(mid–late Nov)*. This Khmer festival in the Mekong Delta dedicated to the moon starts in the temples and culminates in canoe races on the river.

A BRIEF
HISTORY

Vietnam's long and turbulent past is written in its landscape. Having experienced much conflict across the millennia, including a long struggle for independence, it has been re-born a united and prosperous nation.

Origins and the Era of Hung Kings

Although evidence indicates that this area has been inhabited since the Neolithic age, the Viet people are believed to have originated in present-day southern China. According to legend, in the late 29th century BC the loosely allied tribes of the region were led south to the Red River Delta by deity Viem De. His son, Hung Vuong, declared himself ruler of a kingdom called Xich Qui and so founded the Hong Bang Dynasty of Hung kings (2879–258 BC). The people of this period advanced rice cultivation, with the Red River Delta a key agricultural center.

[1] A traditional grass script with calligraphy, or *caoshu*, dating from the Ming Dynasty.

[2] Folk painting of the Trung Sisters at war with the fleeing Chinese.

[3] Hindu temple ruins at My Son.

Timeline of events

9000–6500 BC
Neolithic period

2879 BC
Foundation of the Hung Dynasty kingdom of Xich Qui, later renamed Van Lang

1000 BC
Van Lang prospers under the Hung kings; development of wet rice cultivation and bronze casting

258 BC
Thuc Phan ends the Hung Dynasty and absorbs the region into the state of Au Lac

Chinese Domination

The Hung Dynasty ended in 258 BC when tribesmen from southern China overthrew the kingdom. The land was absorbed into the southern Chinese kingdom of Nam Viet, in 207 BC, ushering in a period of Chinese rule that lasted almost a millennium. In spite of this, the Viet people refused to accept Chinese political domination and there were numerous revolts. They did, however, adopt Chinese writing, architecture, and administration, as well as Buddhist, Taoist, and Confucian beliefs.

The South

Meanwhile, in the south, India was the main influence and two Indic kingdoms emerged – Funan and Champa. A precursor to the Khmer Empire, Funan was a trading nation that had links as far as the Mediterranean. The kingdom of Funan reached Northern Thailand, and was famed for its art and archictecure. Champa was based on agriculture and fishing, with seafaring at the heart of its economy, and stretched from Vinh to the Mekong Delta.

WHERE TO SEE EARLY VIETNAM

The later Hung kings' temples can be seen a little northwest of Hanoi; a public holiday in April is named in their honor. The most famous remains of the Cham comprise towers and Hindu temples in My Son, around Nha Trang, and across the Mekong Delta.

111 BC–939
Nam Viet becomes the Chinese province of Giao Chi; parts of Chinese culture are adopted

1st Century
Foundation of the Funan Empire

207 BC
Chinese General Trieu Da annexes Au Lac into his state of Nam Viet

2nd Century
Foundation of the Champa Empire

The Creation of Dai Viet

China's Tang Dynasty collapsed in the early 10th century. Led by military man Ngo Quyen, the Vietnamese finally achieved independence as Dai Viet in 938, but descended into civil war after his death. Warlord Dinh Bo Linh reunified the country in 968. He made peace with China as a tributary state, renamed the land Dai Co Viet, and proclaimed himself emperor. His dynasty lasted only 12 years, however, after which the throne was seized by Le Dai Hanh who established the Le Dynasty (980–1009).

The Ly Dynasty

At the death of the last Le emperor, a dutiful and enlightened palace guard commander called Ly Thai To was elected by the court as the new emperor. He started the Ly Dynasty (1010–1225), which laid the foundations for the country today and is generally considered the golden age of Vietnam. Although based upon Chinese culture, the bureaucratic Ly Dynasty nation of Dai Viet saw the development of civil infrastructure, a professional army, the elevation of women's and commoners' status, increased education, plus a flowering of art and culture.

1 Ngo Quyen (897-944), king of the Ngo Dynasty.

2 The Battle of the Bach Dang River, which saw the end of the Ly Dynasty and start of the Tran.

3 Intricate red doors in Hue's Imperial City.

Did You Know?

Dinh Bo Linh was killed while sleeping, and succeeded by his 6-year-old son

Timeline of events

939
Ngo Quyen expels the Chinese and founds the Ngo Dynasty

1009–1225
Vietnamese art and culture thrive during the Ly Dynasty

1407–1428
China seizes control of northern Vietnam, but Le Loi drives them out

1428–1788
Later Le Dynasty

3

The Tran Dynasty

After a ruthless coup by powerful clan leader Tran Hung Dao, in 1225, the Ly Dynasty ended. The Tran Dynasty followed, and with it the territory of Dai Viet extended further south into Champa lands. The Tran also defeated three significant Mongol invasions.

The Later Le and Nguyen Dynasties

The Tran were toppled in a coup d'etat, which led to invasion by Ming China and the region once again became a province of China. However, an uprising under the leadership of Le Loi established the Later Le Dynasty and Dai Viet became a strong regional state. From 1539 onward, power was divided between the warring Nguyen and Trinh families, which left the country weakened and the Le rulers in name only. European fleets began to arrive, carrying traders seeking wealth and missionaries intent on converting locals to Christianity. After a period of civil war, the Nguyen were overthrown and forced to flee. Nguyen Anh returned in 1788 and, supported by the French, reclaimed Saigon. In 1802, he declared Hue the new national capital and himself the first ruler of the Nguyen Dynasty.

↑ Military commander Tran Hung Dao (1228–1300)

1471
Dai Viet conquers most of the southern kingdom of Champa

1773
Tay Son armies seize control of southern Dai Viet from the Nguyen lords

1802
Nguyen Anh defeats Tay Son armies, unifying what is now Vietnam

1802–1945
Nguyen Dynasty, with its capital at Hue

1

2

The French Colonial Period

The Nguyen rulers that followed Nguyen Anh reintroduced feudalism and suppressed Catholicism. These anti-French measures prompted France to attack Danang in 1858. By 1887 all of present-day Vietnam, Laos, and Cambodia were unified as French Indochina, which was exploitatively ruled by France. In 1940 the Japanese invaded, but after liberation in August 1945, the wartime resistance leader Ho Chi Minh declared independence on September 2. He renamed the country the Democratic Republic of Vietnam (DRV) and set up a Communist government.

The First Indochina War

In September 1945, France reinstated troops in Saigon and set out to regain control of Vietnam, which led to full-scale war. Despite setting up a puppet imperial state in the south in 1949 and receiving support from the US, France was defeated by the Viet Minh in 1954. The Geneva Conference of the same year officially split Vietnam across the 17th Parallel; the north was under Ho Chi Minh's Communist DRV government, while the south was ruled by Ngo Dinh Diem, a US-backed, anti-Communist Catholic.

↑ French military medal from the First Indochina War

Timeline of events

1858–1887
France attacks Vietnam and it becomes part of French Indochina

1940–45
Vietnam occupied by the Imperial Japanese army but administered by the French Vichy Regime

1941
Ho Chi Minh and other Communists establish the Viet Minh resistance

1946
French forces attempt to recapture Vietnam, initiating the First Indochina War

1954
The Viet Minh defeat the French at the Battle of Dien Bien Phu

3

The Vietnam War (The American War)

Repression of Catholics in the North led almost a million to flee south, while similar treatment of Communists in the South triggered the formation of the National Liberation Front (NLF), or Vietcong (VC), who started a guerilla campaign. This escalated into war by 1959. While the US and its allies supported the South, the USSR, China, and other Communist states supported the North in what would be one of the biggest proxy conflicts of the Cold War. A key event was the Gulf of Tonkin incident (1964), which saw the US accuse the NLF of launching an unprovoked attack on two destroyers. President Lyndon Johnson used this as his reason to bomb the North and dramatically increase US troop numbers.

Aided by the Ho Chi Minh Trail *(p163)*, Vietcong fighters waged a guerilla war against the South Vietnamese and Americans. This mobile force consistently outmaneuvered their better equipped opponents, and after the massive Tet Offensive in 1968, it became clear to the Americans that this was a war they could not win. US troop numbers decreased year-by-year, and after much of the north of South Vietnam was taken during the Easter Offensive of 1972, the last US combat troops left in March 1973.

1 Paul Beau, French Governor-General of Indochina, arriving in Saigon, 1902.

2 Viet Minh victory parade in Hanoi, 1954.

3 US Army artillery gun crew, 1968.

Did You Know?

US soldiers extended the range of their radios by using metal Slinkys as antennas.

1959
Rebellion against the South Vietnamese government begins the Vietnam War (Second Indochina War)

1965
US forces land at Danang and begin fighting in Vietnam

1968
Vietcong forces, along with the North Vietnamese army, launch the Tet Offensive

1969
Ho Chi Minh dies

1973
The US ends its military involvement in Vietnam

1

2

Reunification and Isolation

On 30 April, 1975, just two years after US withdrawal, North Vietnamese forces entered Saigon and raised the Vietcong flag above the Palace of Independence. Saigon was renamed Ho Chi Minh City, after the late leader. In July 1976, Vietnam was officially reunited and Le Duan, the new general secretary of the Communist Party, proclaimed the Socialist Republic of Vietnam. His hardline Communist rule would see Vietnam slide into a decade of economic decline as collectivization of industry and commerce in the south and a harsh US trade embargo crippled the economy. Cross-border attacks by the Khmer Rouge in 1977 led the Vietnamese to invade Cambodia and topple the Chinese-backed regime in 1978. The next year, China invaded northern Vietnam in the punitive Third Indochina War, and Vietnam was forced into a closer alliance with the USSR.

↑ Vietnamese Prime Minister Nguyen Tan Dung greets a crowd

Renovation and Rebirth

By Le Duan's death in 1986, Vietnam was on the brink of economic collapse. Up to two million "boat people" had fled the country, and change was needed. New leader Nguyen Van Linh introduced

Timeline of events

1975

South Vietnam surrenders to northern forces; the US initiates a trade embargo

1976

North and South Vietnam officially unifies as the Socialist Republic of Vietnam

1978–9

Vietnam invades Cambodia and removes the Chinese-backed Khmer Rouge government, leading to a brief but bloody invasion by China

1986

Death of Le Duan and launch of the *Doi Moi* economic reforms by Nguyen Van Linh

economic reforms called *Doi Moi*. Private business ownership, foreign investment and economic deregulation were permitted, while the state retained control of strategic industries.

The collapse of the Soviet Union in 1991 allowed Vietnam to mend fences with China and open up to the global economy. In 1994 the US lifted its trade embargo, and normalized diplomatic relations a year later when Vietnam became a member of ASEAN (Association of Southeast Asian Nations).

Nguyen Tan Dung, a determined modernizer, became Vietnam's youngest prime minister in 2006. Vietnam's economy thrived in 2010, with a massive influx of foreign brands and the construction of modern skyscrapers. Since then, and despite hiccups such as the ongoing dispute with China over the South China Sea, Vietnam has continued to flourish.

Vietnam Today

Vietnam has a relatively strong economy today, and its citizens enjoy more freedom and a higher standard of living than at any other time in its history. Tourism has been a big part of that economic success, and visitors are treated well and welcomed.

1 Vietnamese troops invade Cambodia, 1979.

2 South Vietnamese leaving Saigon, 1975.

3 US President Bill Clinton visits Hanoi, 2000.

4 Ho Chi Minh City's modern skyline.

Did You Know?

Nguyen Tan Dung was the first postwar president not to have been part of the independence struggle.

1994

The US ends its long-standing trade embargo and Vietnam becomes a member of ASEAN

2011

President Nguyen Phu Trong is elected

2012

Tensions escalate with China over territorial disputes in the South China Sea

2018

Special Economic Zones set up for foreign investment spark anti-China riots

EXPERIENCE

Girls releasing floating candles on Perfume River, Hue

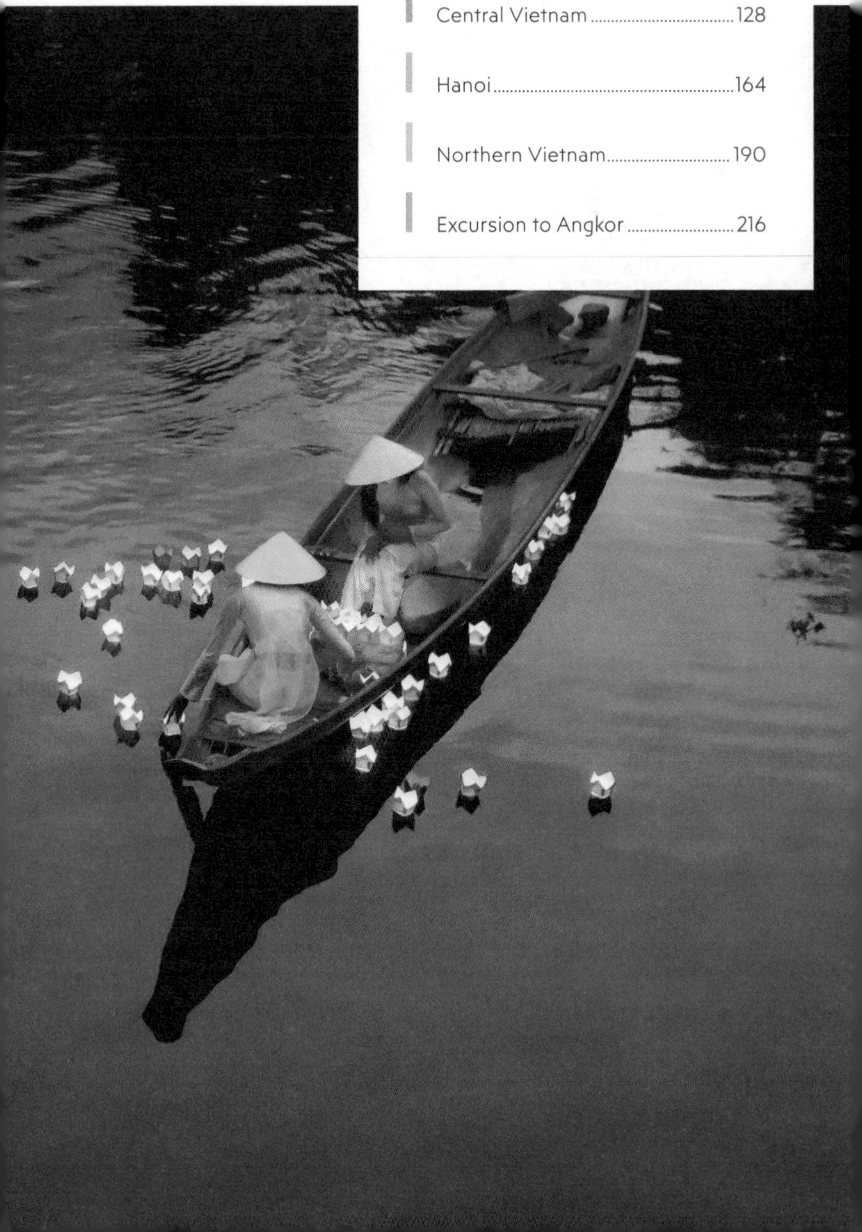

Incense coils hanging from the ceiling in Thien Hau Pagoda

HO CHI MINH CITY

Originally part of the kingdom of Cambodia, Ho Chi Minh City was a small port town until the late 17th century. By the 18th century, it had become part of Vietnam and the city, renamed Saigon, and was the provincial capital of the Nguyen Dynasty. However, in the second half of the 19th century, control over the city passed to the French, and Saigon became the capital of French Cochinchina. This was a period of much infrastructural and architectural development, during which Saigon earned the epithet "Paris of the Orient." In 1954, the city was proclaimed the capital of South Vietnam. The ensuing war between the US and the Communist North lasted until 1975, when North Vietnam took over Saigon and renamed it Ho Chi Minh City. Populated by almost eight million people, the city has long been the hub of manufacturing, entertainment, and cuisine in Vietnam.

HO CHI MINH CITY

Must Sees
1 Jade Emperor Pagoda
2 Cao Dai Holy See

Experience More
3 Municipal Theater
4 Saigon Central Mosque
5 Continental Hotel
6 People's Committee Building
7 Ho Chi Minh City Museum
8 Bitexco Financial Tower
9 Rex Hotel
10 Notre Dame Cathedral
11 Central Post Office
12 Independence Palace
13 Mariamman Hindu Temple
14 Ben Thanh Market
15 Fine Arts Museum
16 Museum of Vietnamese History
17 Le Van Duyet Temple
18 Vinh Nghiem Pagoda
19 Women's Museum of Southern Vietnam
20 War Remnants Museum
21 Xa Loi Pagoda
22 Nghia An Hoi Quan Pagoda
23 Thien Hau Pagoda
24 Quan Am Pagoda
25 Binh Tay Market
26 Phung Son Pagoda
27 One Pillar Pagoda of Thu Duc
28 Cu Chi Tunnels
29 Giac Vien Pagoda
30 Nui Ba Den
31 Vung Tau
32 Long Hai
33 Ho Coc Beach
34 Binh Chau Hot Springs
35 Cat Tien National Park
36 Can Gio Nature Park

Eat
① Xu Restaurant Lounge
② Pizza 4 Ps
③ Bun Cha
④ Noir
⑤ Deng Long

Drink
⑥ EON Heli Bar

Stay
⑦ Caravelle Hotel

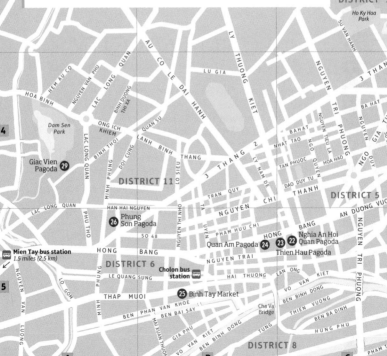

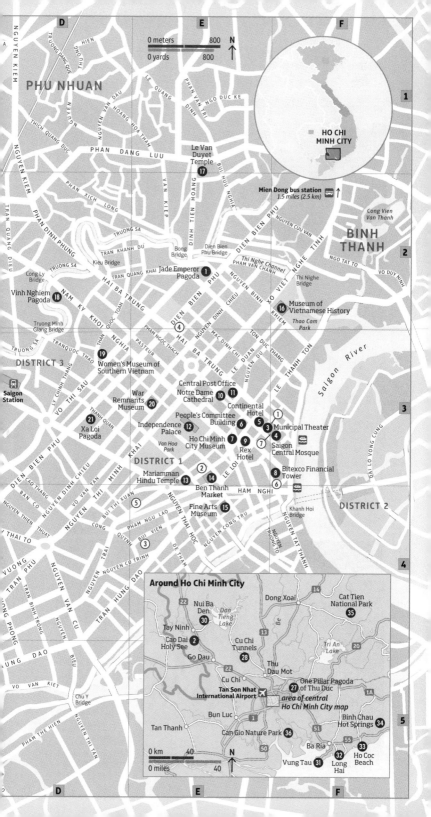

1 People's Committee Building.

2 Bitexco Financial Tower.

3 Nightlife around Ben Thanh Market.

4 Fruit sellers in Binh Tay Market.

5 Prayer slips in Thien Hau Pagoda.

2 DAYS
in Ho Chi Minh City

Day 1

Morning Begin the day in Lam Son Square, in the heart of the city, where stands the elegant neoclassical Municipal Theater between the city's most famous hotels: the Continental and the Caravelle *(pp64–5)*. From here, walk one block west to admire the elaborate facade of the People's Committee Building *(p65)*.
Just two blocks north of here, the Notre Dame Cathedral *(p67)*, with its iconic twin spires, is one of the city's most famous landmarks. Spend the rest of the morning in the sprawling Independence Palace *(p68)*, South Vietnam's wartime command center. Don't miss the basement, with its telecomms center and tunnels.

Afternoon Visit the War Remnants Museum *(p73)*, which recounts the horrors of the Vietnam War. As a welcome contrast, afterward peruse the Ben Thanh Market *(p70)* for some souvenir shopping and hard bargaining. Then head to the Saigon Skydeck at the top of the Bitexco Financial Tower *(p66)* to soak up the panoramic views, and see how many of the city's main sights you can spot.

Evening Have a sundowner at the EON Heli Bar above the Saigon Skydeck, followed by dinner at one of the many fine restaurants around District 1 *(pp67–73)*, then simply wander around and soak up the bustling atmosphere of the street life at night, especially around Ben Thanh Market.

Day 2

Morning Head north of the city center to the ornate Jade Emperor Pagoda *(p60)*. Stop by the Le Van Duyet Temple *(p71)*, dedicated to General Le Van Duyet, one of Vietnam's many national heroes. On the way back toward the center, check out the Museum of Vietnamese History *(p71)* to find out about the country's complex past.

Afternoon Make your way to Cholon, or "big market", the largest Chinatown in Vietnam. Dive straight into the frenetic Binh Tay Market *(p75)* before heading to the ancient and atmospheric temples in the backstreets. Don't miss Quan Am Pagoda *(p75)*, home to a plethora of deities, or the intricately decorated Thien Hau Pagoda *(p74)*. Round off the day with a visit to District 11 and the tranquil lakeside Giac Vien Pagoda *(p78)*, one of Ho Chi Minh City's oldest places of worship.

Evening Take a taxi, or a motorbike taxi if you're feeling adventurous, back to District 1 for dinner at Xu Restaurant Lounge *(p67)*. Then enjoy a stroll along the river before a nightcap at an iconic hotel bar in Dong Khoi, such as the rooftop Level 23 Wine Bar at Sheraton Saigon (88 Dong Khoi).

①

JADE EMPEROR PAGODA

♥ E2 **⌂ 73 Mai Thi Luu St, District 1** **⏱ 7am-6pm daily**

One of the city's most ornate pagodas, this wonderfully atmospheric small house of worship honors the King of all Heavens, Ngoc Hoangor or the Jade Emperor – chief deity of the Taoist pantheon. Built by the Cantonese community in 1909, it is filled with exquisite wood carvings and reinforced papier-mâché statues of various Buddhist and Taoist deities.

The pagoda's pink facade is quite simple. In contrast, the tile roof is an intricate work of art, as are the large wooden doors, richly carved with images of gods and men. Most remarkable, however, are the vibrantly colorful and gilded images of Buddhist divinities and Taoist deities inside the temple, including an elaborate statue of the Jade Emperor himself. Just about every surface is embellished with beautiful tiles and carvings, most of which are dense with religious imagery and symbols, and shrouded in a haze of burning incense.

> 💬 **INSIDER TIP**
> **Le Van Tam Park**
>
> For a peaceful, shady spot, head to Le Van Tam Park with its large trees, on Hai Ba Trung Street, just southwest of the pagoda.

Sculptures of dragons, believed to represent a connection to the divine, rise from the roof peaks made of elaborate woodwork and green ceramic tiles.

The King of Hell and his horse head the Hall of Ten Hells, which is lined with wood reliefs depicting scenes of damnation.

The altar of Phat Mau Chuan De contains her Hindu-style effigy flanked by statues of her five Buddha sons.

The Women's Room is filled with 12 colorful ceramic female figurines. Each represents a lunar year, juxta- posed with a vice or virtue.

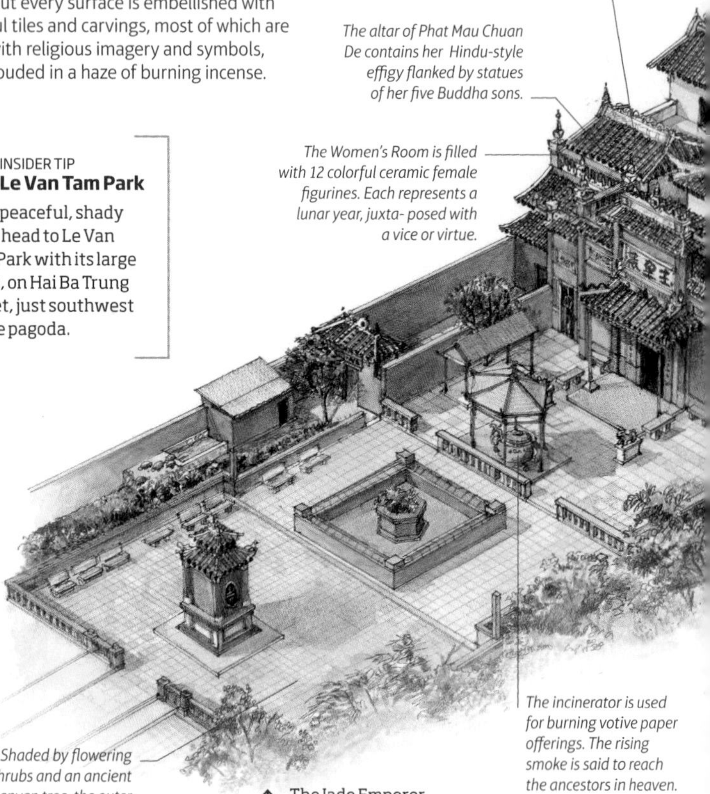

The incinerator is used for burning votive paper offerings. The rising smoke is said to reach the ancestors in heaven.

Shaded by flowering shrubs and an ancient banyan tree, the outer courtyard has benches and a turtle pond.

↑ The Jade Emperor Pagoda and its courtyard

Smoke-filled interior of the pagoda, where worshippers light candles and joss sticks ↑

The main sanctuary is presided over by a statue of the Jade Emperor, attended by guardians and resplendent in flowing robes.

↑ Buddha statues dressed in colorful robes

Made from reinforced papier-mâché, the two large demon guards here are richly painted and robed in finery. One restrains an evil dragon under his foot, and the other a rampant tiger.

This small tortoise shelter is home to several turtles, which are considered symbols of good luck and fortune in Vietnam.

→ The incinerator in front of the entrance to the Jade Emperor Pagoda

②

CAO DAI HOLY SEE

⚲ E5 **⌂ Long Hoa Village, 2.5 miles (4 km) E of Tay Ninh; 59 miles (96 km) NW of HCMC** **ℹ Tay Ninh Tourist: 210B 30 Thang 4 St, Tay Ninh; (091) 843 4329** **⊙ Daily**

As the center of Cao Dai, a religion founded in 1926 comprising a mixture of many Asian and some Christian beliefs, this vast complex draws millions of worshippers. The main attraction is the Great Divine Temple, which has an unusual mix of Asian and European architectural elements.

The spiritual centerpiece of the Cao Dai complex, the Great Divine Temple was built between 1933 and 1955. Its vividly decorated three-tiered roof, stained-glass windows, and kaleidoscope of colors make for an unusual, striking building. Amid the vibrant pinks, greens, and yellows of the decor are carvings of writhing serpents and dragons, lotus motifs, and a multitude of Divine Eyes, gazing from all directions. The chief symbol of Cao Daisim, the all-seeing Divine Eye represents supreme knowledge and wisdom. The prayer services, attended by hundreds of clergy in highly colorful robes, are held four times daily and are a breathtaking sight. Visitors are welcome at the noon prayer service, as long as they are careful not to disturb the worshippers.

As well as the Great Divine Temple, the complex houses administrative offices, residences for hundreds of priests, and a hospital of traditional Vietnamese herbal medicine that attracts people from all over the country for its treatments.

↑ The long, brightly colored prayer hall, with elaborately carved columns

Intricate carvings adorn the pillars.

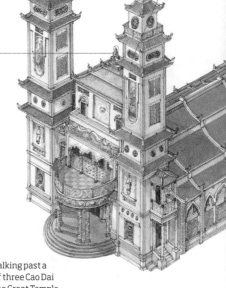

Dominating the central tower of the temple's front facade is a statue of the Buddha, reflecting the Cao Dai reverence for Buddhism.

← Visitors walking past a painting of three Cao Dai saints in the Great Temple

The massive Great Divine Temple, one of Vietnam's most photographed structures ↑

The all-seeing Divine Eye, the symbol of Cao Dai, is painted on a large, star-speckled blue globe that adorns the main altar.

Behind the main altar is a statue of one of the founders of Cao Dai, Phan Cong Tac.

Statues of the Cao Dai pantheon, including Jesus, the Buddha, and Confucius, dominate the area above the altar.

A mural depicts the three Cao Dai saints, Chinese leader Sun Yat Sen, French poet Victor Hugo, and Vietnamese poet Nguyen Binh Khiem, as earthly signatories to the "Third Alliance Between God and Man."

The garishly colored prayer hall is split into nine levels, represent-ing the steps to heaven.

↑ The Cao Dai Great Divine Temple, with a blend of Asian and European styles

Did You Know?

The Divine Eye symbol is a left eye as God is Yang (opposite of Yin) and Yang represents the left side.

EXPERIENCE MORE

 3

Municipal Theater

📍 E3 🏠 7 Lam Son Sq, District 1 🕐 Opening times vary; check website 🌐 hbso.org.vn

A superb French colonial building, the Municipal Theater, or Nha Hat Thanh Pho, was built in 1899 as a concert hall for the French. Sometimes still referred to as the Saigon Opera House, the hall also served temporarily as the headquarters of the South Vietnam National Assembly in 1956. A graceful staircase leads to the entrance, flanked by two huge columns shaped like Greco-Roman goddesses. Winged figures and exquisite scrollworks grace the eaves, and the grounds are scattered with lovely fountains and statues.

While the interior is not as ornate, it is a fine setting for a range of performances, from traditional Vietnamese theater and Western classical music to rock concerts and a regular hour-long cultural show. Program details are posted on the box office billboards and online.

 4

Saigon Central Mosque

📍 F3 🏠 66 Dong Du St, District 1 🕐 8am–8pm daily

Although the four gilded minarets of this neat white and pastel-blue mosque can be seen from the streets surrounding Dong Du, most passersby miss this hidden gem. Built in 1935 by South Indian Muslims, it offers a glimpse into the lives and beliefs of Vietnam's 75,000 Muslims and provides a peaceful rest stop while visiting Dong Khoi. Visitors are welcome to sit inside its cool, well-tended interior, or on the shaded verandah outside. Just remember to take off your shoes before you enter and to dress modestly. There are a number of halal street food stalls just outside the mosque.

 5

Continental Hotel

📍 E3 🏠 132–134 Dong Khoi St, District 1 🕐 Daily 🌐 continentalsaigon.com

In Lam Son Square, the historic center of Ho Chi Minh City, adjacent to the Belle Époque Municipal Theater, is

> It was British author Graham Greene who immortalized the Continental in his atmospheric novel *The Quiet American*. He was a resident for several months.

The grand People's Committee Building on Lom Son Square, an elegant reminder of the city's colonial past

Did You Know?

The Hôtel de Ville became known as the People's Committee Building in 1975.

the famous Continental Hotel. With its stately facade, the Continental is the grande dame of hotels built during French rule and retains the majesty of its past. It is set around a courtyard, which is well-shaded by frangipani trees. Inside, the red-carpeted staircases retain their original tropical hardwood. The structure, for the most part, has been spared the "modernization" visited upon some other historic buildings in the city, and wears its elegant patina of age well.

The hotel has earned a place in the annals of history for attracting many illustrious visitors since its completion in 1886. During the Vietnam War, top-flight journalists, including Walter Cronkite (1916–2009), would stay here and spend many hours on the famous terrace bar, which they dubbed "The Continental

Shelf." The great Indian poet Rabindranath Tagore (1861–1941), French author André Malraux (1901–76) and British writer W. Somerset Maugham (1874–1965) are other guests of note. It was British author Graham Greene (1904–91) who immortalized the Continental in his atmospheric novel *The Quiet American* (1955). He was a resident of the hotel for several months so it is no surprise that he captured the spirit of the time and place so well.

6 People's Committee Building

🅴E3 🏠 Intersection of Le Thanh Ton and Nguyen Hue sts, District 1 🚫 To the public

Designed by French architect P. Gardes and completed in 1908, the People's Committee Building, once known as the Hôtel de Ville, is one of the city's most iconic landmarks. It was outside this building in 1945, that thousands of

people congregated to establish the Provisional Administrative Committee of South Vietnam. Today, it is still the house of the city government and sits regally at the city's center. Contrary to popular belief, this striking building has never been a hostelry, nor is it open to the public. Modeled on the City Hall in Paris, it comprises two stories, with two wings off a central hall and a clock tower. It is capped with a red-tile roof, and its fanciful yellow-and-cream-colored facade is most often described as "gingerbread." Though it retains an obviously Parisian appearance, the building fits in well with the cityscape, especially at night when it is magnificently floodlit.

Unfortunately, there is no way for the general public to see the chandelier-bedecked interior today. However, the square in front of the hall, featuring a statue of Ho Chi Minh cradling a child, is a popular vantage point from which to take photographs of this beautiful building.

7

Ho Chi Minh City Museum

E3 **65 Ly Tu Trong St, District 1** **7:30am–6pm daily** **hcmc-museum.edu.vn**

Once the French governor general's residence, this, like many of the city's buildings, looks as though it may have been shipped in pieces from France and reassembled here. In a neoclassical style and painted in light grey with white trim, the museum generates a commanding presence. The spacious halls, with high ceilings and chandeliers, are a popular backdrop for wedding photographs.

Spread over two rambling floors, the museum purports to represent 300 years of the city's history. However, its original name, Revolutionary Museum, is a more accurate indicator of what to expect. The first floor has somewhat scattered displays of pictures of Saigon during French rule, old maps, and crumbling documents from the time the city was founded in the 17th century. Also here are relics from Vietnam's natural history and traditional wedding costumes. The second floor is devoted to Vietnam's struggle against imperialism. Weapons such as AK-47 rifles and improvised bombs are showcased here, along with photographs of soldiers, letters from the front, and political manifestos. Many of the obligatory engines of war, including a Huey helicopter, a jet fighter, and an American-built tank, can be seen on display in the gardens outside. The museum also has an extensive collection of Vietnamese currency.

8

Bitexco Financial Tower

F3 **2 Hai Trieu St, District 1** **9:30am–9:30pm daily** **bitexcofinancialtower.com**

Since opening in 2010, this has become a major landmark and an emblem of the city's rejuvenation. Once the tallest building in HCMC, its slender, tapered shape with a helipad jutting near the top is visible from everywhere in the city center. The main attraction is the Saigon Skydeck on the 49th floor, which offers panoromic views of the city center and the Saigon River flowing through it. The observation deck provides information about the history and culture of the city. Binoculars are fitted in the glass walls for visitors to use. From this vantage point, 584 ft (178 m) above the ground, many of Ho Chi Minh's best-known sights are easily seen, including the Municipal Theater, the People's Committee Building,

> Saigon Skydeck in the Bitexco Financial Tower, offering great views

---

BOAT TOURS

Two-hour breakfast and sunset river cruises run in Ho Chi Minh City. There are also one-day boat trips to Cao Dai and the Cu Chi Tunnels, and one-to three-day boat tours of the Mekong Delta. Most leave from the Passenger Ferry Port. Tours are best booked through a tour agency, and include transportation to and from your hotel.

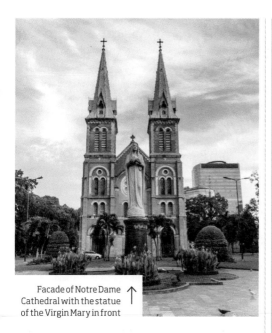

Facade of Notre Dame Cathedral with the statue of the Virgin Mary in front ↑

EAT & DRINK

EON Heli Bar

The highest bar in the city draws crowds for the views, though the drinks are pricey. There is nightly live music. Arrive early to secure a window seat.

⊙F3 ⌂52F Bitexco Financial Tower, 2 Hai Trieu St, District 1 ⓦeon51.com

$ $ $

Xu Restaurant Lounge

Modern Vietnamese cuisine is perfectly presented in this ultra-chic venue. Gastronomes will enjoy the tasting menu, while the downstairs lounge is great for cocktails.

⊙F3 ⌂71-75 Hai Ba Trung, District 1 ⓦxusaigon.com

$ $ $

and Ben Thanh Market. The bird's-eye view also gives an idea of the frantic pace of the city's development, with new high-rise blocks appearing all around. The tower also has many high-end stores for shopping enthusiasts as well as a range of fine restaurants, cafés, and a cinema.

---

⑨ Ⓨ ⍰ ⌂

Rex Hotel

⊙E3 ⌂141 Nguyen Hue Blvd, District 1 ⊙Daily ⓦrexhotelvietnam.com

Located in the center of the city, the Rex Hotel has played an important part in Ho Chi Minh City's history ever since its construction in the 1950s. Originally built by French colonial developers, it quickly became a focus of the social and military activities of American soldiers during the Vietnam War. It was from here that US military officers gave the daily press briefings that became known as "The Five O'Clock Follies," due to their blatantly self-serving nature.

Today, with its very popular rooftop bar, the Rex continues to serve as an important gathering place. Plenty of corporate conclaves are held here, gamblers flock to its popular casino, and there are innumerable weddings celebrated in the central court.

---

⑩

Notre Dame Cathedral

⊙E3 ⌂1 Cong Xa Paris Sq, District 1 ⊙8-10:30am, 3-4pm Mon-Sat

The basilica-style Notre Dame Cathedral, or Nha Tho Duc Ba, is the largest church ever built during the French Empire. When it was completed in 1880, its 40-m (120-ft) spires made it the tallest structure in the city. At first glance it seems to be brick-built, but in fact, the facade is made of red tiles brought over from Marseilles and attached to granite walls. Stained-glass windows from Chartres were installed, but destroyed during World War II and later replaced with plain glass. The two bell towers,

added in 1895 and topped with crosses, each house six bronze bells. The cathedral's interior remains relatively unadorned, but the ambient lighting creates a beautifully calm atmosphere.

In front of the cathedral is a statue of the Virgin Mary. Made in Rome, it was brought to Vietnam in 1959 and given the name Holy Mary Queen of Peace, in the hope that she would bring peace to the war-torn country.

While the city's Roman Catholic community is no longer a political force, droves of worshippers still throng the church. The belfry, open on Sundays, affords lovely views.

↑ The airy interior of the Central Post Office with its cool tiled floor and high vaulted ceiling

Central Post Office

📍E3 🏠2 Cong Xa Paris Sq, District1 📞(028) 3829 3274 🕐7am-7pm Mon-Fri, 7am-6pm Sat, 8am-6pm Sun

Designed by the French architect Marie-Alfred Foulhoux between 1886 and 1891, Buu Dien Trung Tam or the Central Post Office is one of the most attractive buildings in the city. Its massive facade is bright yellow with a cream trim and features carvings of the faces of famous philosophers and scientists, below which are finely engraved inscriptions. In all, the building is no less than a temple to the art of communicating by mail.

The interior is vaulted like the inside of a railroad station, and supported by wrought-iron pillars painted green, with gilded capitals. The floor tilework is intricate, especially in the foyer where huge antique maps illuminated by chandeliers depict the city and the region. One of the maps shows the city in 1892, and another portrays the region in 1932. A large portrait of Ho Chi Minh gazes over the daily bustle. Wooden writing benches are available for patrons' use, as is a kiosk selling souvenirs and stamps. The entire hall is cooled by overhead fans.

Independence Palace

📍E3 🏠135 Nam Ky Khoi Nghia, District1 🕐7:30-11am, 1-4pm daily (except during official functions) 🌐dinhdoclap.gov.vn

Set in spacious grounds, the historic Independence Palace (also known as Reunification Palace) is a prominent symbol of the country's political history. During the 19th century, the building was the site of the Norodom Palace, former residence of the French governor general. It was later occupied by South Vietnam's President Ngo Dinh Diem, and named the Presidential Palace.

In 1962, much of the building was destroyed when Diem's own air force bombed it in a failed assassination attempt. It was rebuilt soon after, but Diem was killed before he could move in. It was in this former palace's International Reception Room that succeeding President Van Thieu received potentates and presidents, until he boarded a chopper from the rooftop heli pad and fled before North Vietnamese troops took over Saigon. In 1975, the South surrendered to the North, and the palace gates were knocked down by a North Vietnamese Army tank. The photograph of this event has become emblematic of the reunification of Vietnam.

Today, the interior remains largely unchanged, with high and wide corridors that open onto cavernous lobbies and reception rooms. The living

> **INSIDER TIP**
> **Gong Vien Van Hoa Park**
>
> To escape the traffic and hustle and bustle of the city center, head to this park next to the Independence Palace. With benches and greenery, it is a lovely space in which to relax.

quarters, built around a sunny atrium, are lavishly furnished with glittering chandeliers and elaborate antiques. Not to be missed is the lacquer painting depicting scenes from the Le Dynasty.

In the basement is a bunker and military operations center, with radio transmitters and maps. Oddly, the third floor also has a gambling room.

---

⑬

Mariamman Hindu Temple

⦿ E3 **⌂** 45 Truong Dinh St, District 1 **☎** (028) 3823 2735
⊙ Sunrise-sunset daily

Dedicated to Mariamman, an incarnation of Shakti, the Hindu Goddess of Strength, the incense-filled Mariamman Hindu Temple caters not only to the small community of Hindus in Ho Chi Minh City, but also to the many local Vietnamese Buddhists, who worship here either courting good luck or driven by superstition.

Built in the late 19th century, the temple is quite small but still beautiful, and superbly maintained by the government. The bright, coral-colored wall of the facade is surmounted by numerous images of deities, cows, and lions, all painted vividly in pink, green, and blue. Over the entrance, a stepped-pyramidal tower covered with more sculpted images, mostly depicting female deities, rises from the rooftop.

Inside, an imposing statue of a red-robed lion guards the entrance, which opens into an uncovered portico that surrounds the main sanctuary. Three of the courtyard's walls are inset with altar nooks in which images of various gods and goddesses rest. Set in the center of the portico, the sanctuary itself is slightly raised. Made of stone, it recalls the architectural style of Angkor Wat (p224), and forms the setting for the multi-armed representation of Mariamman. The goddess is surrounded by many attending deities, including Ganesha, the Hindu Elephant God, as well as two female deities on either side of her. Two *lingam* (Hindu phallic symbols of Shiva) also stand before her.

The altar is surrounded by numerous incense burners and brass figurine oil lamps. Worshippers hold incense sticks in both hands while praying. In the rear of the sanctuary is a prayer wall where the faithful press their heads in the hope that the goddess will be able to hear their prayers clearly.

→
Statues of Hindu deities on the roof of Mariamman Temple

14

Ben Thanh Market

⟡ E3 ⌂ Intersection of Le Loi and Ham Nghi blvds, District 1 ⊘ 6am–5pm daily; till late outside

One of the most recognizable landmarks in the city, this huge market was built in 1914 by the French, who named it Les Halles Centrales or Central Market Halls. Its most famous feature is the massive clock tower that still dominates the surrounding neighborhood.

Home to several hundred stallholders, the market offers an amazingly extensive and varied selection of merchandise, ranging from food and leather goods to household items and clothing, as well as hardware and livestock. The atmosphere here is one of high energy, noise, and tremendous hustle and bustle (visitors should always be aware of the possibility of pickpockets). Products arrive at the market from around the country and, throughout the day, merchants sing out their wares while shoppers wander in search of great deals. It used to be common practice to haggle here but bargaining is no longer allowed and prices are fixed.

On entering through the main portal situated on Le Loi Boulevard, general merchandise is on the left. To the right is clothing and textiles. You will find plenty of souvenirs here too. Moving farther in, to the right are dry goods, such as tea, coffee, and spices, as well as packaged foods. Halfway in, fresh foods are on the right, and food stalls, where meals are available, to the left. The eateries both here and outside the building

↑ Main entrance to Ben Thanh Market; piles of produce inside the market (inset)

are famous for their quality and low price. Since the signage is written in English as well as Vietnamese, patrons can easily point to the posted menu when they are ready to make their order.

15

Fine Arts Museum

⟡ E4 ⌂ 97A Pho Duc Chinh St, District 1 ☎ (028) 3829 4441 ⊘ 9am–5pm Tue–Sun

Located next to Ben Thanh Market, this former private colonial mansion is an interesting combination of French and Chinese styles. It features columns and wrought-ironwork on windows and balconies, topped with a Chinese-style tiled roof.

Inside, the museum is home to three floors of Vietnamese art, which includes ceramics, lacquerware, sculptures, and oil paintings by Vietnamese and foreign artists. There is no air-conditioning so it is better to go early in the day. The first floor hosts rotating exhibits of contemporary art. The second floor is given over largely to political art, almost all of it related to the Vietnam War, and paintings by some of the leading artists of the country. This floor also has a fine selection of ceramics, mostly of Chinese style or origin. The museum's most interesting collection is on the third floor. Cham, Funan, Khmer, Chinese, and Indian works of art are well represented here. On display are many antiques, Oc Eo pottery and sculptures, Chinese objets d'art and wood carvings, and Cham statues. A highlight is a set of wooden funeral statues from the Central Highlands dating from the early 20th century.

The museum often holds exhibitions by local artists, while two galleries behind the museum offer pieces of contemporary art for sale and there are a few private galleries in the courtyard.

> **Products arrive at the market from around the country and, throughout the day, merchants sing out their wares while shoppers wander in search of great deals.**

representation of the Hindu deity Shiva used for worship). Another key exhibit is the mummy of a patrician woman along with her possessions, uncovered in Cui village. The mummy dates back to 1869 during the Nguyen Dynasty,

The museum hosts a fun daily water puppet show. Next to the museum is the Botanical Garden, which provides an ideal setting for a relaxing meander.

Did You Know?

The birds in cages sold near Le Van Duyet Temple are bought and released by pilgrims to gain merit.

Museum of Vietnamese History

⊙ F2 ⌂ 2 Nguyen Binh Khiem St, District 1 ☎ (028) 3829 8146 🕐 8–11am, 1:30–5pm Tue–Sun

Built in a classic pagoda style, this very attractive museum, also known as Bao Tang Lich Su, contains a vast collection of artifacts, spanning almost the entire history of Vietnam. Relics from the beginning of the nation's cultural evolution can be seen in the form of prehistoric implements and tools. These are followed by bronze artifacts from the Hung Kings era. Stand-out exhibits include bronze drums belonging to the Dong Son civilization, and tokens from the Oc Eo culture, including a 2nd-century AD Roman coin.

Farther on are remnants belonging to the Nguyen Dynasty, with a rich collection of garments and jewelry. Also on display are numerous Cham and Khmer relics, such as ceramics and a stone *lingam* (an abstract

→

Brightly painted porcelain wall tile at Le Van Duyet temple

⑰

Le Van Duyet Temple

⊙ E1 ⌂ 1 Bis Phan Dang Luu St, Binh Thanh District ☎ (028) 3841 2517 🕐 Sunrise–sunset

Dedicated to General Le Van Duyet (1763–1831), this is perhaps the best example of a temple devoted to a national hero rather than to a deity or religion. Le Van Duyet helped suppress the Tay Son Rebellion (pp46–7), and was lauded by Emperor Gia Long. After Van Duyet's death, he was repudiated by Emperor Minh Mang (r. 1820–41), but was restored to favor in the 1840s, and the temple was built to honor him.

The main sanctuary is bereft of any images other than a large portrait of Le Van Duyet, reminding devotees that they are worshipping a mortal. Also inside is a fascinating collection of the general's personal effects, such as crystalware, weapons, two life-size horse statues, and a stuffed tiger. The patrons are mostly locals who come here to meditate and make offerings. Over the years, the temple has grown into a complex of inter-connected buildings, cloisters, patios, and courts. From the street, a gate leads into a large parkland, with tall trees shading the benches. The temple exterior is remarkable for its mosaic wall panels and reliefs. By contrast, the outer sanctuary is unique in its lack of embellishment. All the pillars and altars are made of carved and polished wood, as are the giant cranes and the life-size horse seen here. The inner sanctum adjoining it is a blaze of color, with bright red-and-gold dragon pillars. Le Van Duyet's tomb, as well as that of his wife, is also to be found in the peaceful temple grounds.

There are celebrations held here during Tet and on the thirtieth day of the seventh lunar month every year – with a chance to hear trad-itional *boi* singing – to honor the anniversary of Le Van Duyet's death.

18

Vinh Nghiem Pagoda

📍 D2 🏠 339 Nam Ky Khoi Nghia St, District 3
📞 (028) 3896 6798
🕒 Sunrise-sunset daily

Completed with aid from the Japan-Vietnam Friendship Association in 1971, this is, by some measures, the largest pagoda in the city. Certainly, its eight-story tower, located immediately to the left of a high gate, is the tallest. Each side of the tower is adorned with an image of the Buddha in high relief. To the right of the gate is a smaller, 16-ft- (5-m-) high tower, built of concrete blocks. The concrete is of such quality and color that the structure appears to be made of granite.

Across a 65-ft (20-m) courtyard is the large, squat main building. A steep staircase leads up to the sanctuary where five massive lacquerware doors lead into the vast

first room. The walls here are lined with clear paintings showing scriptural scenes and explanatory notes are posted alongside. Farther in is the main altar with a huge, seated Buddha, flanked by disciples.

Behind the sanctuary lies a solemn room, filled with photographs and memorials to the departed. A statue of the goddess Quan Am sits on the altar here. On the second floor, a cloister leads into an art gallery where local artists show their works.

Rock and topiary gardens flank the building.

VIETNAM ON FILM

The setting for more Hollywood films than any country in the region, Vietnam features in many famous movies, with themes ranging from warfare and politics to romance. Both versions of Graham Greene's *The Quiet American*, in 1957 with Audie Murphy and in 2002 with Michael Caine, were set in Ho Chi Minh City. Francis Ford Coppola's allegorical *Apocalypse Now* (1979) and Oliver Stone's realistic *Platoon* (1986) are two of the best known war movies. Regis Wargnier's *Indochine* (1993) is a sensuous romp in colonial Vietnam, while Tran Anh Hung's *Cyclo* (1996) is a gritty portrayal of poverty and the criminal underworld in 1990s Ho Chi Minh City.

19

Women's Museum of Southern Vietnam

📍 D3 🏠 202 Vo Thi Sau St, District 3 📞 (028) 3932 0322 🕒 7:30am-noon, 1:30-5pm daily

To bring to light the cultural and military contributions made by South Vietnamese women over the ages, the Women's Museum of Southern Vietnam or Bao Tang Phu Nu Nam Bo was established in 1985. The ten rooms here span three stories and are filled with fascinating displays, ranging from military plaques and medals to a selection of beautiful ethnic costumes.

The tour usually begins from the third floor. The exhibits in this set of rooms are dedicated to women who were involved in the 20th-century Communist struggle for independence and unification. Their photographs line the walls, and some of their personal effects are displayed in glass cases, providing a reminder that Vietnamese women were no strangers to combat. The second floor continues the theme, with the addition of statues and large paintings of historical events involving women. There is also

←

Tiered tower of the historically important Xa Loi Pagoda

a re-creation of the prison cell that once held a national heroine captive.

The first floor, with its focus on traditional crafts and customs, is the most colorful. The anteroom, with a mock-up of a temple entrance bedecked with many artifacts, is dedicated to the ancient Vietnamese practice of goddess worship. In the next room, faux terraces feature mannequins dressed in exquisite regional costumes. In a large room to the left is a detailed exhibit about the production of cotton cloth and rush mats. These products are woven by women in craft villages of the south.

The museum complex also boasts a movie theater, a small library, and a boutique.

↑ Military helicopters and vehicles in the grounds of the War Remnants Museum

EAT

Noir
One of the city's most famous concept restaurants, Noir offers great Vietnamese, Asian, and European dishes, served by blind waiting staff in a pitch-black dining room.

⊠E2 **⌂Lane 178-180D, District 1** **Ⓦnoirdininginthe dark.com**

⑤⑤⑤

Deng Long
Local, home-style dishes here include ginger chicken hotpot and coconut shrimp salad. There are plenty of vegan options too.

⊠E4 **⌂130 Nguyen Trai, District 1** **☎(090) 994 9183**

⑤⑤⑤

20

War Remnants Museum

⊠E3 **⌂28 Vo Van Tan St, District 3** **Ⓞ7:30am-noon, 1:30-5pm daily** **Ⓦwar remnantsmuseum.com**

Located in the former US Information Service building, this exhibition shows films, pictures, and other items that document war atrocities committed by US, Chinese, and French soldiers in grim detail. Events are from a Vietnamese perspective and are thought-provoking. Among the most disturbing exhibits are the formaldehyde-filled jars of foetuses deformed due to the chemical defoliants used in the Vietnam War. Also displayed are photographs showing the effects of torture and a video of a prisoner being thrown from a helicopter by Vietnam's aggressors, along with US weapons, military vehicles, and even a guillotine.

21

Xa Loi Pagoda

⊠D3 **⌂89B Ba Huyen Thanh St, District 3** **☎(028) 3930 0114** **Ⓞ7-11am, 2-5pm daily**

This was one of the most important pagodas during the Communist revolution. Built

in 1956, it was a center of resistance to Ngo Dinh Diem's notoriously corrupt and anti-Buddhist regime in the early 1960s. Three of its monks immolated themselves publicly as a gesture of protest, and on one occasion, about 400 worshippers and clergy were arrested here. These powerful actions were crucial in galvanizing wide-spread opposition to the Diem regime, ultimately leading to the coup that resulted in his assassination in 1963.

Today, few traces of these tumultuous events remain. The pagoda's colorful seven-tiered tower rises above the temple complex. The roof soars to 49 ft (15 m), and large painted panels at the top of the walls depict scenes from the life of the Buddha.

The monks' quarters are on the first floor of the two-storied main building, and the sanctuary, which is unusual for its minimal decor, is located on the floor above. The ample space is devoid of furnishings, pillars, censers, and displays so that the visitor can simply contemplate the massive bronze statue of the Buddha, which is seated behind the solitary altar.

↑ Incense sticks burning in pots at the Thien Hau Pagoda

 22

Nghia An Hoi Quan Pagoda

📍C5 🏠678 Nguyen Trai St, Cholon 📞(028) 3853 8775
🕐Sunrise–sunset daily

Built in the 19th century, this is one of the oldest pagodas in Ho Chi Minh City. Renowned for its intricate carvings, the temple is dedicated to Quan Cong, a deified Chinese general, and Nghia An, his horse's faithful groom.

On entering, to the left are large wooden statues of Quan Cong's red horse and Nghia An. Devotees stop to pray at these statues, touching them to collect blessings. Of the two, the horse is considered more sacred. Devotees ring the bell around its neck, and crawl under it to the other side, symbolically wiping up blessings along the way.

To the right is a glass encased altar to Ong Bon, Guardian of Happiness and Virtue. The main sanctuary, entered through wooden folding screen doors, features friezes of a tiger and dragon. The glass cases behind the

main altar have images of Quan Cong and his assistants; Quan Binh, his chief mandarin, is on the right and Chau Xuong, his chief general, is on the left. On the fourteenth day of the first lunar month, unicorn, lion and dragon dance groups perform in front of the temple. After worship, a few nights of various artistic activities take place to demonstrate the admiration of the Hoa community for Quan Cong.

 23

Thien Hau Pagoda

📍C5 🏠710 Nguyen Trai St, Cholon 📞(028) 3855 5322
🕐8am–4:30pm daily

Also named Hoi Quan Tue Thanh, but commonly known as Chua Ba, or Lady's Pagoda, this temple is dedicated to Thien Hau, Goddess of the Sea

> **Devotees make a donation and then affix a label with their name onto one of the images. With each turn of the column their prayer is heard.**

and Patroness of Sailors. Built in the early 1800s by the Cantonese congregation, this is one of the most popular and richly embellished temples in the city. The front courtyard is surrounded by high walls, topped by intricate friezes and carved tableau. The entrance ceiling is even more complex, with wood-work and gilt reaching half-way down to the floor.

Inside, the atrium, with its exquisite friezes and reliefs, has giant censers billowing fragrant smoke. The spacious central room has a display case of the nozzles of the fire hoses used to extinguish a serious fire that threatened the temple in 1898. The walls of this room are covered with prayer flags – red strips of paper on which devotees write their prayers. It is believed that as the breeze rustles the paper, the prayers waft to Thien Hau.

Banks of incense coils grace the main sanctuary ceiling, while three statues of Thien Hau, each flanked by two attendants, preside at the altar. Hanging from the ceiling is a carved wooden boat that recalls Thien Hau's connection to the sea. To the right is an image of Long Mau, Goddess of Mothers and Newborns.

 24

Quan Am Pagoda

9 B5 **📍** 12 Lao Tu St, Cholon **📞** (028) 3855 3543 **🕐** 8am–4:30pm daily

This pagoda, also known as Ong Lang, was built by Chinese merchants in 1816 and honors Quan Am (or Kwan Yin), the Chinese Goddess of Mercy. The unusual pagoda is set in two parts, separated by a street. On the south side is a small plaza that adjoins a grotto set in a fish and turtle pond, while the north side houses the main temple complex. The eye-catching roof and entryway are richly adorned with paintings of saints, gilded scrollwork, and carved wooden panels depicting dragons, houses, people, and scenes from traditional Chinese life and stories. Inside, the first altar is dedicated to the Buddha, and leads into the main sanctuary, featuring two rotating lotus-shaped prayer wheels inset with scores of Buddha images. Devotees make a donation and then affix a label with their name onto one of the images. With each turn of the column their prayer is heard.

Next to the main altar is a representation of Quan Am, surrounded by the images of several other deities, including Amida, or the Happy Buddha, who represents the future; A Di Da, the Buddha of the Past; and Thich Ca, the Historical Buddha, Siddhartha. On either side of the altar are small incinerators. Paper money is burnt here for the benefit of departed souls. The pagoda maintains a large and unusual collection of live turtles for good luck. In a courtyard behind the sanctuary are more altars and images of gods and goddesses. The entire complex is filled with oil lamps and votive candles imbuing the air with the fragrance of incense.

Did You Know?

Cholon is Vietnam's largest Chinatown, with roots dating back to 1778.

  25

Binh Tay Market

9 B5 **📍** Thap Muoi St, Cholon **🕐** 8am–5pm daily **🌐** chobinhtay.gov.vn

This huge marketplace in Ho Chi Minh City's Cholon (Chinatown) – *cho lon* means "big market" – is a pagoda-style tribute to trade. Originally a small collection of open-air stalls, a Chinese merchant took the initiative to build a permanent structure in 1826. Over time, it evolved into today's huge emporium.

The yellow building has four wings joined in a square, with a courtyard and a fountain in the middle. A tall clock tower looms in the center of the complex. Stacked pagoda-like roofs cover the bustle of commerce. Primarily a wholesale market, it is less touristy than Ben Thanh Market *(p70)* and has a wide range of items and services available, from medicinal herbs and imported Chinese toys, to tailors and mechanics.

→

Rooftop and exterior of the large Binh Tay Market in Cholon

26

Phung Son Pagoda

◉ A5 ⌂ 1408 3 Thang 2 St, District 11 ☎ (028) 3969 3584 ◷ 5am-7pm daily

Also known as Go Pagoda, the present complex was built between 1802 and 1820 on the remains of an ancient site. Local lore and, more recently, archaeological findings suggest that this was once the site of a complex belonging to the Funan Empire (p45).

According to legend, at one time the temple was to be moved to a new site. But, as valuables were loaded upon a white elephant, the animal stumbled. This was taken as an omen that it was better that the pagoda remain at its present location.

The complex includes the monks' living quarters, while the main sanctuary is situated over to the left and contains statues of various Buddhas. Connected to it is an atrium with images of Quan Am, Goddess of Mercy, and the Buddha, as well as a bronze bell and ceremonial drum.

↑ Woman praying while holding incense sticks at Phung Son Pagoda

support provided by the monks kept the structure safe and intact.

Like its Hanoi counterpart, the building can be seen rising from a lotus pond. A narrow staircase leads from the pond's edge to the porch-like entrance. The facade has many windows, and an almost unbroken 360-degree view.

28

Cu Chi Tunnels

◉ E5 ⌂ 25 miles (40 km) NW of HCMC ☎ (028) 3794 8768 ▭ 13 to Cu Chi town, then by taxi ◷ 7:30am-5pm daily

The small town of Cu Chi is famous for its elaborate network of tunnels, located at

a distance of around 9 miles (15 km) from the town itself. There are two different tunnel systems here. The one at Ben Dinh village was used by the Vietcong during the Vietnam War. The guided tour begins in a briefing room, where maps and charts display the extent of the tunnel network in this district northeast of Ho Chi Minh City. Following an audio-visual presentation on the tunnels' history, describing the living quarters, kitchens, storage areas, armoury, and hospital within the tunnel network, visitors are led to an area set with faux booby traps and mannequins of Vietcong fighters. Close by are trapdoors that lead down into narrow tunnels. Although these have been widened, many visitors still find them claustrophobic. Deep down in the depths, the chambers have been restored to the way they might have been, with beds, stoves, and caches of ammunition.

The second set of tunnels is at Ben Duoc. Created mainly for tourism purposes, the tunnels here are better equipped than the actual ones used by the Vietcong.

Cu Chi town is known for its shooting galleries, but there is also a memorial pagoda, which features murals and a striking sculpture in the shape of a tear. The rather plain war cemeteries all over the area can be seen from the road.

27

One Pillar Pagoda of Thu Duc

◉ F5 ⌂ 100 Dang Van Bi St, Thu Duc District ☎ (028) 3896 0780 ◷ Sunrise-sunset daily

This little pagoda, based on the earlier Lien Phai Pagoda in Hanoi (p179), was built by monks who fled from there after the country was partitioned in 1954. During the Vietnam War (p50), the temple was used by the Vietcong as an undercover camp. Despite President Diem's efforts to destroy the pagoda, local

→

A guide revealing a well camouflaged entrance to the Cu Chi Tunnels

TUNNEL COMPLEXES

Elaborate tunnel complexes, such as those at Cu Chi and Vinh Moc *(p161)*, have been used by the Vietnamese for centuries. The tunnels were a key part of guerilla warfare during the Vietnam War *(p41)*, and played a major role in defeating American soldiers. Claimed to extend more than 125 miles (201 km), the tunnels were dug by local people using shovels.

TUNNEL DWELLINGS

Built at many levels, they had living spaces, kitchens, and clinics. Here, the Vietnamese could escape bombings, hide from the enemy, and mount surprise attacks. Tunnel entrances were small and well camouflaged with leaves. The American soldiers knew of the tunnels, and used infrared imaging and sniffer dogs in their search for them. They did not often succeed in finding them since the tunnels were rerouted and enlarged to avoid detection. Cramped and narrow passageways were made as tight and constricted as possible so that the larger American soldiers would find it difficult to pass through the tunnels. Ingenious booby traps, using everything from bamboo and iron staves to explosives, made the tunnels potential death traps for the unwary.

ANATOMY OF THE TUNNEL SYSTEM

While most tunnels were fairly small and simple, the major ones had three levels, and could be up to 33 ft (10 m) deep. Nonetheless, they were hot, cramped, and damp, making life underground difficult.

"TUNNEL RATS"

"Tunnel rats" was the nickname given to the special teams of US soldiers deployed for entering and disabling the tunnels. They wore masks as protection when releasing gases in the tunnels to drive out the Vietnamese. One method they used to find the tunnels was by listening to subterranean activity through stethoscopes.

Well-hidden firing posts helped the Vietnamese shoot at the enemy and then disappear.

A cooking area used highly creative ways to keep smoke from rising to the surface.

Bunker for strategy and planning

Air-raid shelters, located at the lowest level of the tunnels, protected the Vietnamese from intense bombing.

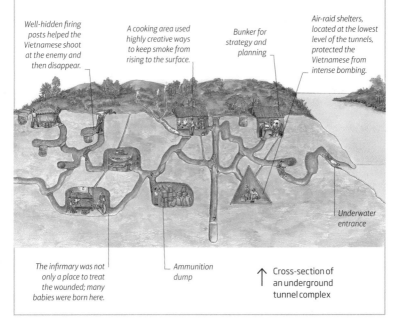

Underwater entrance

The infirmary was not only a place to treat the wounded; many babies were born here.

Ammunition dump

↑ Cross-section of an underground tunnel complex

↑ Wooden Buddha statues in the altar of Giac Vien Pagoda

Giac Vien Pagoda

Q A4 **🚗** 161/35/20 Lac Long Quan St, District 11 **🕐** 7am-7pm daily

Established by the monk Hai Tinh Giac Vien in 1744, this temple is located on the outskirts of the city, and is one of the most peaceful places around. Well known for its collection of more than 150 wooden statues, the pagoda seems to serve mainly as a dedication to the departed. Several large, beautifully carved tombs lie to the right of the entrance, as do some photographs of the dead. A columbarium houses funerary urns. Although the interior is dark, strategically placed apertures in the roof allow the sunlight to pierce the gloom.

The sanctuary's altar is a riot of several Buddha statues in varying sizes, some gilded, others plain wood or ceramic. A large A Di Da Buddha sits at the back and two small Bodhisattvas are perched in front; more than a dozen sit between. A stepped conical structure with small Buddhas on every level fronts the altar, and is lit by fairy lights. On either side of the sanctuary are cloisters filled with bonsai trees and grottos.

Close by is the **Dam Sen Water Park**, especially popular with children. Water slides and rides, an artificial river and lake, and shady rest spots all make for a fun-filled day. The park also has landscaped gardens, lagoons, pagodas, and unusual animal sculptures.

Dam Sen Water Park
 3 Hoa Binh St, District 11 **🕐** 9am-6pm Mon-Sat, 8:30am-6pm Sun **w** damsenwaterpark.com.vn

---

Nui Ba Den

Q E4 **🚗** 66 miles (106 km) NW of HCMC on Hwy 22; 10 miles (15 km) NE of Tay Ninh town **🚌** 4 to An Suong, then minibus to Tay Ninh town

There are two major attractions in Tay Ninh province, Cao Dai Holy See (p62) and Nui Ba Den or the Black Lady Mountain. Few visitors visit Nui Ba Den, as it is off the beaten track and cannot be reached directly by public transportation. However, those who make the trip are well-rewarded. Once a Vietcong camp, the mountain was bombed and sprayed with deadly chemicals during the Vietnam War. Its caves, used as Buddhist sanctuaries, have regained their beauty.

Despite the amusement park atmosphere at the base, the real attraction here is the lovely forest-clad mountain itself. Set amid shimmering lakes and a vibrant green landscape, Nui Ba Den rises above the surrounding plains at a steep 3,235 ft (986 m). The summit has stunning views, as well as a shrine to the Black Lady, a pious woman named Huong who died while defending her honor. It is possible to hike up the mountain to visit the temple, but there is also a cable car for those who prefer

→

A woman catching fish off Long Hai beach, with boats in the distance

a relaxed mode of transport. An annual festival honors the spirit of Nui Ba Den, with offerings, singing, and dancing.

Vung Tau

Q F5 **🚗** 81 miles (130 km) E of HCMC on Hwy 51 **🚁** Helicopter from HCMC **🚤** Hydrofoil from HCMC **ℹ** 29 Tran Hung Dao St; www.vungtau tourist. com.vn

The peninsula town of Vung Tau was once a pristine beach resort, known by the French as Cap St Jacques. It is still a very popular seaside getaway, but now that it is developed and home to an offshore oil industry, the quality of the water and beaches has been somewhat affected. On weekends it is crowded, noisy, and expensive. During the week, however, the area is quieter, and its proximity to Ho Chi Minh City makes it a convenient beach destination. The two main beaches here are Bai Truoc (Front Beach) on

Set amid shimmering lakes and a vibrant green landscape, Nui Ba Den rises above the surrounding plains at a steep 3,235 ft (986 m).

the west side and the long and wide Bai Sau (Back Beach) on the east side of the South China Sea peninsula. Bai Truoc has the greater concentration of expensive hotels, bars, and restaurants, while Bai Sau has a wider range of accommodations and more beach facilities.

In the vicinity of Vung Tau, two promontories, Nui Lon (Big Mountain) and Nui Nho (Little Mountain), are both worth visiting for splendid views. Nui Nho features a giant statue of Jesus; visitors can climb up to the top or take a cable car to the top of Nui Lon. Vung Tau Lighthouse, about a mile from the ferry landing, also offers a superb vantage point.

The local museum, **Bach Dinh**, or White Villa, was the residence of Emperor Thanh Thai while he was under house arrest by the French. Inside are many interesting exhibits dating from the Chinese Qing Dynasty. The relics on display were salvaged from a 17th-century shipwreck.

Bach Dinh
 ⌂ 12 Tran Phu St 📞 (064) 351 2258 🕐 7–11:30am, 1:30–5pm daily

---

㉜

Long Hai

📍 F5 ⌂ 81 miles (130 km) E of HCMC on Hwy 19; 30 miles (40 km) NE of Vung Tau 🚌 from HCMC ℹ Vung Tau Tourist, 29 Tran Hung Dao St; (064) 385 7527

While the two settlements grew, the stretch of coastline between Vung Tau and Phan Thiet was virtually deserted, but today it is lined with a number of large resorts. Home to the small town of Long Hai, this area is now rather exaggeratedly referred to as Vietnam's Riviera. Nonetheless, the beaches are relatively unspoiled, prices are low, the seafood is fresh, and the atmosphere is very relaxed.

A point of interest near Long Hai is the Mo Co Temple, where hundreds of boats from all over the region converge during the Fisherman's Festival in June. Farther east is one of Bao Dai's villas, now the upmarket resort Alma Oasis, as well as several cheaper resorts. Although there is no direct public transportation or hydrofoil from Vung Tau, the drive to Long Hai is pleasant, with several charming Catholic churches lining the highway as well as a number of interesting temples.

Did You Know?

Vung Tau has a nutritious delicacy, *tiet canh tom hum*, a lobster dish unique to the town.

↑ Verdant Crocodile Lake and a bar-bellied pitta (inset) in Cat Tien National Park

33 Ho Coc Beach

📍 F5 🏠 118 miles (190 km) E of HCMC; 22 miles (36 km) NE of Long Hai 🚌 From Mien Dong bus station

The relative seclusion of Ho Coc Beach is its best feature. While popular with the Vietnamese as a weekend destination, it is otherwise little visited and there is limited public transportation. However, there is a growing range of accommodations options, as well as various cafés and restaurants serving fresh seafood. The beach is superb, with 3 miles (5 km) of clean, white sand, studded here and there with massive boulders.

Ho Coc lies adjacent to the Binh Chau - Phuoc Buu Nature Reserve. The trees come right up to the beach, and several trails leading into the wooded area start from the sand itself. The reserve was once home to many large animals, but most of these have now been relocated for reasons of conservation and safety. Nevertheless, it is still inhabited by several species of monkeys and birds. The greenery and the tranquil surroundings are soothing. Guides may be hired from Ho Chi Minh City for walking tours, for a small fee.

34 Binh Chau Hot Springs

📍 F5 🏠 93 miles (150 km) SE of HCMC; 31 miles (50 km) NE of Long Hai 🌐 saigonbinhchau.com

With more than 100 natural mineral-rich hot springs reputed to have therapeutic properties, this area has historically been popular with those seeking curative treatments. Today it is also a very attractive holiday destination, with a resort, playground, water park, golf course, and tennis courts.

Public and private facilities for hot spring baths are on offer. The private baths are enclosed by wooden screens for dressing and overhead coverings for shade. These can accommodate two to ten people, and incur a higher charge than the public facilities. The highlight of the public baths is a large outdoor pool whose water averages 99 °F (37 °C). The water temperature is said to be beneficial to bones and skin. The hottest of the springs at Binh Chau is a simmering 180 °F (82 °C). The spring is surrounded by large statues of chickens; dotted around it are baskets containing eggs for sale, which you boil in the spring. For an even more relaxing spa experience, there are also therapeutic mud baths.

Amid the hot springs are verdant marshlands, and there are also some well-marked walking trails around the area where visitors can take a stroll.

Cat Tien National Park

📍 F4 🚗 100 miles (160 km) NE of HCMC 🚌 From Mien Dong bus station to Dalat - the park is halfway) 🌐 namcattien.org

Cat Tien is easily one of the most abundant, biologically diverse reserves of its kind. This is remarkable in light of the fact that it was subjected to sustained bombardment by defoliants during the Vietnam War. Even farther back in time, it was a place of pilgrimage, as evidenced by the discovery of ancient religious artifacts around the area traced to both the Funan and Champa empires (p46).

📷 PICTURE PERFECT
Tree-mendous

A marked trekking route goes past many of the giant trees in Cat Tien's primary rain forest. Take a photograph of yourself looking very small next to towering Tung trees, which are hundreds of years old.

Today, this lush 277-sq-mile (718-sq-km) park is home to a wide range of flora and fauna. There are more than 1,600 varieties of plants, and new ones continue to be discovered. This was once the habitat of the now-extinct Javan rhinoceros, but it continues to be the home of many other animals, including elephants, deer, and over 360 species of birds. Colonies of monkeys, including rare douc langurs, populate the trees, while 440 species of butterfly flutter amid wildflowers. Not surprisingly, Cat Tien is one of the most popular adventure destinations in Vietnam. Accommodations in the park are minimal but adequate, and are reached by crossing the Dong Nai River.

Can Gio Nature Park

📍 F5 🚗 37 miles (60 km) from HCMC 🚌 From Ben Thanh Market 🚤 Binh Kanh 🚌 90

This coastal area by the Dong Nai River is home to a large mangrove forest nature reserve, regarded as the "green lungs" of Ho Chi Minh City. It can easily be visited on a day trip. Wetlands, mud flats, and salt marshes support a huge variety of mangrove plant species and more than 200 animal species, including seabirds such as the spotbilled pelican, saltwater crocodiles, fishing cats, and several thousand wild macaques.

After entering the park, a boat takes visitors upriver past ramshackle villages that give an unsanitized view of local rural village life, before going up through the humid mangrove forest to Monkey Island. Here, troops of wild macaques descend from the forest to steal snacks, drinks, and anything they can grab from tourists, so keep a firm hold of your possessions. It pays to be wary of the monkey circus show that unfortunately takes place here on holidays and weekends, which has been widely denounced by wildlife experts and animal advocates. The boat continues through the waterways to reach the interesting reconstructed Vietcong Rung Sac guerilla camp.

A SHORT WALK
DONG KHOI

Distance 0.5 mile (0.8 km) **Time** 15 minutes

The lively area around Dong Khoi Street is the very nerve center of Ho Chi Minh City. Dong Khoi Street itself became famous during the French era, and was then known as the Rue Catinat. Home to stately hotels, elegant boutiques, and cozy cafés that coexisted with bars and brothels, it was at the heart of most of the action in Graham Greene's novel *The Quiet American*. The subsequent Communist regime shut down most of these establishments, but Vietnam's economic liberalization in 1986 gave the area a new lease on life as smart hotels, restaurants, and shops slowly made a reappearance. Today, Dong Khoi's vibrancy is unparalleled in the country, and it does justice to the city's old nickname, "Paris of the Orient."

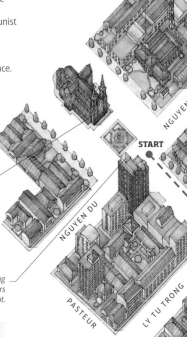

One of the most handsome French colonial buildings in the city, the massive Central Post Office has a cavernous interior with comfortable benches, providing a cool respite from the heat outside.

START

NGUYEN D

NGUYEN DU

The tall, late 19th-century Notre Dame cathedral is built of locally quarried stone and covered with red ceramic tiles shipped in from France. The statue of the Virgin Mary was added to the lawns in front of the building in the 1950s.

The Metropolitan Building is home to HSBC's headquarters and is a popular café spot.

PASTEUR

LY TU TRONG

The erstwhile Hôtel de Ville now houses the office of the People's Committee of Ho Chi Minh City. It is one of the most magnificent and photogenic colonial buildings in the entire city.

←

Interior of the Central Post Office, with its high, arched ceiling and portrait of Ho Chi Minh

↑ The imposing French colonial
People's Committee Building

Locator Map
For more detail see p56

0 meters 100
0 yards 100
N ↑

Did You Know?

The Central Post Office
has a public writer who
pens letters for those who
are unable to do so
themselves.

The Vincom Shopping Center
(Vincom Towers) is one of the
largest modern shopping
centers in Vietnam, selling a
variety of imported brands.

Constructed in classic French colonial
style, the elegant Continental Hotel is
a serene haven amid the bustle of the
city. The central atrium is popular for
afternoon tea and the patio offers
al fresco dining in summer.

The lovely Neo-Classical
Municipal Theater, known as
the Opera House in colonial
times, was once the heart
of French high society.

DONG KHOI

LE THANH TON

NGUYEN HUE

LE LOI

FINISH

The Lower Dong Khoi area has
become one of the city's most
fashionable spots for boutique
shopping. Local brands such as
Khai Silk can be found here,
alongside well-known international
brands including Louis Vuitton.

A popular base for several journalists during the
Vietnam War, the Rex Hotel is one of the best known
landmarks in the city. The hotel's rooftop bar offers
superb views of the street below.

A WALK AROUND
CHOLON

Distance 1 mile (2 km) **Walking time**
30 minutes **Road safety** Traffic can be
heavy along Hung Vuong, so take care
when walking here

Home to Chinese traders and merchants for
more than three centuries, Cholon, which
means big market, has long been one of Ho
Chi Minh City's most vibrant commercial
centers. Also known as District 5, its markets
are always busy and brimming with a wide
range of specialty shops selling everything
from silks, spices, and medicinal herbs to hats,
jade curios, and ceramics. With much of the
city's vast ethnic Chinese or Hoa community
concentrated here, Cholon is a religious hub
and home to several Chinese-style pagodas
and temples. These striking buildings are
concentrated on and around Cholon's main
street, Nguyen Trai, which runs through the
heart of the area. The narrow streets of this
bustling district are best traversed on foot.

Locator Map
For more detail see p56

*The Fujian
community built the
Phuoc An Hoi Quan
Pagoda in 1902,
dedicating it to Quan
Cong. The ancient
spears displayed
before the main
altar represent the
cardinal virtues.*

*The electronics
market is a one-stop
destination for
TVs, toasters,
air conditioners,
and more.*

Phuoc An Hoi
Quan Pagoda

START

HONG BANG

Quan Am
Pagoda

LUONG NHU HOC

CHAU

VAN

LIEM

NGUYEN
TRAI

TRAN
HUNG DAO

HAI THUONG
LAN ONG

*The only temple
complex in the city
bisected by a street,
the Quan Am
Pagoda, also known
as Ong Lang, has a
colorful façade and an
exquisitely detailed
ceramic-tiled roof (p75).*

↑ Ancient spears in front of the main altar
in the Phuoc An Hoi Quan Pagoda

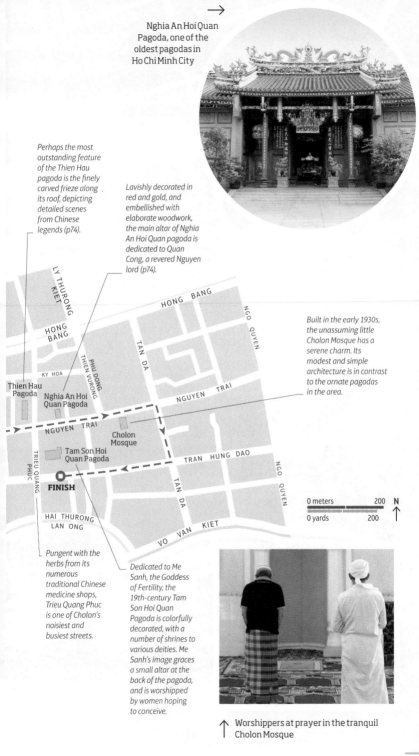

Nghia An Hoi Quan Pagoda, one of the oldest pagodas in Ho Chi Minh City

Perhaps the most outstanding feature of the Thien Hau pagoda is the finely carved frieze along its roof, depicting detailed scenes from Chinese legends (p74).

Lavishly decorated in red and gold, and embellished with elaborate woodwork, the main altar of Nghia An Hoi Quan pagoda is dedicated to Quan Cong, a revered Nguyen lord (p74).

Built in the early 1930s, the unassuming little Cholon Mosque has a serene charm. Its modest and simple architecture is in contrast to the ornate pagodas in the area.

Thien Hau Pagoda

Nghia An Hoi Quan Pagoda

Tam Son Hoi Quan Pagoda

Cholon Mosque

FINISH

LY THUONG KIET

HONG BANG

HONG BANG

KY HOA

PHU DONG THIEN VURONG

TAN DA

NGO QUYEN

NGUYEN TRAI

NGUYEN TRAI

TRAN HUNG DAO

TAN DA

NGO QUYEN

TRIEU QUANG PHUC

HAI THUONG LAN ONG

VO VAN KIET

0 meters 200
0 yards 200
N

Pungent with the herbs from its numerous traditional Chinese medicine shops, Trieu Quang Phuc is one of Cholon's noisiest and busiest streets.

Dedicated to Me Sanh, the Goddess of Fertility, the 19th-century Tam Son Hoi Quan Pagoda is colorfully decorated, with a number of shrines to various deities. Me Sanh's image graces a small altar at the back of the pagoda, and is worshipped by women hoping to conceive.

↑ Worshippers at prayer in the tranquil Cholon Mosque

Rural village along the lush Mekong Delta

MEKONG DELTA AND SOUTHERN VIETNAM

With its origins on the high plateau of Tibet, the mighty Mekong River's tentacled waterways bestow Vietnam's southern plain with rich alluvial soil that has made it a "rice basket," as well as a "fruit basket" filled with coconut, longan, and mango trees. The Delta has long been laid claim to by Cambodia, and in 1978, the Khmer Rouge orchestrated a savage massacre at numerous villages. Nevertheless, the Delta and its people are extremely resilient, having survived the ravages of frequent floods, French and Cambodian occupation, many bombings, and the devastating effects of the chemical defoliant, Agent Orange.

Despite this legacy of conflict and upheaval, life on the Delta ebbs and flows to an age-old rhythm. Everywhere are attractive Khmer, Vietnamese, and Chinese-style pagodas that reflect the Delta's ethnic diversity.

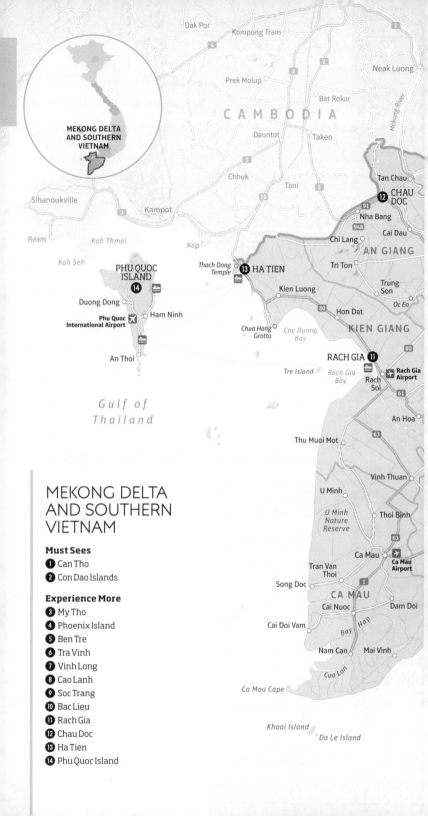

MEKONG DELTA
AND SOUTHERN
VIETNAM

Must Sees

1 Can Tho
2 Con Dao Islands

Experience More

3 My Tho
4 Phoenix Island
5 Ben Tre
6 Tra Vinh
7 Vinh Long
8 Cao Lanh
9 Soc Trang
10 Bac Lieu
11 Rach Gia
12 Chau Doc
13 Ha Tien
14 Phu Quoc Island

←

1 Fisherman casting nets at sunrise on the Mekong River.

2 Fruit-sellers at a floating market near Can Tho.

3 Khleang Khmer Pagoda, with resident monks, in Soc Trang.

While the most famous sights in Vietnam are to be found between Hanoi and Ho Chi Minh City, a trip through the largely rural Mekong Delta will show you the authentic side of Vietnam – and it's a jumping-off point to visit the world-famous Angkor Wat in Cambodia.

10 DAYS

in the Mekong Delta with an Excursion to Angkor

Day 1: HCMC to Vinh Long

Head out early from Ho Chi Minh City to Vinh Long *(p103)*. Here you can get a real taste of rural life on the Mekong Delta by taking a day-long boat tour *(p110)* along the Co Chien River and through the network of canals around the town. You'll pass through traditional villages that have remained largely unchanged for centuries, sweet-smelling orchid gardens, and fruit orchards. For dinner, take a taxi to Mr Kiet's Historic House *(p102)* for excellent local food in gorgeous, atmospheric surroundings.

Day 2: Can Tho

It's a short hop from Vinh Long to Can Tho *(p96)*. You'll want to make another early start so you get there in time to visit one of its famous floating markets. Hire a sampan boat to take you to Cai Rang market, where a chaotic mass of floating traders paddle around in sampans overflowing with produce. After lunch, head to the Can Tho Museum to escape the worst of the day's heat and learn about the history of the province and the Delta's largest city. After it's cooled off a bit, check out the impressive Khmer Munirangsyaram Temple, with its Angkor-like tower and welcoming monks.

Day 3: Soc Trang

A bus ride south is Soc Trang *(p104)*, the religious center of the Delta and home to dozens of Khmer, Chinese, and Vietnamese religious buildings. Start off at the Khmer Museum to get a flavor of the local culture, then head to the 16th-century Khleang Khmer Pagoda. Stroll around its beautiful grounds, and have lunch at one of the vegetarian restaurants outside. A short walk east, you'll find Clay Pagoda, so named for the hundreds of fantastical clay figurines and statues that festoon its interior. Then, at sunset, take a taxi to Chua Doi, or Bat Pagoda, when thousands of bats emerge from the temple to blacken the darkening sky. →

1

Day 4: Ha Tien

Next make the five-hour trip by road up to Ha Tien *(p107)*, which overlooks the Gulf of Thailand by the Cambodian border and is surrounded by dramatic limestone promontories. It is one of the most attractive towns in the Delta. After checking in at a hotel and having lunch, hire a taxi to take you to the many sights around the town, such as the Buddhist cave temples at Thach Dong, or the Hang Pagoda in Hon Chong, where a grotto contains "musical" stalactites. Enjoy the absolutely stunning scenery around the town during your drive.

Days 5 and 6: Phu Quoc Island

Hop on a ferry and head to golden beaches and swaying palms on Phu Quoc Island *(p108)*, an ideal setting for some rest and relaxation. There are plenty of resorts and hotels to stay in on the beautiful beaches, including Bai Truong, or less developed ones such as the lovely Bai Sao and Bai Dam. If you get bored with lazing on the beach, you could easily spend a day on the several hiking trails that wend through the jungle past unspoiled beaches and coves in the Phu Quoc National Park, or take a snorkeling or diving trip out to Hon Doi Moi, whose coral reefs teem with colorful marine life.

Day 7: Chau Doc

After taking the boat back to Ha Tien, head up to the waterside border town of Chau Doc *(p106)*. After lunch, take a wander down the riverfront to see the fascinating stilt and floating houses where most of the people here live and work, and the lively riverside market, which is one of the busiest in the region. Then spend the afternoon at Sam Mountain, a short taxi ride away, whose slopes are crowded with temples,

Ha Tien overlooks the Gulf of Thailand by the Cambodian border and is surrounded by dramatic limestone promontories.

grottoes, pagodas, and ancient tombs ripe for exploration; from here there are spectacular views across the countryside.

Days 8, 9 and 10: Siem Reap and Angkor

It's a long (about 12 hours) but interesting journey to Angkor – take a boat across the border into Cambodia and upriver to Phnom Penh, and then a bus to the town of Siem Reap *(p237)*. This will take up most of the day, but it's a good chance to see the Cambodian landscape.

Allow two full days to explore the mysterious and magnificent Angkor Wat *(p224)* and Angkor Thom *(p228)* nearby, which you can do either on a tour, or independently by bike. A great way to end your trip, Angkor Wat is the single largest religious monument in the world, while the nearby ruined city of Angkor Thom is somewhat less visited but equally awe-inspiring. The tourist hub of Siem Reap has an airport, from which you can fly out home or to your next destination.

1 Phu Quoc Island.

2 Traditional stilt house in Chau Doc.

3 Dragon heads decorating a pagoda at the base of Sam Mountain.

4 South Gate of Angkor Thom.

Birds of the Delta

The Delta's rich environment provides sustenance for a huge range of both migratory and sedentary avian species. The painted stork and the sarus crane, as well as a wide variety of egrets, spend time here in migration, but many colorful tropical species, such as the green bee-eater, can be seen year round. Some excellent bird sanctuaries have revived local populations. The mangrove forests of the Bac Lieu Bird Sanctuary attract some 46 bird species. Tram Chim National Park, accessible only by boat, is a migratory stop for storks and cranes, as is the Bang Lang Stork Garden near the town of Can Tho.

↑ Green bee-eaters, which nest in tunnels in the riverbank

THE MEKONG DELTA'S
FLORA AND FAUNA

The rich soil and lush green habitat of the dense mangrove swamps and tropical forests of the Mekong Delta are home to a wide variety of plant and animal species, with new ones still being discovered. The region is truly a wonderland of biodiversity.

Coconut Trees Lining Delta Waters

Coconut palms are an intensively cultivated source of food, eco-friendly packaging, and building materials. The nuts provide cooking oil, are used to make candies, form a vitamin-rich beverage, and are used in curries. The leaves are woven into baskets, as well as roofing materials. Coconut tree roots in canals provide a habitat for fish.

←

Banks of the Mekong Delta, with hundreds of coconut palms

Reptiles

Reptilian life, such as snakes and lizards, abounds in the rich eco-system of the Mekong Delta. Indigenous snakes include the feared king cobra and the giant python. Crocodiles are now rarely seen in the wild but are raised on crocodile farms to preserve them from extinction.

$\rightarrow$

Swimming crocodiles in one of the numerous crocodile farms

Colorful Orchids

Many species of orchids flourish naturally in the Delta region, and have been supplemented by imported varieties and hybrids, which are cultivated. Most orchids attach themselves to the trunks of larger plants, so in the wild you will need to look upward to spot them. Nurseries around Sa Dec town have live specimens and rhizomes for re-cultivation.

$\leftarrow$

Purple orchids, one of the orchid species abundant in the Delta

$\rightarrow$

The beautiful nocturnal fishing cat, very much at home near water

💬 INSIDER TIP
Tra Su Bird Sanctuary

Fifteen miles (23 km) west of Chau Doc, the huge Tra Su Bird Sanctuary is a habitat for a large number of wading birds. The best time to visit is between September and November. Travel through the park is mostly by boat. Even if you're not an avid bird-watcher this is a beautfully tranquil spot to spend a day in a stunning setting.

Mammals

The best-known mammal living in the wilds of the Delta is the crab-eating macaque. These monkeys are omnivorous, eating crabs, insects, and plants, and will happily raid local fruit orchards. Less common is the fishing cat, which will actually dive into the water in pursuit of prey. The hairy-nosed otter is one of the endangered species under protection at the U Minh Nature Reserve in the southern Delta province of Ca Mau.

 Cai Rang, a floating market, southwest of Can Tho

 ❶

CAN THO

🅰 C7 🏠 105 miles (169 km) SW of HCMC ✈ 6 miles (10 km) S 🚌 🚉 ℹ 50 Hai Ba Trung St; (0710) 382 7674 🌐 canthotourist.vn

The largest city on the delta, Can Tho is one of the most delightful destinations in the south. Bordering six provinces, it serves as a transportation hub for the region, as well as a major agricultural center, with rice milling as its main industry. The city is also an ideal base for day trips, especially to the floating markets – the highlight of a visit here.

① Ong Pagoda

🏠 32 Hai Ba Trung St
📞 (0292) 382 3862

Devotees come to this small pagoda to pray before Than Tai, God of Fortune, and Quan Am, Goddess of Mercy.

② Can Tho Museum

🏠 1 Hoa Binh St 📞 (0292) 382 0955 🕐 8-11am, 2-5pm Tue-Thu; 8-11am, 7-9pm Sat & Sun

This excellent large museum illustrates life in Vietnam and the history of the city and province. Exhibits include reproductions of buildings, including a traditional teahouse, a lifelike tableau of a herbalist tending to a patient, and many artifacts. There are also some harrowing war photographs.

③ Munirangsyaram Temple

🏠 36 Hoa Binh St 📞 (0292) 381 6022 🕐 8am-5pm daily

An Angkor-like tower rises over this Khmer Theravada Buddhist temple. Inside, Doric columns blend beautifully with Asian features, such as seated Buddhas and ceramic lotuses.

④ Floating Markets

Can Tho is central for at least two floating markets, which provide a glimpse into a unique commercial culture. Traders paddle from boat to boat, selling a variety of goods amid a traffic jam of sampans.

The morning market of Cai Rang is the closest and largest, located just 4 miles (7 km) southwest of the city. A bridge nearby offers great views, but nothing compares to exploring the market by boat. A farther 9 miles (14 km) west, Phong Dien market possesses an endearing simplicity. Sampans can be

 Munirangsyaram Temple, built in 1946 to serve Can Tho's Khmer community

rented for both these markets from the riverfront off Hai Ba Trung Street or from local tour operators. About 32 miles (52 km) north of Can Tho is a sanctuary for storks, the Bang Lang Stork Garden. The trees attract thousands of storks in the evening: a wonderful sight as they settle down to roost.

---

⑤

Binh Thuy Communal House

🏠 Bui Huu Nghia 📞 (0292) 384 1127 🕐 8am-5pm daily

Built in 1893, this historic building is an interesting fusion of architectural styles, with a French facade and ceilings, a Chinese roof, and

---

Did You Know?

Devotees at the Ong Pagoda often pen their prayers onto scrolls, which are hung on the wall.

Vietnamese wood carvings. Its dark interior is crammed full of antique Chinese furniture and *objets d'art*. Once used for community meetings and religious rites (there are several shrines within the grounds), it has been the residence of the same Chinese family for five generations. As there is no ticket office, the small fee to enter should be paid to whichever household member is present, but visitors are welcome to wander around the oriental-style gardens for free.

---

⑥

Tarot Museum

🏠 44 Nguyen Khuyen St
🕐 9am-10pm daily
🌐 museum-tarot.com

This small museum provides a quirky break from the usual attractions. Housed in a beautiful old building and run by multilingual tarot expert Philippe, it is crammed with tarot cards, historical books, decorative occult objects, and healing stones. Reserve online at least two days in advance.

STAY

Victoria Can Tho

This peaceful resort and spa is housed in a beautiful colonial building on the banks of the Hau River and features two outdoor pools set in a garden.

🏠 Cai Khe Ward
🌐 victoriahotels.asia

$$$

Nam Bo Boutique Hotel

Located near the main pier, this tiny, quirky hotel has seven suites. All have beautiful Asian decor and living rooms with river views. The two roof-terrace restaurants also overlook the river.

🏠 1 Ngo Quyen
🌐 nambocantho.com

$$$

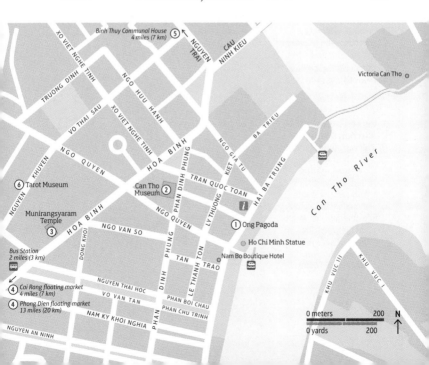

❷
CON DAO ISLANDS

🗺 C7 🕒 62 miles (100 km) off the southern tip of Vietnam ✈ From HCMC
⛴ From Vung Tao ℹ Nguyen Hue St; (0254) 383 0115; www.condao.com.vn

A cluster of 16 islands, Con Dao may be remote but, with its remarkable dense jungles, wildlife, and beaches, it is one of the most astounding destinations in Vietnam. Still relatively little visited other than by Vietnamese tourists, it is a beautiful tropical paradise.

CON SON ISLAND

Often referred to as "Bear Island" because of its shape, Con Son is the largest island in the group and the only permanently inhabited one. About 6 miles (10 km) in length, and with well-marked trails, the entire island can be walked in a day, and has beautiful beaches, coral reefs, and lovely bays.

The idyllic surroundings of Con Son hold the remnants of a sad history. It became a devil's island of sorts after the French built the Phu Hai Prison here in 1862. The abandoned prison can now be visited, a poignant and eerie reminder of the past. Many political dissidents and revolutionaries were imprisoned under horrifically cruel conditions, often kept shackled to the floor.

← Sun setting over the sea of Con Dao; visitors embarking on a snorkeling tour *(inset)*

EAT

Thu Ba Seafood Restaurant
A step up in price and quality from the beach-side seafood shacks, this modern eatery serves delicious, well-presented seafood - try the hotpot.

📍 7 Vo Thi Sua, Con Son Town 📞 (098) 480 1505

Villa Maison Con Dao Kitchen & Wine Bar
This restaurant serves a mix of sublime Vietnamese and international dishes. From local lobster to lemongrass chicken to fillet mignon, you won't be disappointed.

📍 46 Nguyen Hue, Con Son Town 📞 (064) 383 0969

SEA TURTLES

The Con Dao National Park is renowned for its large population of visiting sea turtles, which lay their eggs on many of the islands between April and September. These include endangered species such as the green and hawksbill. Visits to the nesting sites can be arranged. For more information, contact the Con Dao Tourism information office.

A re-creation of this is displayed in one of the cell blocks. In 1954, Phu Hai was handed over to the South Vietnamese, who carried on the tradition. The most inhumane cells were "tiger cages" – tiny holes in the ground with steel bars for roofs. Members of the insurgent Communist party were routinely kept here.

Photographs and exhibits relating to this harrowing past can also be seen at the Bao Tang Con Dao Museum, which has displays on the whole of the islands' history.

For much more cheerful pursuits, the islands boast many spectacular beaches; Dat Doc on Con Son is the most popular. To see the brown booby, a rare bird, visit Hon Trung, an hour's boat ride from Con Son. Tre Nho Island is a great picnic spot.

CON DAO NATIONAL PARK

Declared a nature preserve in 1993, Con Dao National Park covers a massive portion of the archipelago, stretching across 154 sq miles (400 sq km) and offering fantastic wildlife-watching opportunities. About two-thirds of the park is on land, while the rest, including the beautiful coral reefs, is water. These seas are home to more than 1,300 aquatic species, such as sea turtles, dolphins, and dugongs – a mammal belonging to the manatee family. On land are more than 130 species of fauna and 880 types of flora, including orchids unique to the islands. The only home of the pied imperial pigeon, this park is a bird-watcher's dream.

There are several lovely, wild beaches in the Con Dao National Park. Sandy Ong Dung Beach is the most easily accessible from the park entrance, while remote Bang Beach and Dat Tham Beach are more of a trek.

With more than 200 fish species and other marine life, Con Dao is great for diving and snorkeling. The best time to visit, when the seas are calmest, is March to July.

EXPERIENCE MORE

3

My Tho

🗺 C7 **📍** 45 miles (72 km) SW of HCMC on Hwy 1 **🚌** From HCMC to Mien Tay bus station **🚢🛈** Tien Giang Tourist, 8, 30/4 St; www.tiengiangtourist.com

Because of its proximity to Ho Chi Minh City, My Tho, on the northernmost tributary of the Mekong River, is the most popular day-trip destination in the delta. It is an ideal base from which to hire a boat and cruise along the canals, stopping along the way to explore the surrounding islands.

A stroll through My Tho's wide tree-lined boulevards and bustling waterfront market is almost a walk back in time. In fact, the town was founded by Chinese immigrants from Formosa (now modern-day Taiwan) in the 17th century. The French also had a garrison here to oversee the rice and fruit crops production. Wooden boats and barges crowd the shore, as vendors sell an impressive array of goods, from food to hardware and domestic items such as the giant earthenware urns used for bathing. The pungent aroma of dried fish and the fragrance of pineapple, coconut, and jackfruit fill the air.

In addition to commerce, My Tho is also a religious center, with **Vinh Trang Pagoda** being one of its most noteworthy edifices. The temple's facade is embellished with mosaics made from broken pottery, a custom followed throughout Southeast Asia. Lily ponds and stone tombs surround the beautiful complex, and an image of the Buddhist goddess Quan Am is set into the heart of a banyan tree.

Serving the city's large population of Christians, **My Tho Church** functions both as a diocese and a Catholic school. Originally established in the 19th century, the current massive yellow building, with a high-vaulted ceiling and a red-tile roof, sits on sprawling grounds that are covered with trees and shrubs.

A short distance northwest of My Tho is the small but historically significant hamlet of Ap Bac. This was the site of the battle which resulted in the first major victory of the Vietcong against the US-backed South Vietnamese army in 1963.

Did You Know?

Built in 1879, My Tho's Nguyen Dinh Chieu High School was the first in south Vietnam.

Vinh Trang Pagoda
🏠 60 Nguyen Trung Truc St
📞 (0273) 387 3427
🕐 9–11:30am, 1:30–5pm daily

My Tho Church
🏠 32 Hung Vuong St
📞 (0273) 388 0075
🕐 7am–6pm daily

↓ The Vinh Trang Pagoda complex in My Tho, with its pretty gardens

4

Phoenix Island

C7 **2 miles (3 km) from My Tho**

Midway between My Tho and Ben Tre are numerous small islands, with Con Phung or Phoenix Island the best known. This was the lonely bastion of the Coconut Monk. On this small spot of dry land, he built his quaint little **Sanctuary**. On a circular base, about 75 ft (25 m) in diameter, are several free-standing blue-and-gold dragon columns, supporting nothing but the air above them. Nearby is a lattice-work structure resembling a roller coaster flanked by minarets and the monk's impression of a moon rocket. On the upriver side, a huge funerary urn lies on the back of a giant tortoise sculpture. A small coconut candy factory operates on the perimeter of the island.

Nearby are islands that make good picnic venues: Con Tan Long or Dragon Island, home to beekeepers and boatwrights (p103); Thoi Son or Unicorn Island, full of narrow canals that irrigate lush longan orchards; and Con Qui or Tortoise Island, known for its coconut candy and potent banana liquor. Pineapples, jackfruit, and mangoes are grown here in abundance. Each of these islands is served by a scheduled ferry.

Sanctuary
8:30–11am, 1:30–6pm daily

 5

Ben Tre

C7 **53 miles (86 km) SW of HCMC; 9 miles (14 km) S of My Tho** **From HCMC** **From My Tho** **65 Dong Khoi St; (0275) 382 9618**

Somewhat off the tourist trail, Ben Tre does not get as many visitors as other Delta towns,

thus providing a rare glimpse into an ancient river town still living by its traditional ways.

The capital of Ben Tre Province, this town is famous for its coconut candy, and is lush with vast plantations yielding huge amounts of coconuts. To make the candy, the fruit's milk and flesh are boiled down to a sticky mass that is allowed to harden, then cut into small pieces and wrapped in edible rice paper. The process is fascinating to watch and the results delicious.

A "country" market in every sense of the word, the town's central market offers little finery, with preference given to hardware, cloth, and food. The most interesting stalls

↑ Traditional wooden boats plying the waters of the delta near Ben Tre

belong to the fishmongers, who sell a variety of fresh and dried fish.

A notable religious site in Ben Tre is **Vien Minh Pagoda**. Established around 1900, it is now the head office of the provincial Buddhist association. The sparse interior is enlivened by colorful wall hangings and images sporting neon halos.

Vien Minh Pagoda
156 Nguyen Dinh Chieu St
(0275) 381 3931
Sunrise–sunset daily.

COCONUT MONK

The given name of the Coconut Monk was Nguyen Thanh Nam (1909–90). A student of chemistry, he eventually discarded the trappings of his comfortable life and dedicated himself to meditation and abstinence. Subsisting on a diet of coconuts and water, he even started his own religion known as Tinh Do Cu Si, a whimsical blend of Buddhism and Christianity. He challenged the authorities on how to reunify the nation and restore peace after its partition in 1954, and often ended up in jail as a result of his views. The somewhat bizarre temple complex headquarters on Phoenix Island remain the Coconut Monk's most enduring legacy.

→
Red-clad Khmer monks
praying in the sanctuary
of a temple in Tra Vanh

6

Tra Vinh

 C7 ⏱ 62 miles (100 km)
W of Can Tho 🚌 From Vinh
Long and Can Tho 🛈 Phan
Chau Trinh St; (0294) 385
1819

With its large Khmer, Christian,
and Chinese population, Tra
Vinh is distinguished by the
diversity of its places of
worship. Of the many Khmer-
style religious buildings, Ong
Met Pagoda is distinctive for
its portico posts surmounted
by four-faced images of the
Buddha. The 10-ft- (3-m-) tall
gilded *stupas*, mound-shaped
reliquary monuments, are
dedicated to deceased
monks. One of the most
vibrant Chinese pagodas in
town is Ong Pagoda, which
was consecrated in 1556 and
dedicated to the deified
Chinese general Quan Cong of
the 3rd century. The pagoda is
known for its wildly colorful
rear courtyard, one wall of
which is engraved with red
dragons dancing between
blue mountains and a green
sea. A highlight is a fish pond
where richly painted sculpted
carp are shown in mid-leap as
they break through the

surface. These are all the
works of Le Van Chot, who
has a sculpture studio in
the grounds.

However, it is the Tra Vinh
Church that best captures the
spirit of the town's religious
eclecticism. Although its
exterior has a colonial-style
design, a close examination of
the eaves reveals "dragon
flames," typically seen on
Khmer-style temples.

About 4 miles (7 km) south
of town, Hang Pagoda is a
simple structure. Whose main
attraction is the hundreds of
storks that nest here. The
**Khmer Minority People's
Museum** has some interesting
exhibits but there is no
English signage. While household items, costumes, and
jewelry are self-explanatory,
religious items might need a
guide. The museum is located
beside the tree-ringed Ba Om
Pond, about 4 miles (7 km)
southwest of Tra Vinh, which is
ideal for picnics. Also close by
is the Ang Pagoda, a religious
site since the 11th century.
A pride of sculpted lions
guard the entry, flanked by
murals depicting the Buddha's
life. Not far from here is the
small green-and-white
painted Mosque Hoi Giao.

EAT

Meo U Kitchen
This cute Japanese-
Vietnamese fusion
café-restaurant serves
Asian rice and noodle
dishes, including vegan
options and great juices.

 C7 ⏱ 1/7 Hoang Thai
Hieu, Vinh Long
📞 (0270) 222 0168

$⑤$⑤$⑤

**Mr Kiet's Historic
House**
Around 7 miles (11 km)
outside Vinh Long, this
restaurant in a building
dating to 1838 serves
delicious local cuisine,
including "elephant ear"
fish wrapped in rice
paper. Eat in its
authentic interior, or
outside in the garden.

 C7 ⏱ 1924, Phu Hoa
Village 📞 (0273) 382
4498

$⑤$⑤$⑤

The mosque belongs to the region's Cham community and was originally built in 1921.

About 3 miles (5 km) north of Tra Vinh is the small President Ho Chi Minh (Uncle Ho) Temple, built in 1971, just two years after the death of Ho Chi Minh. There is a small museum of his life, with pieces of military equipment placed around its leafy compound.

Khmer Minority People's Museum

4 miles (7 km) SW of town on 3 SEB Luong Hoa St **C** (0294) 384 2188 **O** 7–11am, 1–5pm Fri–Wed

---

Vinh Long

A C7 **Q** 84 miles (136 km) SW of HCMC; 46 miles (74 km) SW of My Tho **E I** Cuu Long Tourist, 1 Thang 5 St; (0270) 382 3656

A big town on the bank of the Co Chien River, Vinh Long is mostly used by tourists as a base for exploring the islets dotting the waters around it. The town's substantial,

French colonial Catholic church shows that the area was once a target for Christian missionaries. On the outskirts of town, **Van Thanh Mieu Temple** is an elegant, simple structure dedicated to Confucius in 1866. In 1930, a new building was added to it in honor of Phan Thanh Gian, who led a rebellion against the French.

Boat tours are a popular way to take in the dramatic sweep of the river and the charm of the offshore islands, most of which have lovely flower gardens. An Binh and Binh Hoa Phuoc are popular amongst visitors as idyllic picnic spots. Just north of the ferry landing at An Binh, is the unassuming Tien Chau

Pagoda. Inside, however, are startlingly lurid murals depicting the horrors of Buddhist Hell – perdition for the lapsed includes being trampled by horses, devoured by serpents, and decomposing eternally.

Vinh Long is an ideal place to experience life on the delta. Surrounded by orchards, sampans, and monkey bridges, the boatwrights, candymakers, beekeepers, and artisans ply their trades. Homestays, where visitors can eat, sleep, and work with a local family, are recommended.

Floating markets are common throughout the delta. Cai Be Floating Market, about an hour from Vinh Long by boat, is the easiest to get to. Open in the early morning, it is both a wholesale and a retail market, with large boats selling to merchants and small boats serving householders. Traders maneuver their boats agilely, loading fruit, coffee, and even hot noodles from one vessel to another.

Van Thanh Mieu Temple

A 2 miles (3 km) S of town on Tran Phu Rd **C** (0270) 383 0174 **O** 8am–sunset daily

↓ Boats carrying their wares at Cai Be Floating Market

8

Cao Lanh

🅰 C7 🚗 100 miles (162 km) from HCMC 🚌ℹ️ Dong Thap Tourist, 6 Do Cong Tuong St; www.dongthaptourist.com

Although a somewhat unremarkable town, Cao Lanh is a pleasant stopping off point on the way to Chau Doc (p106). The **Dong Thap Museum**, which displays many of the implements used by delta farmers and fishermen, is worth a visit. The Soviet-style **War Memorial** is a big clamshell structure, festooned with hammers, sickles, and flags. The cemetery is filled with the graves of Vietcong soldiers. A mile southwest of town is Nguyen Sinh Sac Tomb, a memorial to Ho Chi Minh's father, surrounded by plaques stating his revolutionary credentials.

Stretching away to the north of Cao Lanh, the rich swamplands of Dong Thap Muoi, or Plain of Reeds, are home to many birds. The Tram Chim National Park, 28 miles (45 km) northwest of town, once drew legions of bird-watchers who braved the long boat ride to see the red-headed cranes (spotted from December to May only and an increasingly rare sight). Vuon Co Thap Muoi, about 27 miles (44 km) northeast of Cao Lanh, is home to many white storks.

Southeast of Cao Lanh, the Rung Tram Forest once housed a hidden Vietcong base, Xeo Quyt. This restricted site can be reached by a 30-minute boat ride with permission from the tourist office.

Dong Thap Museum

📍 162 Nguyen Thai Hoc St 📞 (0277) 385 1342 🕐 7–11am, 1–4pm daily

War Memorial

📍 Off Hwy 30 at the eastern edge of town 🕐 Daily

9

Soc Trang

🅰 C7 🚗 39 miles (63 km) SE of Can Tho 🚌ℹ️ Soc Trang Tourist, Ton Duc Thang; (0299) 382 2024

This lively town is famous for its festivals and religious sites. Of the ten annual festivals held in the town, the largest event is the carnivalesque

Khmer festival, Oc Om Boc (p43), in mid-November, with its famous boat racing. Once part of the Angkor Empire, the entire province is home to 90 Khmer, 47 Chinese, and 30 Vietnamese pagodas, many of which are in Soc Trang itself.

Set in beautiful grounds, Khleang Pagoda is a Khmer temple topped by a peaked roof with gables, and festooned with colorful gargoyles. The sanctuary is lit by lotus-motif chandeliers,

HOUSES IN THE MEKONG DELTA

Home to thousands of people who live not only beside the river, but on it, the Mekong Delta is known for two of Vietnam's most distinct forms of house - stilt and floating. While stilt houses line the steep banks, villages of floating homes occupy the river, completely independent of land. Resting on tall bamboo poles, the stilt houses are firmly anchored to the ground. Floating houses, in contrast, sail adrift on pontoons or empty oil drums. Both types of houses are often connected to the shore by a monkey bridge - a crossing made from wooden poles tightly tied together, with only the barest of footholds.

↑ Fishermen casting their v-shaped nets in Bac Lieu

and a splendid gilt Buddha dominates the altar. About 356 ft (200m) east of the Khleang Pagoda is Chua Dat Set, or Clay Pagoda, populated by fantastic clay figures sculpted by Ngo Kim Tong, also known as the Clay Monk, between 1930 and 1970. Standing guard at the door is an almost life-size statue of an elephant, while there is imagery of a golden lion, giant phoenix, and numerous other beasts inside the pagoda.

The **Khmer Museum** doubles as a cultural center, hosting traditional dance and music recitals. The exhibits at the museum include ethnic clothing, crockery, statues, and even a couple of boats. The building itself is a peculiar blend of Khmer and French colonial architecture.

Earning its nickname from the legions of fruit bats living in its dense groves, Chua Doi

or Bat Pagoda is 2 miles (4 km) west of town on Le Hong Phong Street. At sunset, the bats fill the sky like a great screeching cloud. The pagoda also has friendly monks, and vibrant murals inside showing scenes from the Buddha's life.

Xa Lon Pagoda, 9 miles (14 km) west of town, was almost destroyed in 1968 by the intense combat of that year. Today a stout building, with exquisite exterior tile-work, it serves as a pagoda and a Sanskrit school. Also worth a stop is the handsome, Khmer-style Im Som Rong Pagoda, located about one mile (1.6 km) east of Soc Trang.

Khmer Museum

🏠 23 Nguyen Chi Thanh St
📞 (0299) 382 2983 🕐 7:30–11am, 1:30–5pm Mon–Fri

10

Bac Lieu

🅰 C7 🏠 174 miles (280 km) from HCMC; 31 miles (50 km) SW of Soc Trang
 🛈 2 Hoang Van Thu St; www.baclieutourist.com

This small town is primarily an agricultural center, with a major part of its revenue coming from the shrimp and salt farms located along the coast. Most visitors use the place as a base from which to explore the region, including the Bac Lieu Bird Sanctuary a little way out of town.

Bac Lieu also features some fine French colonial buildings, such as the impressive Cong Tu Bac Lieu, once the palace of the prince of Bac Lieu Province. It is now an upscale hotel, the building having been restored to its 1930s splendor, taking visitors on a journey back in time.

The Bac Lieu Bird Sanctuary is about 3 miles (5 km) south of town. Its mangrove forests are home to a splendid variety of species. More than 50 types of birds either reside here or use it as a way station during their annual migrations. There are large, beautiful flocks of white herons, which are the main attraction for most visitors. Guides should be hired at the entrance to the sanctuary. The best months to visit here are between July and December, when bird populations are at their peak, as there is little to see for the rest of the year.

Traveling though the towns and villages of the Mekong Delta by fast boat

outside Rach Gia indicate that Funan's traders had made contact with many nations of the region from the 1st to the 5th centuries AD. A Roman coin has also been unearthed in this area. There is not very much to see at the excavation site, apart from a few foundations.

Kien Giang Museum

 27-D Nguyen Van Troi St ☎ (0297) 386 3727 ⏰ 7:30–11am & 1:30–5pm

---

⓫ Rach Gia

⬛ B7 ⬛ 72 miles (116 km) from Can Tho ⬛ From HCMC ⬛⬛⬛ ⓘ Kien Giang Tourist, 11 Ly Tu Trong St; (0297) 386 2103

A prosperous port town, Rach Gia boasts many religious buildings, such as Sac Tu Tam Bao Tu Pagoda, with its many statues, and the charming Pho Minh Pagoda, which houses an order of mendicant nuns. Its Twin Buddhas, one of which is in Thai style and the other Vietnamese, sit companionably in the sanctuary. The sprawling 200-year-old Phat Lon Pagoda has a unique sanctuary, surrounded by many small altars. The main altar holds images of the Buddha in Khmer regalia. The pagoda has its own crematoria for the disposal of its monks' bodies, and tombs for those chosen for veneration.

The colorful Nguyen Trung Truc Temple is dedicated to a revered national hero who sacrificed his life in the struggle against the French in the mid-19th century. He was executed in Rach Gia's market

square on October 27, 1868. In addition to the pagodas, the town also hosts the **Kien Giang Museum**, with an interesting collection of Oc Eo artifacts and pottery.

The ancient city of Oc Eo was a major trading center of the Indianized Funan Empire, which once extended from southern Vietnam to as far as Malaysia. Artifacts recovered from an archaeological site located 6 miles (10 km)

↑ Statue of militia leader Nguyen Trung Truc, Sac Tu Tam Bao Tu Pagoda

⓬ Chau Doc

⬛ B7 ⬛ 152 miles (245 km) SW of HCMC; 74 miles (119 km) NW of Can Tho ⬛ From HCMC, Can Tho, and Ha Tien ⬛ From Phnom Penh, Cambodia ⬛

Life and commerce in Chau Doc, a bustling border town, centers on the water. Many people live not only by the river in stilt houses, but on it in floating houses (p104). The town's exceptionally busy market is also located along the riverfront.

During a period of several centuries, control over Chau Doc has passed between the Funanese, Cham, Khmer, and Vietnamese. Consequently, it is no surprise that this is one of the most ethnically and religiously diverse towns in the region. It is also home to the Hoa Hao sect, an indigenous Buddhist order founded in the 1930s, and based on the rejection of religious practice and the intercession of priests. The small community of Cham Muslims residing in Chau Doc worship at the green Mubarak Mosque across the Hau Giang River and the larger Chau Giang Mosque.

Neither has a proper address, but boatmen will know how to reach them.

In the town center, the Bo De Dao Trang Plaza is dominated by a statue of Quan Am, Goddess of Mercy, standing in a gazebo. Behind the deity, a statue of the Buddha sits under a tree facing a small pagoda. Close by, Chau Phu Temple is dedicated to a Nguyen lord, and also serves as a tribute to the dead, with many memorial tablets amid colorful artworks.

A sacred site for hundreds of years, Sam Mountain lies 4 miles (6 km) southwest of town. Its slopes are covered with shrines, grottos, pagodas, and ancient tombs. At the northern base lies the Phat Thay Tay An Temple, packed with statues of elephants and monsters – all painted in lurid colors. Close by is Ba Chua Xu Temple, dedicated to a Vietnamese heroine, Lady Xu. Her statue is bathed and clad in finery every May. The view from the mountain's summit is stunning, with the rice fields of Vietnam to the east and the plains of Cambodia stretching away on its west side.

Ha Tien

A B7 **⏱** 190 miles (306 km) W of HCMC; 57 miles (92 km) NW of Rach Gia **🚌** From HCMC and Chau Doc **⛴** From Phu Quoc Island

Overlooking the idyllic shores of the Gulf of Thailand, and surrounded by limestone promontories, Ha Tien is one of the more attractive Delta towns. With its riverfront substantially refurbished and a vast new suburb growing to the west, it is also one of the fastest developing areas. It became a part of Vietnam after a battle with the Thai in 1708. The hero of the war, Mac Cuu, is buried with his family in the Mac Tombs, which are located on a hillside, Nui Lang, just west of town. On the northern side of Nui Lang, the Phu Dung Pagoda contains elegant 18th-century tombs and its sanctuary features fine high-relief panels.

Sitting snugly in a system of caves, halfway up a karst formation about 2 miles (4 km) west of town, Thach Dong Temple goes all the way through the limestone. There are altars everywhere, but the religious focus is on the stone pagoda in the largest cave. A statue of Quan Am stands near its entrance, and a short distance away is the Stele of Hatred. This monument is dedicated to the 130 people killed here by the Khmer Rouge in 1978.

About 18 miles (30 km) to the southeast of Ha Tien lies the secluded beach resort of Hon Chong. At the southern end of the beach is the Hang Pagoda, a grotto with stalactites that resonate like organ pipes when struck. Offshore, Nghe Island has many caves and shrines. At just about an hour away by boat, the island is ideal for a day trip.

Did You Know?

Hac Cuu (1655–1736), a Chinese adventurer, was the founder of Ha Tien.

↑ Boat vendor carrying refreshments on the Mekong River at Chau Doc

EAT & STAY

Mango Bay Resort

Offering a comfortable rustic getaway, this resort's 44 rooms and villas are individually designed and built from natural materials. There are hammocks on the verandas, though the hotels eco-ethic means there are no TVs or air-conditioning.

B7 ☐ Ong Lang Beach
ⓦ mangobay
phuquoc.com

$⑤$⑤$⑤$⑤$

Pepper Tree

One of the finest restaurants on the island, and with the best wine list, Pepper Tree serves high-end Vietnamese and international food in an elegant, sophisticated setting. Perfect for a romantic dinner on the veranda overlooking the beach.

B7 ☐ La Veranda,
Long Beach
ⓦ laverandaresorts.com

$⑤$⑤$⑤$⑤$

Crab House

This is one of the best restaurants in town for seafood lovers. Crab is the obvious choice, but there are excellent, generous dishes of mixed seafood too, all served with delicious dipping sauces. Book ahead.

☐ B7 ☐ 21 Tran Hung Dao, Duong Dong
ⓒ 0773 84506

$⑤$⑤$⑤$⑤$

---

⑭
Phu Quoc Island

☐ B7 ☐ 28 miles (45 km) W of Ha Tien ✈ From HCMC 🚢 From Rach Gia and Ha Tien ⓦ phuquocisland guide.com

Around 31 miles (50 km) long and just 12 miles (20 km) wide, the island of Phu Quoc is developing fast, with most tourist facilities concentrated on Bai Truong (Long Beach). The main town, Duong Dong, is home to a lighthouse and central market. The Vietnamese staple, *nuoc mam* (fish sauce) is produced on Phu Quoc by around 85 manufacturers and connoisseurs can attest to its quality. A fish sauce factory in the town offers tours.

Almost 70 percent of the main island is occupied by the Phu Quoc National Park. Established in 2001, it is covered with tropical forest, waterfalls, and peaks. At present, there are just a few hiking trails, but the pools at the park's southern end are very scenic and make a good

↑ The sandy beach of Bai Truong (Long Beach)

place for swimming. Halfway between Duong Dong town and the park is the Khu Tuong black pepper plantation. Phu Quoc is also blessed with many unspoiled beaches, known in Vietnamese as *bai*. Bai Truong, along the south-west shore, is the best known; lined by many hotels, it offers wonderful sunset views. To its north is the rugged Bai Ong Lang, with other tiny resorts nestled in its coves. Just off-shore is Hon Doi Moi, with a pretty coral reef teeming with marine life, including fish, mollusks, and even turtles and dugongs. It is

Did You Know?

The Phu Quoc Ridgeback, a breed of dog unique to the islands, has webbed feet for swimming.

also great for snorkeling and diving. The An Thoi island group at the southern tip also has a coral reef though this area is now connected to Phu Quoc by a 5-mile- (8-km-) long cable car, which whisks visitors from An Thoi town to Hon Thom Nature Park in 8.5 seconds.

The southeastern shore of the island hosts the barely developed but stunning white-sand Bai Sao and Bai Dam beaches. Scuba gear, island trips, and fishing equipment can be arranged at most resorts. The southwest coast of Phu Quoc is also the home of a fascinating cultured pearl farm with a gallery.

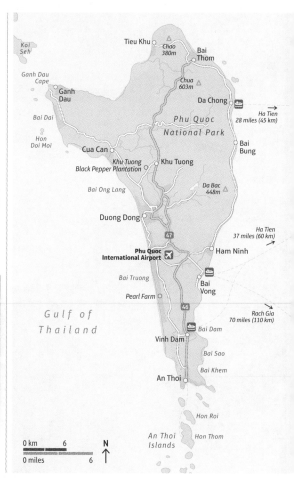

↑ Snorkeling off the An Thoi island group to the south of Phu Quoc

The lush green hills and turquoise blue waters of the Phu Quoc Island ↓

Boats laden with produce at Cai Be floating market

A BOAT TOUR
VINH LONG

Length 5 to 6 hours **Stopping-off points** Binh Hoa Phuoc village is an ideal place to stop for a quick and tasty meal **Boat rentals** Book a boat tour via www.cuulongtourist.com

Possibly the best way of experiencing the timeless, bucolic character of the Mekong Delta is by taking a boat ride along the dense network of narrow canals around Vinh Long. A typical tour makes its way through the small islands of An Binh and Binh Hoa Phuoc, offering a close look at life on the river. Thatched houses sit amid luxuriant orchards and gardens interlaced with the sights and sounds of a colorful and bustling floating market.

MEKONG DELTA AND SOUTHERN VIETNAM

● Vinh Long boat tour

Locator Map
For more detail see p88

A tiny village of farmers, orchardists, and boatmen, Dong Phu has barely changed over the centuries.

Cai Be

The orchards on An Binh island nurture a variety of fruits, including longan, jackfruit, rose apple, and uglifruit, which tastes far better than it looks.

Mekong River

The lively Cai Be floating market is packed with vendors selling a range of goods on boats.

Dong Phu

Hoa Ninh

Phu Phung

An Binh

Binh Hoa Phuoc

Co Chien River

53

Vinh Long

Hoa Ninh is known for its flower gardens filled with jasmine plants, as well as apricot, mango, and longan trees.

Located on an island by the same name, Binh Hoa Phuoc village is known for its bonsai orchards. It also offers cozy homestay facilities.

0 kilometers 2
0 miles 2

N

Surrounded by a patchwork of canals and several islets, Vinh Long is almost an island itself. Situated on the banks of the Co Chien River, it is an ideal base for exploring the region.

↑ Suggested boat tour on the canals around Vinh Long

← Baby jackfruit, picked from orchards on An Binh island

SOUTH CENTRAL VIETNAM

Covering much of the ancient Kingdom of Champa, South Central Vietnam has a densely populated coast scattered with fishing towns and beaches, and a hinterland inhabited by indigenous peoples.

Under the steady influence of seaborne trade, Champa emerged during the 4th century AD as a powerful kingdom. At its peak, it extended from the Ngang Pass in the north to present-day Ho Chi Minh City and the Mekong River Delta in the south. From AD 1000, its power dwindled. By the late 18th century, only tiny Panduranga, extending from Phan Rang to Phan Thiet, held out, but it too fell to the Vietnamese in 1832. Today, Champa's remains, in the form of towers and temples, cluster in the hills of the South Central region. Cham peoples still live in the old region of Panduranga.

SOUTH CENTRAL VIETNAM

Must Sees
1 Nha Trang
2 Dalat

Experience More
3 Dambri and Bo Bla Falls
4 Buon Ma Thuot
5 Lak Lake
6 Ta Cu Mountain
7 Phan Thiet
8 Mui Ne Beach
9 Phan Rang-Thap Cham
10 Yok Don National Park
11 Kontum
12 Quy Nhon
13 Sa Huynh
14 Quang Ngai

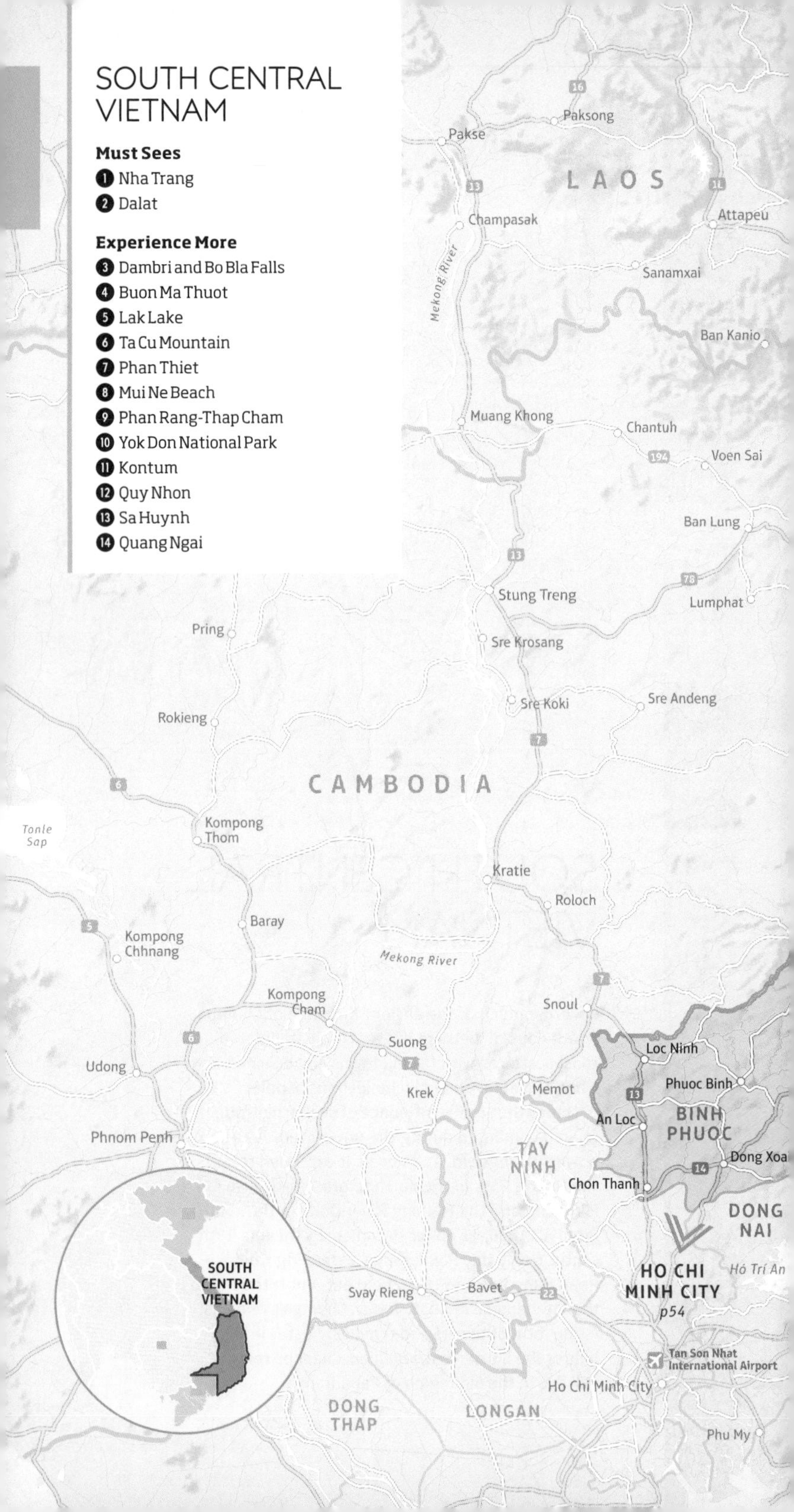

LAOS

Pakse
Paksong
Champasak
Attapeu
Sanamxai
Ban Kanio

Mekong River

Muang Khong
Chantuh
Voen Sai

Ban Lung

Stung Treng
Lumphat

Pring
Sre Krosang

Rokieng
Sre Koki
Sre Andeng

CAMBODIA

Tonle Sap

Kompong Thom

Kratie
Roloch

Baray

Kompong Chhnang
Mekong River

Kompong Cham
Snoul

Loc Ninh
Suong
Phuoc Binh

Udong
Krek
Memot
An Loc
BINH PHUOC

Phnom Penh
Dong Xoa
TAY NINH
Chon Thanh
DONG NAI

SOUTH CENTRAL VIETNAM

Svay Rieng
Bavet
HO CHI MINH CITY
p54
Hó Trí An

Tan Son Nhat International Airport

DONG THAP
LONG AN
Ho Chi Minh City
Phu My

Nha Trang city and its promenade lining the bay

 1

NHA TRANG

🅰 D6 🏠 280 miles (450 km) N of Ho Chi Minh City
✈ 21 miles (34 km) S at Cam Ranh ℹ Khanh Hoa Tourism,
61 Yersin St; www.nhatrang-travel.com

A bustling city and major fishing port, Nha Trang is also Vietnam's primary beach resort. The busy Cho Dam market is at the city's heart, while outside town are the hot springs of Thap Ba and Ba Ho.

①
Long Son Pagoda

🏠 Thai Nguyen St 📞 (0258) 381 6919 🕐 8am–5pm daily

The most revered pagoda in Nha Trang, Long Son sits on the summit of Trai Thuy Hill. Destroyed by a typhoon at the beginning of the 20th century, it was restored several times, most recently in 1940. It is dedicated to the memory of the numerous Buddhist monks who were killed during or died protesting against the repressive regime of South Vietnam's President Ngo Dinh Diem (1955–63). Today, it remains a functioning pagoda, with monks in residence.

The pagoda is distinctly Sino-Vietnamese in style and is decorated with elaborate dragons and ceramic tiles. The main sanctuary is dominated by a giant white sculpture of the Buddha, dating from the 1960s. Seated behind the temple at the top of the hill, the sculpture is reached via 150 steep steps. From here, there are panoramic views over Nha Trang and the neighboring countryside. Another large white Buddha, this time reclining, is located halfway up the steps on the right. It was sculpted by an artisan from Thailand in 2003.

②
Nha Trang Cathedral

🏠 31 Thai Nguyen St
📞 (0258) 382 3335

The seat of the Catholic Diocese of Nha Trang, this church was built in provincial French Gothic style in the 1930s. Stained-glass windows look onto colonnaded cloisters running the length of each side of the building. The three cathedral bells, cast in France in 1786, are still in fine working order.

③
Municipal Beach

Nha Trang has a fine beach, almost 4 miles (7 km) long and sheltered by headlands to its north and south. Tran Phu Street follows its entire length, providing a lovely promenade with great views

↑ The elegant Gothic Nha Trang Cathedral, located near the train station

across the bay. The esplanade area has many hotels and restaurants on the inland side, and numerous cafés and food stalls between the road and the sea. Note that in high season the beach may be less pristine than at off-peak time.

---

④

Alexandre Yersin Museum

🏛10D Tran Phu St ☎(0258) 382 2355 🕓8–11am, 2–4:30pm Mon-Sat

The Swiss physician Alexandre Yersin (1863–1943) moved to Vietnam in 1891 after studying in Paris under the renowned microbiologist Louis Pasteur. He quickly became fluent in Vietnamese and was involved in the founding of Dalat as a hill station in 1893. Yersin introduced cinchona trees to the country for the production of the anti-malarial drug quinine. His most significant achievement came in 1894, when he identified the microbe that causes bubonic plague.

The museum, located in Yersin's former office within the Pasteur Institute, displays his lab equipment, desk, and books. Still operational, the institute produces vaccines and conducts medical research.

---

⑤

Po Nagar Cham Towers

🏛2 Thang 4 St ☎(0258) 383 1569 🕓7:30am–5pm daily

Dedicated to the goddess Yang Ino Po Nagar and one of the most important Cham sites in Vietnam, Po Nagar dates to the 8th century, when it was built by the kings of the Cham principality Kauthara. Although a Cham goddess, Yang Ino Po Nagar is now very much a patron goddess of Nha Trang, venerated by ethnic Viet and Chinese Buddhists, as well as by local Cham Hindus. Of the original eight towers, four remain standing. Built in 817, Thap Chinh, the North Tower, is the most impressive. It houses an image of the Hindu goddess Uma in her incarnation as Po Nagar. At the entrance, her consort, the Hindu god Shiva, dances on the back of his holy mount, the sacred bull Nandi. The columns of a ruined meditation hall also still stand and a small museum displays Cham artifacts.

EAT

Lanterns
Decorated with pretty paper lanterns, this friendly rooftop eatery serves fresh, tasty Vietnamese and Western dishes, and is noted for its seafood claypots. Brilliantly ethical, it caters to veggies, sources ingredients from nearby villages, and supports local charities.

🏛30A Nguyen Thien Thuat 🌐lanternsvietnam.cf

$$$

Sandals
A sophisticated fine-dining venue right on the beach inside the Sailing Club's compound, Sandals has a menu of Vietnamese-Mediterranean fusion dishes. Enjoy superb views of the sun setting over the sea as you dine.

🏛72–74 Tran Phu 🌐sailingclub nhatrang.com

$$$

[Map of Nha Trang showing Cai River, Po Nagar Cham Towers ⑤, Ha Ra Bridge, Dam Market, Long Son Pagoda ①, Bus station 3 miles (4.5 km), Nha Trang Station, Nha Trang Cathedral ②, Alexandre Yersin Museum ④, Municipal Beach ③, Lanterns, Sandals]

0 meters 800
0 yards 800
N

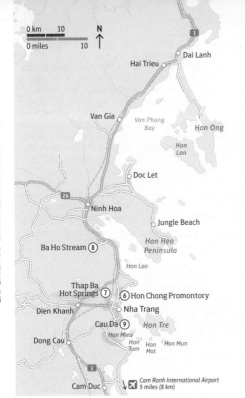

 Dai Lanh
Hai Trieu
Van Gia
Van Phong Bay
Hon Ong
Hon Lon
Doc Let
26
Ninh Hoa
Jungle Beach
Hon Heo Peninsula
Ba Ho Stream ⑧
Hon Lao
Thap Ba Hot Springs ⑦ ⑥ Hon Chong Promontory
Dien Khanh Nha Trang
Dong Cau
Cau Da ⑨
Hon Tre
Hon Mieu
Hon Tam
Hon Mot
Hon Mun
Cam Duc
Cam Ranh International Airport 5 miles (8 km)

0 km   10
0 miles   10
N

AROUND NHA TRANG

⑥
Hon Chong Promontory

 2.5 miles (4 km) N of Nha Trang

Just north of Nha Trang, a stack of boulders named Hon Chong thrusts into the sea, creating a headland that shelters the beach. One of the rocks bears five indentations, said to be the handprint of a giant. The bay is picturesque – though unsuitable for swimming because of several fishing villages in the area – with views of Nha Trang Bay to the south and the mountainous coastline to the north. Nui Co Tien, or Heavenly Woman Mountain, said to resemble the female physiognomy, is to the west. As well as superb views, Hon Chong is a great place for affordable seafood.

⑦
Thap Ba Hot Springs

6 miles (10 km) NW of Nha Trang ⏰ 7am–7:30pm daily 🌐 thapbahotspring.com.vn

Locals and visitors alike gather to wallow in the hot, muddy waters of Thap Ba. The mud is full of sodium silicate chloride and is thought to be beneficial in the treatment of arthritis and rheumatism. It is also said to promote general relaxation. Bathers make a point of rubbing the curative mud all over their bodies, and sit in the sun until it dries and cracks. They then wash the mud off with clean, hot mineral water. Various types of water massage are also on offer, and mineral water swimming pools are available for a post-mudbath dunk.

⑧
Ba Ho Stream

15 miles (25 km) N of Nha Trang

A terrific spot for a picnic, Ba Ho Stream or Suoi Ba Ho rises on the flanks of Hon Long Mountain and then runs east to the South China Sea. The river widens into three adjoining pools, which make for excellent but cold swimming, and each pool is linked to the next by a tumbling cascade of water. There are very few facilities, so take along food and drink. On weekends, the area here can be very busy as it is popular with locals.

⑨
Cau Da

2 miles (3 km) S of downtown Nha Trang

Sheltered in the lee of Chut Mountain or Nui Chut, Cau Da is a suburb of Nha Trang and is the main pier for ferries and boat trips to the islands. Boat trips are operated by many companies and can cost less than $10 including lunch and snorkeling equipment (this does not include extra fees to go ashore on some islands, and boats are often crowded).

The **Oceanographic Institute**, housed in a colonial mansion near the pier, displays an extensive collection of marine specimens.

Oceanographic Institute
1 Cau Da 📞 (0258) 359 0036 ⏰ 6am–6pm daily

350

The number of species of coral found in the area around Nha Trang to date.

BEACHES AROUND NHA TRANG

① Dai Lanh

At the northern end of a long sandy peninsula, Dai Lanh is an idyllic, practically deserted beach mostly surrounded by mountains. It has clear, calm water, which offers safe swimming conditions.

Hon Ong

Sheltered by Van Phong Bay, Hon Ong, or Whale Island, is isolated, pristine, and known for fine diving. It's a good place to see plenty of marine life.

Doc Let

Still relatively untouched by tourism, Doc Let is a magnificent white-sand beach. Jungle Beach, popular with backpackers, is a short motorbike ride away.

Hon Lao

About 1 mile (2 km) off the coast, Hon Lao, popularly known as Monkey Island due to its large population of wild monkeys, has a lovely beach with calm water.

② Hon Tre

Dominated by a 600-ft (180-m) hill, Hon Tre or Bamboo Island is the largest of the islands near Nha Trang. On the northeast coast, the white sands of Bai Tru Beach are home to the luxurious Vinpearl Resort.

Hon Mieu

Regular ferries link Cau Da with the fishing village of Tri Nguyen on Hon Mieu, the closest of the islands in the archipelago. The local aquarium is more of a fish farm, with a café serving seafood overlooking the concrete pools. A gravel beach is nearby at Bai Soi.

③ Hon Mun

Renowned for the best snorkeling in the archipelago due to the large number of coral reefs, Hon Mun is the place to see a wide variety of tropical sealife.

④ Hon Tam

Also known as Silkworm Island due to its green silkworm-shaped appearance, this island of tropical forests, stunning beaches, and clear water, is home to a large eco-resort.

⑤ Hon Mot

The smallest island in the Nha Trang gulf, Hon Mot is popular for snorkeling due to its shallow waters and coral reefs.

↑ The beautiful Xuan Huong Lake in the center of Dalat

DALAT

🗺D6 🏠191 miles (308 km) N of Ho Chi Minh City ✈🚌
ℹ️Dalat Trip, 27 Truong Cong Dinh St; (0263) 351 6888;
www.dalattrip.com

With its cool climate, Dalat was a popular summer retreat for French colonists seeking an escape from the heat of the plains in the early 20th century. Today it draws tens of thousands of Vietnamese honeymooners and holidaymakers, who come for the clean air and beautiful scenery, plus the abundant fresh produce, wine, and local crafts. A short drive away are several impressive waterfalls.

①
Xuan Huong Lake

This crescent-shaped lake right in the town center was created by a dam in 1919 and rapidly became the central promenade for the Dalat bourgeoisie. Once called Le Grand Lac by the French, it was later renamed in honor of Ho Xuan Huong, the celebrated 18th-century Vietnamese female poet whose name means Essence of Spring. Paddling around the waters in a swan-shaped pedal-boat or a more traditional kayak is the most popular activity on the lake. A pleasant walk or cycle along the 4-mile (7-km) shore passes the town's Flower Gardens on the north shore.

②
Dalat Cathedral

🏠Tran Phu and Le Dai Hanh sts 📞(0263) 382 1421
🕐Daily

Dedicated to St Nicholas and adding yet another French touch to this Gallic-inspired hill station, Dalat's Catholic cathedral was established to meet the spiritual needs of the colonists and the many local converts. Construction began in 1931 and was not complete until the Japanese invasion of the 1940s, an event which signaled the beginning of the end of French Indochina. The church has a 155-ft (47-m) spire and vivid stained-glass windows manufactured in 1930s France.

③
Hang Nga (Nga's Crazy House)

🏠3 Huynh Thuc Khang St
🕐8:30am–7pm daily
🌐crazyhouse.vn

You will either love or hate the "Crazy House," as this striking guesthouse is called by locals. Constructed first of wood and wire, it was then covered with concrete to form a treehouse. With giant toadstools, oversized cobwebs, tunnels, and ladders, it is a monstrosity to some and a charming miniature Disneyland to others, especially children. For a small fee, visitors can poke around unoccupied rooms, including one in the belly of a concrete giraffe. Dr Dang Viet Nga, the owner and architect, is the daughter of the former senior Communist Party hardliner Truong Chinh.

④ Bao Dai's Summer Palace

🏠 1 Trieu Viet Vuong St
☎ (0263) 382 6858
🕐 7am–5pm daily

The last Nguyen Emperor, Bao Dai, regarded as a powerless puppet of the French, lived in Dalat from 1938 until 1945, where he spent much of his time hunting and womanizing.

The Summer Palace was built in 1933–8 in a curious, semi-nautical Art Nouveau style, and, with just 25 rooms, it is far from palatial. Visitors can browse the memorabilia on display, which includes Bao Dai's desk and an etched-glass map of Vietnam.

⑤ Dalat Train Station

🏠 1 Quang Trung St, off Nguyen Trai St ☎ (0263) 383 4409

Built in 1932 in imitation of the station at Deauville in France, Dalat Train Station retains its original Art Deco

> Paddling around the waters in a swan-shaped pedal-boat or a more traditional kayak is the most popular activity on the lake.

design. Bombing during the Vietnam War closed the line, but after restoration a Russian engine now travels the picturesque 5-mile (8-km) route to the village of Trai Mat four to five times daily if there are sufficient passengers.

⑥ Lam Dong Museum

🏠 4 Hung Vuong St ☎ (0263) 381 2624 🕐 7:30–11:30am, 1:30–4:30pm Mon–Sat

This museum traces the rich history of Dalat and its surroundings. Exhibits include pottery from the Funan and Champa kingdoms, musical instruments, traditional local costumes, and photographs. The museum is located in front of a 1935 French-style villa, which was the home of Bao Dai's wife, Empress Nam Phuong.

⑦ Thien Vuong Pagoda

🏠 2.5 miles (4 km) from Dalat center on Khe Sanh St

Built by the local Chinese community in 1958, this hilltop pagoda, which has monks in residence, comprises three low, wooden buildings set attractively amid pine trees. In the main sanctuary stand three big sandalwood statues, with Thich Ca, the Historical Buddha, forming the centerpiece.

Did You Know?

"Da Lat" means "river of the Lat tribe" in the language of the local hill people.

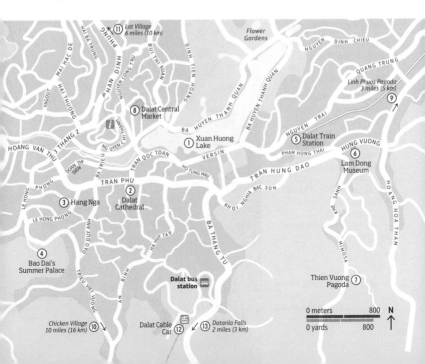

↑ Dalat Cable Car, hanging above mountain forest

(8) Dalat Central Market

⌂ Town center **⊙ Daily**

Nestled in the lee of a tall hillside and surrounded by rows of cafés, Dalat Central Market is among the largest in the country. Food vendors sell grilled corn, meat on skewers, sweet potatoes, hot soy milk, and sweet waffles stuffed with pork and cheese.

(9) Linh Phuos Pagoda

⌂ 3 miles (5 km) NE of Dalat, 120 Tu Phuoc, Trai Mat District **☏ 091 772 12 80** **⊙ 7am-6pm daily**

This temple fuses Buddhist architecture with surreal elements reminiscent of Gaudí's buildings. The whole pagoda is covered in bright mosaics. Within the grounds you'll find a large dragon with scales made from 12,000 empty beer bottles. The tall bell tower is inlaid with broken rice bowls and contains what is believed to be the heaviest bell in Vietnam.

→

Linh Phuos Pagoda, whose every surface is covered in stunning mosaics

(10) Chicken Village

⌂ 10 miles (16 km) S of Dalat, just off Hwy 20

Renowned for the large and rather bizarre statue of a cockerel that stands at its center, Chicken Village, known locally as Lang Ga, draws a large number of sightseers. It is inhabited by the K'ho people, who eke out a living growing fruit and coffee, and making textiles. The village lies just off the highway between Dalat and the coast, and tour buses stop regularly to allow visitors to watch the K'ho women weave and to buy their wares.

(11) Lat Village

⌂ 6 miles (10 km) N of Dalat

Made up of nine hamlets, Lat Village is inhabited mainly by members of the Lat ethnic minority, part of the K'ho tribe, but also by the Ma and Chill. The villagers, once impoverished, are now better off as a result of tourism. The

> **INSIDER TIP**
> **Adventures**
>
> Due to its cool climate and varied landscape, the area around Dalat offers great trekking, rock climbing, cycling, abseiling, and canyoning opportunities. Local tour operators can help organize these.

attraction here is the local weaving and embroidery. There are some fine bargains, but be prepared to haggle.

(12) Dalat Cable Car and Thien Vien Truc Lam

⌂ 2 miles (3 km) S of Dalat, off 3 Thang 4 St/Hwy 20 **⊙ 7:30-11:30am, 1:30-5pm daily**

The Dalat Cable Car hangs across 1.5 miles (2.4 km) of picturesque villages, farmland, and majestic mountain forests, providing panoramic views all the way to Thien Vien Truc Lam, or Bamboo Forest

Meditation Center. This Zen monastery was built in 1993 and houses about 180 monks and nuns. The temple overlooks Paradise Lake, which offers an abundance of free picnic tables and chairs.

---

 (13)

Datanla Falls

🏠 2 miles (3 km) S of Dalat, Hwy 20 ⏱ Daily

Set in the pine-forested hills to the southwest of Dalat, Datanla Falls are only a short distance from town, and a pleasant 15-minute walk from Highway 20. The falls, which tumble down a ravine in two cascades, are a popular destination with Vietnamese tourists. You can either walk down to the falls or ride a roller coaster – for some, this is the chief attraction – that brings you lower into the waterfall area. The surrounding countryside of primitive rain forests is stunning. Note that it is not worth making the visit during the dry season.

EXPERIENCE MORE

3

Dambri and Bo Bla Falls

🅰 D6 🏠 Dambri: 52 miles (85 km) SW of Dalat, off Hwy 20; Bo Bla: 50 miles (80 km) SW of Dalat on Hwy 28 ⏱ 7am–5pm daily

The most spectacular falls in South Central Vietnam are at Dambri, where the water cascades down a 295-ft (90-m) drop. It is a steep climb down but there is an elevator. Above the falls, there is a small lake where boat rides are available. A visit can easily be combined with a stop en route at Bo Bla Falls, another beauty spot.

4

Buon Ma Thuot

🅰 D6 🏠 118 miles (194 km) NE of Nha Trang 🚌 ℹ 3 Phan Chu Trinkh; www.daklak tourist.com.vn

The capital of the Central Highlands province of Dak Lak, Buon Ma Thuot makes a great base for exploring the lakes, rain forests, waterfalls, and hilltribe villages of the surrounding areas. Indigenous minority peoples, the Ede and Mnong, still live in villages throughout the province. The interesting **Dak Lak Ethnology Museum** is a good place to gain an insight into their culture, traditions, and handicrafts, and those of other hilltribes in the region.

The town is Vietnam's coffee capital, ranking second only to Brazil for exports. The coffee plantations here are interesting to visit, but elephant rides in the area should be avoided as there are concerns over the welfare of the animals. Buon Ma Thuot is also significant for being the site of the last major battle of the Vietnam War on March 10, 1975.

Tur, a village located 9 miles (14 km) southwest of Buon Ma Thuot, is inhabited by the Ede minority; their society is matrilineal so property is owned by the women. It is a good place to see Ede wooden longhouses.

Dak Lak Ethnology Museum
 🏠 12 Le Duan ☎ (0262) 385 0426 ⏱ 8am–4pm daily

5

Lak Lake

🅰 D6 🏠 20 miles (32 km) S of Buon Ma Thuot on Hwy 27 ℹ Dak Lak Tourist, 3 Phan Chu Trinh; www. daklak tourist.com.vn

Located in the center of the scenic Dak Lak Plateau, this large, serene freshwater lake was once a favorite retreat of Emperor Bao Dai, who built a hunting lodge on its banks. Although the surrounding hills have been largely stripped of forest, there are still stunning views across the lake. The area is an excellent place to stop for refreshments on the highway between Buon Ma Thuot and Dalat. The people living around Lak Lake are mainly from the Central Highland's Mnong minority.

↑ Canoes floating on the still waters of Lak Lake

↑ The catch of the day being brought in at Phan Thiet

STAY

Xin Chao

A lovely, small family-run hotel a short walk from the beach, Xin Chao has just ten rooms set around a relaxing courtyard, swimming pool, and garden. Providing great value for money, it offers friendly service and has a good restaurant.

🄰D6 🄲129 Nguyen Dinh Chieu, Phan Thiet Ⓦxinchaohotel.com

$$$

Sandunes

A little way out of the centre of Mui Ne Village, the secluded Sandunes has comfortable, stylish rooms and bungalows just a few yards from a quiet area of the beach. With a spa, good restaurant, and a shaded pool, this resort is ideal for recharging the batteries.

🄰D6 🄲5 Quarter, Mui Ne Ward Ⓦsandunesbeach.com

$$$

Ta Cu Mountain

🄰D7 🄲18 miles (30 km) S of Phan Thiet Pagodas and park 🄸(0252) 386 7484

The scenery around Ta Cu is flat and arid, and the mountain, although only 2,100 ft (650 m), affords spectacular views of the coast on clear days. Linh Son Truong Tho Pagoda and Linh Son Long Doan Pagoda, both established in the mid-19th century, are important sites for the many Buddhist pilgrims who come to this holy mountain. However, the main attraction for most visitors is a white Reclining Buddha, 160 ft (49 m) long and claimed to be the largest in Vietnam. It was sculpted in 1962. A cable car, located near Highway 1, is available to carry visitors up the mountain to the huge Buddha; alternatively, it takes two hours to reach the site on foot.

Phan Thiet

🄰D6 🄲125 miles (200 km) E of Ho Chi Minh City 🄱🄴🄴🄸 Binh Thuan Tourism; (0252 381 0801)

This pleasant seaside town has an active fishing fleet and a port along both banks of the Ca Ty River. For visitors staying at nearby Mui Ne Beach, the town is convenient for both shopping and exploration.

Phan Thiet was once at the heart of Panduranga, the last semi-independent Cham principality, which was finally absorbed by the Nguyen Emperor Minh Mang in 1832. The town's Cham name is Malithit, and there is still an appreciable Cham element among the local population. Locally, it is chiefly celebrated for its *nuoc mam* (fish sauce), as is Phu Quoc Island.

Located just 4 miles (7 km) from Phan Thiet, on a hill overlooking the town, stands Thap Poshanu, the southernmost collection of Cham religious buildings within the former Kingdom of Champa. There are three *kalan*, or sanctuary towers, with other supplementary structures dating back as far as the 8th century AD, making them some of the oldest Cham archaeological remnants in the country.

Mui Ne Beach

🄰D6 🄲E of Phan Thiet 🄴🄸 (090) 111 1666; www.muine-phanthiet.com

A 12-mile (20-km) strip of palm-shaded white sand, Mui Ne Beach (Ham Tien) curves

from just east of Phan Thiet to the small fishing village of Mui Ne. The coast is backed by two good roads running parallel for the full length of the beach.

As one of the best beaches south of Nha Trang, Mui Ne's growing reputation inevitably led to constant and ever-increasing development. Almost the entire length of the beach is now overrun with resorts and upscale bars and restaurants. Today the area has become an enclave for Russian tourism. A number of resorts, bars, and restaurants are Russian-owned and street signs can be in Vietnamese, Russian, and English. Above the beach, at Sealinks, is a golf course and there are plans to construct several other courses here.

Activities at Mui Ne include swimming, sunbathing, and, between November and March, kitesurfing and wind-surfing. However, the sea is not suitable for diving.

About halfway along the road to Mui Ne Village, Suoi Tien or Fairy Stream flows through the sand dunes to the sea. Farther east, where the road leaves the beach and curves inland, a track to the north leads to Mui Ne's celebrated sand dunes, where children rent out tray-like bobsleighs for "sand sledding." At Mui Ne Village, maturing vats of quality *nuoc mam* (fish

Shiva statue at the entrance to the largest temple at Po Klong Garai

sauce) fill backyards and gardens. The fishing fleet land their catch in the early mornings, and it is fascinating to wander along the beach by the village, watching the fish merchants from Phan Thiet and farther afield park their pickups on the sand and bargain with the fishermen for the freshly landed catch. Unsurprisingly, the whole area offers great seafood.

9
Phan Rang–Thap Cham

🅰D6 🅰65 miles (105 km) S of Nha Trang 🚆🚌

A twin city located on an arid coastal strip known for its grape and Cham textile production, Phan Rang–Thap Cham is an important road junction linking the coastal provinces with Dalat and the Central Highlands. Thap Cham means Cham Towers, and three of the country's best-preserved Cham religious complexes are situated here.

Po Klong Garai is a group of three brick temple-towers that are remarkably well preserved. Located on a hilltop, the temple was built in the 13th century by King Jaya Simhavarman III. Inscriptions in Cham script are engraved on the entranceway. The temple has a *mukha lingam* with the face of King Jaya Simhavarman III in the main

White sands of the large Mui Ne Beach, lined with palm trees

kalan or sanctuary. A statue of the bull Nandi, Shiva's mount, receives regular offerings. During the Kate Festival each autumn, traditional Cham musical ensembles play here, and folk dancers perform in the temple precincts.

Po Ro Me was built in the 17th century when the Cham principality of Panduranga was in decline. It is one of the biggest towers of the Champa people and also its last. It too sits on a hilltop, but is more difficult to access than Po Klong Garai and a motorbike is recommended to reach the temple. The tower is dedicated to King Po Ro Me, and there is an image of him on a *mukha lingam* inside. A third temple complex, Hoa Lai, is located a few miles north of Phan Rang.

Pleasant Ninh Chu Beach, shaded by casuarina trees, is located 4 miles (6 km) east of Phan Rang. During his regime (1967–75), it was reserved for President Nguyen Van Thieu and his cronies.

Po Klong Garai
♿ 🅰Route 27, 4 miles (6 km) W of Thap Cham 🕐Sunrise-sunset daily

Po Ro Me
🅰6 miles (9 km) S of Thap Cham 🕐Sunrise-sunset daily

Yok Don National Park

D5 26 miles (40 km) NW of Buon Ma Thuot Or minibus from Buon Ma Thuot yokdonnational park.vn

The largest of Vietnam's national parks, Yok Don covers almost 470 sq miles (1,200 sq km), extending along the Cambodian frontier and cut through by the Dak Krong or Serepok River. The park is home to leopards, tigers, and wild elephants, but of the 67 species of mammal, 38 are endangered, and the chances of seeing the larger mammals are slight. The once large herds of wild elephants have diminished to fewer than 20 animals, and the number is falling.

Half-day treks include a visit to a Mnong village, the main attraction for most visitors. Shops selling handicrafts and sealed pots of *ruou can*, rice liquor, complete with bamboo drinking straws, are clustered around the park's entrance. Accommodations are available just beyond the northern limits of the park, and difficult to access without a private vehicle and government guide, Thap Yang Prong is the most remote of all Vietnam's Cham towers, and an indication of the outposts and settlements of the former Kingdom of Champa during the 13th and 14th centuries.

Kontum

D5 125 miles (200 km) NE of Quy Nhon 2 Phan Dinh Phung St; www.komtumtourism.com

This remote, laid-back town receives relatively few visitors. Despite being heavily bombed during the Vietnam War, Kontum has retained two beautiful French colonial wooden churches and a few French-style shopfronts. However, most visitors come here to explore the surrounding countryside and the many minority villages, with their trademark *nha rong* or communal houses. East of town, the **Seminary Museum**, within an old French Catholic seminary, displays minority handicrafts and clothing.

Ethnic groups, including Jarai, Sedang, Rongao, and Bahnar, inhabit villages in the region, many of which can be easily accessed from Kontum.

Within walking distance, the Bahnar village of Kon Kotu is about 3 miles (5 km) east of town. This community's *nha rong* is made of bamboo and wood, with an immensely tall thatched roof. Kon Hongo, 2.5 miles (4 km) to the west of Kontum, is home to the Rongao minority.

Seminary Museum

56 Tran Hung Dao St 7:30–11am, 2–5pm Mon–Fri

Quy Nhon

D5 137 miles (220 km) N of Nha Trang 187 Phan Boi Chau; www. binhdinhtravel.com.vn

A fishing port with reasonable beaches, Quy Nhon sees few visitors. Long Khan Pagoda, Quy Nhon's most revered Buddhist temple, dates back to the early 18th century, and is dedicated to Thich Ca, the Historical Buddha. Quy Nhon also has many ancient Cham temples. There is a busy beach in town, but better stretches of sand are located 3 miles (5 km) to the south, including Quy Hoa Beach. Quy Nhon is, however, an excellent place to see Vietnamese martial arts; there are many dojos in and around the city (these are listed on the tourism website).

The Thap Doi Cham or Double Cham Towers, thought

← Typical *nha rong* or communal house of the Jarai minority

↑ Quy Nhon beach, scattered with small fishing boats

to date from the second half of the 12th century, are 1 mile (2 km) west of the town center. One of the major surviving works of Cham architecture, Banh It, or Silver Tower, stands on a hilltop near Highway 1, about 12 miles (20 km) north of Quy Nhon. Farther north along Highway 1 are the few remains of Cha Ban. Called Vijaya it was capital of the Cham principality. Founded in AD 1000, the city was razed to the ground in 1470 by the Dai Viets, signalling the end of Champa as a kingdom.

---

⑬ Sa Huynh

D5 ⬛37 miles (60 km) S of Quang Ngai 🚌

Known for its palm-fringed beach and salt pans, this attractive little fishing port is the site of the pre-Champa culture of Sa Huynh, which flourished around 2,000 years ago. In 1909, 200 burial jars were unearthed in the area. Unfortunately, no artifacts of this Bronze-age society are on show here; the remains can be seen in the National Museum of Vietnamese History in Hanoi (p178), and at the Museum of

Sa Huynh Culture in Hoi An (p134). The town's laid-back atmosphere is what attracts visitors. It is a great place for seafood and the beach is relatively deserted, with sufficiently strong waves for surfing.

---

⑭ Quang Ngai

D4 ⬛110 miles (177 km) N of Quy Nhon 🚌🚌 ℹ310 Quang Trung St; www. quangngaitourist.com.vn

This sleepy provincial capital is a hidden gem, with ancient archaeological finds a short drive away. Five miles (8 km) northeast of the city, the 1,200-year-old Chau Sa

citadel is evidence that the Cham once controlled the area. Closer to the western mountains, an ancient wall stretches 79 miles (127 km). It was built in 1819 by the Vietnamese for security and trade regulation between the Hre minority and the Viets.

Motorbike taxis in Quang Ngai also make the 9-mile (15-km) trip east to Son My, the site of the appalling My Lai Massacre of 1968. A chilling Memorial Park has been set up in the sub-hamlet of Tu Cung, and a dark granite museum documents the events in horrific detail. On display are the photographs of the atrocity that shocked the world and contributed substantially to American disillusionment with the war.

MY LAI MASSACRE

During the Vietnam War, the area around Quang Ngai was considered sympathetic to the Vietcong. On March 16, 1968, a strong force of US infantry moved into the area, seeking revenge for the deaths of colleagues there. Over the next four hours, in the worst documented US war crime of the Vietnam War, about 500 Vietnamese civilians were systematically murdered, half of them women and children, as the US soldiers ran out of control. Lieutenant William Calley, who organized the massacre, was convicted of murder but released pending appeal on the orders of President Nixon. No others were convicted.

Multicolored lanterns in a shop in Hoi An

CENTRAL VIETNAM

The ancient Kingdom of Champa began in this region in the 2nd century and flourished for more than 1,000 years. The Cham temple complex at My Son, which was constructed between the 4th and 12th centuries AD, is the most famous Cham site. The Vietnamese defeated Champa in the 15th century, and in the following centuries Chinese, Japanese, and French traders established a foothold in Hoi An, which still houses structures dating to the 16th century. In 1802, Vietnam's last royal dynasty, the Nguyens, set up court at Hue, which became the center of intellectual excellence and spiritual guidance, exemplified by the Citadel and Royal Tombs. Not far north of Hue, Vietnam was partitioned into North and South in 1954, to form a Demilitarized Zone, which witnessed some of the bloodiest battles during the Vietnam War, and stands as a grim reminder of the vicious struggle of that era. Battle sites such as Khe Sanh and Vinh Moc have become poignant places of pilgrimage and mourning for both the Vietnamese and Americans.

CENTRAL VIETNAM

Must Sees
1 Hoi An
2 My Son
3 Hue Citadel
4 Hue
5 Royal Tombs of Hue

Experience More
6 Danang
7 Marble Mountains
8 Monkey Mountain
9 Ba Na Hill Station
10 China Beach
11 Bach Ma National Park
12 Suoi Voi
13 Lang Co Beach
14 Thuan An Beach
15 Khe Sanh Combat Base
16 Demilitarized Zone
17 Vinh Moc Tunnels
18 Dong Hoi
19 Phong Nha-Ke Bang National Park
20 Son Doong Cave
21 Kim Lien

17 VINH MOC TUNNELS

16 DEMILITARIZED ZONE

Vinh Linh

Ben Hai

Gio Linh

Dong Ha

Quang Tri

9

1A

THUAN AN
14 BEACH

HUE
3 4 5

Phu Bai
International Airport

Vinh Thanh

South China Sea

14

A Luoi

49

THUA THIEN
HUE

Phu Loc

SUOI
VOI
12

13 LANG CO BEACH

BACH MA
11 NATIONAL PARK

DANANG

Hai Van Pass

8 MONKEY MOUNTAIN

BA NA
HILL STATION 9

DANANG 6
10 CHINA BEACH
7 MARBLE MOUNTAINS

Prao

604

Da Nang
International Airport

1 HOI AN

14

Dai Lanh

Dai Loc

2 MY SON

Ha Lam

Thanh My

14B

1

QUANG NAM

14E

Tam Ky

Kham Duc

Tien Ky

Chu Lai
Airport

Phuoc Son

Nui Thanh

Tra My

14

Ban Daktiam

Ngoc Linh
8,523 ft (2,598 m)

SOUTH CENTRAL
VIETNAM
p112

1

HOI AN

 **D4** 🏠 **493 miles (793 km) S of Hanoi** 🚌 **From Danang** 🚤
ℹ️ **567 Hai Ba Trung (admission tickets for sights in the Old Quarter can be bought at the Tourist Office)**
🌐 **hoian-tourism.com**

Located on the north bank of the Thu Bon River, the picturesque, historic town of Hoi An was an important trading port from the 16th to the 18th century. Attracting traders from China, Japan, and Europe, the town acquired a rich cultural heritage, rivaled by few other places in Vietnam. A UNESCO World Heritage Site, Hoi An's Old Quarter reflects both indigenous and foreign influences and has a wide array of restaurants and shops.

① 🍴 🛍

House of Phung Hung

🏠 **4 Nguyen Thi Minh Khai St** 📞 **(0235) 386 2235** 🕐 **8am-6pm daily**

Built in 1780 and home to eight generations of the same family, this house shows a Chinese influence in the galleries and window shutters, and Japanese influence in the glass skylights. The general layout and design is Vietnamese in style.

②

Japanese Covered Bridge

🏠 **Intersection of Tran Phu and Nguyen Thi Minh Khai sts** 🕐 **Sunrise-sunset daily**

One of the Hoi An's most prominent landmarks, this rust-colored bridge was constructed in 1593 by the prosperous Japanese trading community, who were based on the west side of the town,

in order to link it with the Chinese quarter farther to the east. However, in 1663, the Tokugawa Shogun Iemitsu issued edicts forbidding the Japanese from trading abroad, thus bringing the community to an abrupt end. In 1719, a Vietnamese temple was built into the northern section of the structure. Although a new name for the bridge, Lai Vien Kieu or Bridge from Afar, was carved over the temple door, locals continue to call it the Japanese Bridge. Roofed in grey tiles, the bridge combines grace and strength in its short span across a tiny tributary of the Thu Bon River. It is a convenient pedestrian link between the art galleries of Tran Phu Street to those in the western part of town.

Did You Know?

The shrine on the Japanese Bridge contains an effigy of Bac De, god of the weather.

↑ Characteristic dark-yellow houses by the Thu Bon River in Hoi An's Old Quarter

STAY

La Residencia
With its fusion of 19th-century Portuguese architecture and traditional Hoi An decor, this boutique hotel will transport you back in time. Though a little short on amenities, it has bags of charm.

🏠 35 Dao Duy Tu St
🌐 laresidenciahotel.com

$$$

Anantara Hoi An Resort
Housed in a colonial-style building by the river, this five-star resort is in a peaceful spot yet only a short walk from the center. The spacious, split-level rooms fuse European and Asian styles. Balconies overlook gardens or the river.

🏠 1 Pham Hong Thai Street
🌐 anantara.com

$$$

③

Cantonese (Quang Dong) Assembly Hall

🏠 176 Tran Phu St
🕐 8am–5pm daily

Quang Dong is the Vietnamese name for the Chinese province of Guangdong, which was formerly known as Canton by Western countries. Built by seafaring merchants in 1786, the Assembly Hall is enlivened by bas-reliefs and colorful hangings. The main altar is dedicated to the great warrior Quan Cong, identifiable by his red face – emblematic of loyalty in Chinese society. Thien Hau, Goddess of the Sea, is also revered here. Look out for the mosaic dragon statue by the entrance hall and an even bigger dragon statue in the garden.

A "boat lady" waiting for her next customer on the colorful quayside outside Tan Ky House ↑

④

Museum of Sa Huynh Culture

🏠 149 Tran Phu St 📞 (0235) 386 1535 🕗 8am-5pm daily

The small port of Sa Huynh, 99 miles (160 km) south of Hoi An, was the site of an eponymous prehistoric culture dating to 1000 BC–AD 200. In 1909, more than 200 burial jars filled with bronze tools, ornaments, ceramics, and the remains of the dead, were unearthed at Sa Huynh. These fascinating artifacts, characterized by a very distinctive style of bronze work, can be admired in this small museum, which is housed in a fine Franco-Vietnamese building.

⑤

House of Tan Ky

🏠 101 Nguyen Thai Hoc St 📞 (0235) 386 1474 🕗 8am-noon, 1:30-5:30pm daily

Perhaps the most celebrated of Hoi An's many traditional abodes, the House of Tan Ky is an excellent representation of an authentic 18th-century Sino-Vietnamese shophouse style of construction. Built around a small courtyard, this two-story structure, as is often the case in Hoi An, is an architectural hybrid. It carries fine Chinese crab-shell motifs on the ceiling, while its roof is supported by typically Japanese triple-beam joists. The floor is made with bricks

imported from Bat Trang in the Red River Delta. Exquisite mother-of-pearl inlay Chinese poems hangs from the columns that support the roof.

⑥

House of Quan Thang

🏠 77 Tran Phu St 🕗 7:30am-5pm daily

This one-story shophouse is a fine example of craftsmanship typical of Hoi An's traditional dwellings. Dating from the 18th century, the house was built by a seafaring trader from Fujian in China, whose family have lived and prospered here for the last six generations. The house has a dark teak facade, and is roofed in curved Chinese-style tiles. It can be accessed via the shop front, which leads into an interior courtyard whose walls are adorned with stucco bas-reliefs of flowers and trees. Beyond this beautiful courtyard is a narrow terrace used for cooking purposes. The wooden windows and shutters are finely carved.

→

The Tran family Chapel, built in 1802, honoring the Tran family ancestors

CULTURAL AND ARCHITECTURAL MIX

A mosaic of cultures, Hoi An has a unique amalgamation of architectural styles, not seen elsewhere in Vietnam. In particular, Japanese, Chinese, and French influences are evident in Vietnamese tube houses, which feature Chinese tiled roofs, Japanese support joists, and French louvered shutters and lampposts.

> In 1909, more than 200 burial jars filled with bronze tools, ornaments, ceramics, and the remains of the dead, were unearthed at Sa Huynh.

Tran Family Chapel

🏠 21D Le Loi St ☏ (0235) 386 1723 ⏰ 7:30am–5pm daily

This ancestral shrine was established more than two centuries ago to honor the forefathers of the Tran family. These venerable ancestors moved to Vietnam from China in the early 18th century, and settled in Hoi An. The current descendants claim that they are the 13th generation since the migration from China. Over time, members of the family intermarried with local Vietnamese natives, and the chapel is appropriately hybrid. Artifacts belonging to the ancestors and memorial tablets decorate the main altar. A forefather who achieved the rank of mandarin is honored in a portrait in the reception hall of the chapel.

Museum of Trading Ceramics

🏠 80 Tran Phu St ☏ (0235) 386 2944 ⏰ 7:30am–5pm daily

Housed in a traditional timber shophouse, with balconies and wood paneling, this museum is dedicated to Hoi An's historic ceramic trade, which flourished from the 16th to 18th centuries. Many pieces on display were recovered from shipwrecks, some near Cham Island off the mouth of Thu Bon River, and include items from China, Japan, and Southeast Asia.

EAT

Morning Glory Original

One of many local eateries run by renowned local chef Trinh Diem Vy, Morning Glory Original is housed in a beautiful yellow colonial building downtown. The outstanding regional street-food-style dishes include *cao lau* (noodles with pork and local greens).

🏠 111 Nguyen Thai Hoc ☏ (0235) 224 1555

$$$

The Sea Shell

Shaded by an old banyan tree, this garden restaurant serves a mix of Asian and Western dishes, and has a good variety of vegan options. Most famous for its *banh bao* (steamed pork) buns, it also serves fresh, modern salad mains and cheesecake.

🏠 119 Tran Cao Van ☏ (091) 429 8337

$$$

The Temple Restaurant

A top Hoi An fine-dining venue, The Temple Restaurant offers sophisticated French and Italian dishes served with an Asian twist in a romantic poolside setting. It's also very popular for its superlative breakfast buffet.

🏠 La Siesta Resort, 132 Hung Vuong Street 🌐 lasiestaresorts.com

$$$

↑ The busy Central Market in Hoi An, selling a vast array of foodstuffs, silks, and handicrafts

Phuc Kien Assembly Hall

🏠 46 Tran Phu St
📞 (0253) 386 1252
🕐 7:30am–5pm daily

A flamboyant building with a lovely garden in front, this assembly hall was founded by merchants who had fled from the Chinese province of Fujian after the downfall of the Ming Dynasty in 1644. The temple complex is dedicated to Thien Hau, Goddess of the Sea, who is regarded as the savior of sailors. She presides over the main altar in the first chamber, and is flanked by attendants who are said to alert her whenever there is a shipwreck. To the right of the altar is a detailed model of a sailing junk, while in a chamber at the back, an altar honors the founding fathers, represented by six seated figures.

> **At Hoi An Artcraft Manufacturing Workshop visitors can watch artisans at work, or make their own lanterns under expert supervision.**

Quan Cong Pagoda

🏠 24 Tran Phu St
🕐 7am–6pm daily

Also known as Chua Ong, this pagoda was founded in 1653, and is dedicated to the 3rd-century Chinese general, Quan Cong, a member of the Taoist pantheon. An impressive gilded statue of him presides over the main altar, accompanied by two fierce-looking guardians, and a white horse, Quan Cong's traditional mount.

Hainan Chinese Assembly Hall

🏠 10 Tran Phu St 🕐 8am–5pm daily

This assembly hall was built in 1875 by Hoi An's immigrant

SHOP

Hoi An is famous for its many tailors. Show them a photograph and they will create an almost identical outfit. It is worth paying a bit more for a good tailor. Allow several days for attending fittings.

Be Be Tailor
One of the town's most established and reputable tailors. You can browse their website for ideas before going to one of the three outlets for a fitting.

🏠 11 Hoang Dieu
🌐 bebetailor.com

Kimmy Tailor
Hoi An's oldest tailoring establishment is owned and run by a Canadian-Vietnamese couple who have a good understanding of Western tastes and fashion.

🏠 70 Tran Hung
🌐 kimmytailor.com

community from Hainan Island in China. It is dedicated to the memory of 108 Hainanese seafarers killed by a renegade Vietnamese pirate-general in 1851. A lacquered board in the entry hall recounts their story in Chinese characters.

Central Market

🏠 Between Tran Phu and Bach Dang sts 🕐 Sunrise-sunset daily

Best visited in the morning, when the pace is not frantic, this lively market occupies two narrow streets that run

→

Sun loungers on the white sands of the popular Cua Dai Beach

south from Tran Phu to the banks of the Thu Bon River. There are stalls selling all kinds of fresh produce, kitchen utensils, and other equipment. To the east of the wharf is the market specializing in fresh seafood and meat. The main draws, though, are Hoi An's popular fabric and clothing stores, which specialize in exquisite and inexpensive silks. Custom-made outfits can be ordered in several days.

 ⑬

Hoi An Artcraft Manufacturing Workshop

🏠 9 Nguyen Thai Hoc St
📞 (0235) 391 0216
🕐 7am–6pm daily

This handicrafts workshop specializes in the production of elegant lanterns, a specialty of Hoi An. The lanterns are handmade, using silk mounted on bamboo frames. Visitors can watch artisans at work, or make their own lanterns under expert supervision. Traditional recitals featuring the *dan bau*, a Vietnamese stringed musical instrument, are also staged in the workshop (at 10:15am and 3:15pm daily), and refreshments are available for visitors in the courtyard.

⑭

Cua Dai Beach

🏠 3 miles (5 km) E of Hoi An

Cua Dai Beach is most easily reached by cycling down Cua Dai Road. The white sands look out onto the islands of the Cham archipelago, making it a much-visited destination. Attractive hotels line the route and front the beach.

MY SON

D4 **25 miles (40 km) SW of Hoi An** **From Hoi An and Danang** **(0510) 373 1757** **6:30am–5pm daily**

The religious and political capital of the Champa Kingdom between the 4th and 13th centuries, My Son contains the remains of a series of spectacular temples, surrounded by mountains.

The unique Champa culture owed its spiritual origins to the Hinduism of the Indian subcontinent. Many of the temples were built to Hindu divinities, such as Shiva, Krishnu, and Vishnu. The site of My Son became known to the world when French archaeologists rediscovered it in the late 1890s. Traces of around 70 temples remain, though only about 20 are in good condition. Today, My Son is a UNESCO World Heritage Site.

Evocative as the complex is, the monuments are rather unimaginatively named after letters of the alphabet; the temples are divided into 11 groups by archaeologists, the most important of which are Groups B, C, and D. Group A was almost completely destroyed by US bombing during the Vietnam War. The most striking edifices are the famous Cham towers, which are divided into three parts: the base represents the earth, the center is the spiritual world, and the top is the realm between earth and heaven.

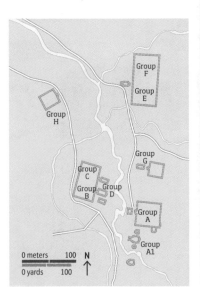

Group F
Group E
Group H
Group G
Group C
Group B
Group D
Group A
Group A1

0 meters   100   N
0 yards   100   ↑

Did You Know?

At one point, the tops of some of the temple towers at My Son were covered in a layer of gold.

←
My Son sanctuary, a fascinating example of Hindu art and architecture

↑ Restored ancient temple ruins in the Group G complex

EXPLORING MY SON

Although centuries of pillage and more recent bombings have taken their toll, the ruins at My Son provide a glimpse into a fascinating Indianized culture. Today, with aid from UNESCO, archaeologists are still struggling to piece together what remains of the site. Although, the French left detailed architectural drawings, the task remains all but impossible, and much of My Son has disappeared forever.

Groups A and A1

Said to be among My Son's most impressive edifices, Groups A and A1 were almost completely destroyed by USAF bombing in 1969. Little remains beyond rubble, but there are plans for restoration. Records show that Group A once featured a striking

tower, A1, said to have been the most important *kalan* (sanctuary) here. Unlike most Cham temples, which only face east, A1 also had a door to the west, usually associated with death. This may have served as a link to

the Cham kings said to be interred in Groups B, C, and D. Also noteworthy is A9, with its winding patterns.

Groups B, C, and D

Situated at the center of the complex, Group B is

 INSIDER TIP
Visiting Hoi Son

Arrive early and carry a hat, sun-screen, and bottled water. Stay on well-trodden paths – the area still has some unexploded mines.

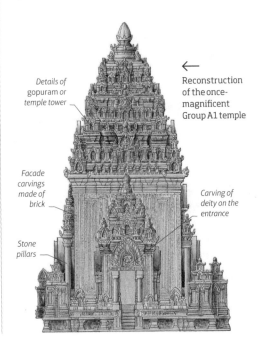

← Reconstruction of the once-magnificent Group A1 temple

Details of gopuram or temple tower

Facade carvings made of brick

Stone pillars

Carving of deity on the entrance

remarkable for exhibiting elements of both Indian and Javanese art. The main sanctuary, built in the 11th century, was dedicated to King Bhadravarman, who built the first temple at My Son in the 4th century, and to Shiva. The *lingam* in B1 is particularly well preserved. A phallic symbol associated with Shiva, the *lingam* is shown within or above the *yoni*, a symbol of the goddess. Water was poured over the *lingam* and flowed through a spout on the *yoni* to symbolize creation. Built in the architectural style of structures at Dong Duong, another Cham city, the ruins at B4 feature religious images carved on stone pilasters and elaborately embellished false doors. Finely carved stone pillars dating from the 8th century distinguish the ruins of B5. The 10th-century tower was used as a repository for temple treasures. It shows traces of the architectural marvel it was, with a boat-shaped roof, carved pilasters, and fine reliefs of Gajalakshmi, Goddess of Prosperity.

Group C forms a contiguous complex with Group B, separated only by a brick wall. Its central tower, C1, combines many elements from the older structures, including the tympanum and lintel. The 8th-century celestial figures on C1 show distinct Javanese influence. The low wide belts worn by the figures are thought to be of Indian origin,

and it is believed that the style came to Cham via Indonesia. Built in the late 8th century, C7 is a squat tower with a stone altar, and is an architectural link between the styles of the Cham cities of Hoa Lai and Dong Duong.

Toward the east of Groups B and C, the *mandapa* or meditation halls of Group D are galleries for sculpture. Shiva *lingam*, as well as statues of Shiva and Nandi, are housed in D1, while D2 contains a stone Garuda, a Dancing Shiva, and *apsaras*.

Groups E, F, G, and H

Although the monuments in the northernmost reaches of the complex are the most damaged, they still offer fragments of beautiful craftsmanship. Built between the

↑ Evocative remains of a Shiva temple in Group B

8th and 11th centuries, Group E differs from the usual design of Cham temples. The main *kalan* has no vestibule, and only one temple faces eastward. Adjoining it, Group F has a finely carved *lingam* in the altar. The 11th-century Group G has been restored. Its tower's base features bas-reliefs of Kala, God of Time. Not much remains of Group H, but a carved stone tympanum of a Dancing Shiva that once adorned the temple is in the nearby Museum of Cham Sculpture *(p155)*.

↑ Kirtimukha (fierce monster) face on a temple in Group G

CHAM ART AND SCULPTURE

The Cham Empire existed in Vietnam for around 1,600 years, from the 2nd century AD to 1832. Today, a thriving Cham community survives, but all that remains of their ancient kingdom is its artistic legacy, which reached its zenith in the 8th to 10th centuries. Part of this heritage is architectural, visible in the red-brick temples scattered across Central Vietnam. Other elements are sculptural, carved chiefly in sandstone and marble or, more rarely, in bronze, at sites such as Tra Kieu, My Son, and Dong Duong. Religious in inspiration, Cham art derives from the Indic tradition and represents Hindu deities with celestial mounts, dancing girls, and demons.

 ③

HUE CITADEL

📍 D4 📍 23 Thang 8 St, Hue ✈️🚉 From HCMC and Hanoi
🚌 From Danang 🛈 11 Nguyen Cong Tru St; (0234) 381 6263
🕐 7am–5pm daily

Built between 1805 and 1832, the vast Hue Citadel formed the capital of the Nguyen Dynasty until 1945. At its very heart lies the once-magnificent Imperial City – a royal fortress and palace, adjoining which was the Forbidden Purple City, with a theater and library.

Designated a World Heritage Site in 1993, the Citadel was established by Emperor Gia Long (r.1802–20). The huge fortress comprises three concentric enclosures – the Civic, Imperial, and Forbidden Purple cities. The Citadel was designed using the rules of Chinese geomancy, along with the military principles

favored by French architect Sebastien de Vauban. The result is an unusual yet elegant complex, where beautiful palaces and temples coexist with massive ramparts, bastions, and moats. Despite the horrific damage caused by the Indochina Wars, restoration work has re-imagined some of the Citadel's lost architectural grandeur.

The Imperial City, also known as Dai Noi or the Great Enclosure, epitomizes the days of royal glory. This historic and particularly evocative part of the Citadel has undergone extensive restoration, allowing more than just a glimmer of its former glory and grandeur to shine through. Entrance to the Imperial City is via the

↑ Entrance to the Thai Hoa Palace, which housed the emperor's throne room

imposing Ngo Mon Gate, beyond which a bridge leads between lotus-filled ponds to the splendid Thai Hoa Palace. Behind this is an open courtyard that overlooks a stretch of land, once home to the Forbidden Purple City.

 ①

Ngo Mon Gate

The majestic main entrance to the Citadel, Ngo Mon is a superb example of Nguyen architecture. Massive stone slabs form the foundation, upon which rests the elaborate Five Phoenix Watchtower.

②

Cot Co or Flag Tower

Looming over the Citadel, the Flag Tower or Cot Co has dominated Hue's skyline since 1809, when Emperor Gia Long erected it over a big 59-ft (18-m) brick redoubt. On January 31, 1968, during the Tet Offensive, Cot Co achieved international recognition

Did You Know?

The golden dragon was the symbol of the Nguyen Dynasty.

when the Communist forces seized the Citadel, hoisting the National Liberation Front's yellow-starred banner on the Flag Tower's mast.

③

Nine Deities' Cannons

Cast by Emperor Gia Long in 1803 as symbolic protection for his new capital, these colossal cannons were made out of bronze. Each weapon is said to represent one of the four seasons and five elements – earth, metal, wood, water, and fire. The cannons can be seen flanking the Ngan and Quang Duc Gates on either side of Cot Co.

④

Five Phoenix Watchtower

This ornate pavilion was where the emperor sat enthroned on state occasions. Viewed from above, it is said to resemble a group of five phoenixes. The middle section of the roof is covered with yellow glazed tiles, and is decorated with dragons, banyan leaves, and bats, while the panels along the eaves are embellished with ceramic orchid, chrysanthemum, and bamboo mosaics. Above the pavillion, a concealed staircase leads up to a room where women of the court could see through finely carved grills.

↑ Dragon relief, a key decorative motif in the imperial enclosure

⑤

Thai Hoa Palace

Originally built by Emperor Gia Long in 1805, the splendid Thai Hoa or Hall of Supreme Harmony housed the throne room of the Nguyen emperors. The most impressive of Hue's remaining palaces, it has been beautifully restored. All of its 80 red lacquered wooden columns are sumptuously decorated with swirling golden dragons. You can easily envisage the hall as the venue for coronations, royal anniversaries, and the reception of foreign ambassadors. The emperor would sit on the resplendent throne, wearing a crown with nine dragons, a gold robe, jade belt, and other attire. Only the most senior mandarins were allowed to stand in the hall, while others waited outside.

⑥

Halls of the Mandarins

On either side of a paved courtyard, just behind Thai Hoa Palace, are the

↑ Cot Co (Flag Tower), Hue Citadel's most distinctive landmark

Halls of the Mandarins. One hall was for the military, while the other was for civil mandarins. In keeping with their ranks, the mandarins would gather at their pavilions to dress in ceremonial robes for imperial functions. Some of these gorgeous, colorfully embroidered vestments and hats with dragon designs are kept on display here.

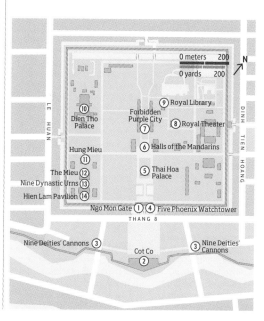

Hien Lam Pavilion, with a finely crafted wooden facade ↑

⑦
Forbidden Purple City

No man except the emperor was permitted to set foot in the 25-acre (10-ha) city-within-a-city known as Tu Cam Thanh or Forbidden Purple City – any male who crossed its threshold was condemned to death. Only the queen, nine separate ranks of concubines, female servants, and court eunuchs were allowed to enter. Built between 1802 and 1833, the Forbidden City once comprised more than 60 buildings arranged around numerous courtyards, but unfortunately, it was damaged extensively by heavy bombing during the 1968 Tet Offensive.

⑧
Royal Theater

Originally built in 1825, the Duyet Thi Duong or Royal Theater is once again a leading venue for traditional entertainment, offering performances of *nha nhac* or court music. Declared a Masterpiece of the Oral and Intangible Heritage of Humanity by UNESCO, *nha nhac* features bamboo lutes, zithers, and fiddles,

accompanied by drums. The beautiful building has a pagoda-style curved roof, and a colorful interior, with lacquered columns etched with the ubiquitous golden dragon motif.

⑨
Royal Library

Constructed by Emperor Minh Mang in 1821, the Royal Library in the northeastern quarter of the Forbidden City served as a retreat where he read in solitude. The building stands before a pond, with a rock garden to its west. Small bridges crossing other lakes and ponds connect various galleries, creating a tranquil atmosphere. The library is sometimes used to stage performances of Hue music, as well as theatrical events.

⑩
Dien Tho Palace

Once the exclusive preserve of the Queen Mothers, Dien Tho or the Residence of Everlasting Longevity was built in 1803 during the reign

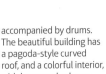

The Mieu

Hung Mieu

Nine Dynastic Urns

of Emperor Gia Long. Inside, the furniture is carefully inlaid with delicate mother-of-pearl, and carved lanterns hang from the ceiling, which is ornamented with fans made from feathers.

⑪
Hung Mieu

Emperor Minh Mang built Hung Mieu in 1821 to honor his grandparents. The temple was seriously damaged by fire

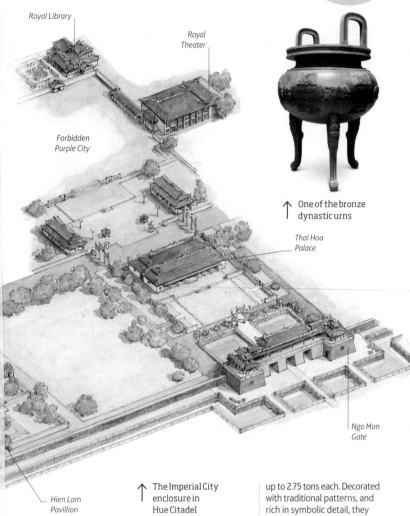

Royal Library

Royal Theater

Forbidden Purple City

↑ One of the bronze dynastic urns

Thai Hoa Palace

↑ The Imperial City enclosure in Hue Citadel

Ngo Mon Gate

Hien Lam Pavillion

in 1947, but has been restored. It is renowned for its refined design and fine roof carvings. Particularly noteworthy are the large gargoyle-like stone dragons keeping vigil over the spacious paved courtyard.

emperors, from Gia Long to Khai Dinh. The building has a roof of yellow glazed tiles. The altars were once stacked high with gold ingots, which today have been replaced with gilt and lacquer ornamentation.

up to 2.75 tons each. Decorated with traditional patterns, and rich in symbolic detail, they represent the might of the Nguyen emperors and play a big role in the cult of imperial ancestor veneration.

 ⑫

The Mieu

Dedicated to the Nguyen Dynasty, the Mieu or the Temple of Generations contains altars honoring

 ⑬

Nine Dynastic Urns

Cast between 1835 and 1837 on the orders of Emperor Minh Mang, these massive bronze funerary urns weigh

⑭

Hien Lam Pavilion

The pyramid-shaped pavilion was built in 1824 by Emperor Minh Mang to honor those who gave the great Nguyen Dynasty its formidable status. As a mark of respect, it was declared that no other building in the Citadel could rise higher than the Hien Lam.

HUE

D4 Capital of Thue Thien Hue Province, 62 miles (110 km) N of Danang Reunification Express from Hanoi and Ho Chi Minh City From Hanoi, Vinh, Danang, Nha Trang, and Ho Chi Minh City 11 Nguyen Cong Tru St; (0234) 381 6263

One of the most significant cultural and historic centers of Vietnam, the former imperial city of Hue is a place of great beauty, renowed for its sophisticated cuisine. Many of Hue's main sights are within the Citadel and Imperial Enclosure *(p142)*. Others are scattered around the city. The scenic Perfume River, superb hotels and restaurants, and a palpably French atmosphere add to the city's many charms.

①

Dong Ba Market

Northeast of Tran Hung Dao St Daily

Hue's bustling covered Dong Ba Market is located to the north of the Perfume River, near the southeast corner of the Citadel. A popular local shopping center, it attracts huge crowds daily. Stalls here overflow with an astonishing variety of goods, from fresh produce and fish to clothing, toys, shoes, and handicrafts. The market is at its busiest and most fascinating in the early hours of the morning, even though it is open all day.

↑ Baskets of fresh fruit and vegetables at Dong Ba Market

HIDDEN GEM
Thanh Toan Covered Bridge

In Thanh Thuy Chan village, 4 miles (7 km) east of Hue, is this little-known but delightful Japanese bridge, similar to the famous Japanese Bridge in Hoi An *(p132)*. The best way to get to it is by cycling through scenic villages.

②

Royal Antiquities Museum

3 Le Truc St (0234) 352 4429 8-11:30am, 1:30-5pm Tue-Sat

East of the Imperial City is the Royal Antiquities Museum, which is housed in Long An Palace. Originally built in 1845, the palace is supported by 128 ironwood columns and features a multitiered roof. The exhibits, which are all from the Nguyen Dynasty (1802–1945), include silver crafts, fine porcelain, antique furniture, costumes from the royal wardrobe, Khai Dinh's bed, and Bao Dai's shoes. Unfortunately, there is little explanation or information offered on this grand collection.

←

The beautiful Perfume River flowing through Hue at dusk

③
Dieu De Pagoda

🏠 102 Bach Dang St
🕐 Sunrise-sunset daily

Built during the reign of Thieu Tri (r.1841–7), and renovated many times since, Dieu De dates from 1953 in its present form. The pagoda features drum and bell towers and a sanctuary dedicated to the Thich Ca Buddha. Dieu De was a stronghold of opposition to the South Vietnamese government in the 1960s.

④
Bao Quoc Pagoda

🏠 Bao Quoc St 📞 (0234) 382 2297 🕐 Sunrise-sunset daily

Giac Phong, a Buddhist monk from China, founded this pagoda in 1670. It was later granted royal status by the Nguyen lord Phuc Khoat (r.1738–65). In the late 18th century, the powerful Tay Son rebel Quang Trung used this house of worship for storing armaments. In 1940, it became a school for Buddhist monks, a function it fulfills to this day. Though it was renovated in the 20th century, the pagoda retains its charm and aura of antiquity even today.

Must See

STAY

Saigon Morin Hotel
Opened in 1901, this landmark French colonial hotel is one of Vietnam's oldest hotels. The renovated, well-equipped rooms retain a nostalgic charm, and many face onto the cool, leafy inner courtyard.

🏠 30 Le Loi Street
Ⓦ morinhotel.com.vn

$ $ $

Tu Dam Pagoda

🏠 Lieu Quan St ⏰ Sunrise-sunset daily

Founded in the 17th century, this temple's chief importance is as a center for supporting Buddhism, a cause that has been at the heart of Central Vietnam's political culture since the 1950s. The temple was a major hub of activity during the Buddhist agitation against President Diem's unpopular Catholic regime during the mid-20th century. As was the disturbing trend at the time, in 1963 a monk burned himself to death in the pagoda's courtyard in protest against the oppressive regime.

Tu Hieu Pagoda

🏠 Thon Thuong 2, Thuy Xuan Village, 3 miles (5 km) SW of Hue ⏰ 6am–6pm daily

Set amid the attractive pine woods to the north of Tu Duc's tomb, Tu Hieu Pagoda is surrounded by a delightful crescent-shaped lotus pond. One of the most serene pagodas in the Hue region, it was established in 1848 by imperial eunuchs. Since they could not have children, the eunuchs financially secured the temple, thus guaranteeing that future generations of monks would always be on hand to perform the necessary ceremonies for their lives in the hereafter. Several monks still inhabit Tu Hieu and hold prayer services daily. The main shrine is dedicated to the Thich Ca Buddha.

Thien Mu Pagoda

🏠 3 miles (5 km) SW of Hue Citadel ⏰ Sunrise-sunset daily

Rising on a bluff above the northwest bank of the Perfume River, Thien Mu or Heavenly Lady Pagoda is an iconic symbol of Hue. Founded in 1601 by Lord Nguyen Hoang, the pagoda is dominated by a seven-story octagonal tower, Thap Phuoc Duyen, which translates as Source of Happiness Tower. A pavilion close by shelters a huge bronze bell cast in 1710. Weighing more than 4,409 lb (2,000 kg), it can purportedly be heard at least 6 miles (10 km) away. A second pavilion houses a stone stele erected in 1715, which eulogises the history of Buddhism in Hue.

Inside, the main shrine is presided over by a laughing

EAT & DRINK

Secret Lounge
This quirky bar has an unusual mix of traditional Vietnamese decor and graffiti art. Drinks are served to a soundtrack of golden oldies.

🏠 15/42 Nguyen Cong Tru 📞 (096) 196 2222

$$$

La Boulangerie Francaise
Established to help train local disadvantaged kids, this French bakery creates warm, crispy filled baguettes, as well as delicious crepes and pastries, served with lashings of good karma.

🏠 46 Nguyen Tri Phuong Street 📞 (0120) 806 3857

$$$

Le Hanh
A long-standing family-run eatery, Le Hanh serves authentic Hue street food, such as *banh beo* (steamed rice cakes) and *lem lui* (ground pork and lemongrass skewers).

🏠 11 Pho Duc Chinh 🌐 banhkhoaihanh.com

$$$

Le Parfum
Gourmet French-Vietnamese dishes are served in an Art Deco dining room or on the terrace by the river.

🏠 La Residence Hotel, 5 Le Loi Street 🌐 la-residence-hue.com

$$$

↑ The peaceful Tu Hieu Pagoda surrounded by pine trees

Did You Know?

Since the 1960s Thien Mu Pagoda has been the site of political demonstrations.

buddha surrounded by statues of the ten kings of hell and 18 *arhat* or holy disciples. Close by is a striking image of the Thich Ca Buddha. The monks' quarters and gardens are at the back of the temple. In an open garage to the west is the car that drove monk Thich Quang Duc to Saigon in June 1963, where he immolated himself in protest against the Diem regime. Images of this horrific event were shown all over the world, provoking widespread shock and outrage.

---

⑧ 🖋
Dan Nam Giao

📍 2 miles (3 km) S of city center, southern end of Dien Bien Phu St
🕙 8am–5pm daily

Built by Emperor Gia Long in 1802, Dan Nam Giao or the Altar of Heaven stands beyond the former French Quarter on the east side of the Perfume River. For more than a century, this was the most important ceremonial site in the country. Approximately every three years, between 1806 and 1945, the Nguyen emperors reaffirmed the legitimacy of their rule through a series of elaborate sacrifices to the Emperor of Heaven. The ritual was modeled on the rites practiced in Beijing by the Chinese emperors at the 15th-century Tian Tan or Temple of Heaven. Today, not much remains of this ceremonial site other than a series of three raised terraces. The first two are square-shaped and are said to represent humanity and earth. The circular terrace at the top symbolizes the heavens. Though there isn't much of the building left, the site has plenty of atmosphere. In this setting, it is easy to conjure up images of the emperors as the rightful Sons of Heaven interceding with the gods on behalf of their subjects.

---

⑨
Royal Arena

📍 Phuong Duc Village, 3 miles (4 km) SW of Hue
🕙 Sunrise–sunset daily

Built in 1830 for the entertainment of the Nguyen emperors and the mandarins, this amphitheater is also known as Ho Quyen or the Tiger Arena. It was used to stage brutal combats between elephants, which were considered noble and symbolized royalty, and tigers, which signified rebellion, in particular the former Champa Kingdom. It is no surprise that these contests were always rigged so that the elephant would win. Fortunately, no fights have been held since 1904, but the eerily quiet arena remains in quite good condition. The viewing platforms are intact, as are the five doors opposite leading to the tigers' cages.

↑ Octagonal tower of Thien Mu Pagoda, seen from the Perfume River

↑ Royal Arena near Hue, the site of wild animal fights in the 1800s

Did You Know?

Khai Dinh, the penultimate emperor of Vietnam, was seen as a puppet of the French.

5

ROYAL TOMBS OF HUE

🅐 D4 🅐 4-10 miles (6-16 km) S of Hue 🚌

Scattered across the scenic countryside south of Hue, the tombs of the Nguyen emperors are among the area's most compelling attractions. Only 7 of the 13 rulers between 1802 and 1945 were given their own mausoleum, as the others died during exile or in disgrace.

①

Tomb of Tu Duc

🅐 4 miles (6 km) SW of Hue 🕑 7am-5pm daily

The supremely elegant mausoleum of Tu Duc (r.1848–83) was designed by the emperor himself. Set on a pine-clad hill, it is flanked by beautiful lotus ponds and aromatic frangipani trees. Tu Duc was known to have preferred the quiet comforts of his future tomb to his own palace. It is said that when the emperor died, he was buried secretly along with great treasure. All involved in his burial were later executed to keep his final resting place safe from desecration.

②

Tomb of Dong Khanh

🅐 0.3 miles (0.5 km) SE of Tomb of Tu Duc 📞 (054) 383 6427 🕑 7am-6pm daily

The smallest of all Nguyen tombs is the mausoleum of Dong Khanh (r.1885–88). French influence is quite prominent in its interior, where images of Napoleon Bonaparte hang from the restored red-lacquered ironwood pillars.

③

Tomb of Khai Dinh

🅐 6 miles (10 km) S of Hue 📞 (054) 386 5875 🕑 6am-5:30pm daily

Khai Dinh (r.1916–25) was the last to be buried in a royal tomb at Hue. His tomb makes use of concrete and is an interesting fusion of European and Vietnamese architectural styles. Built into the side of a hill, the tomb rises steeply through three levels. In the temple at the summit is a bronze bust of the emperor, cast at Marseilles in 1922.

↑ The elaborate tomb of Khai Dinh, built into the side of a steep hill

Tomb of Thieu Tri

◎ 1 mile (1.5 km) S of Tomb of Tu Duc ◎ 7am–5pm daily

The small tomb of Thieu Tri (r.1841–47) features several artificial ponds, although it lacks the usual extensive walled gardens. The complex is divided into two parts. To the east, a delicate temple salutes the deceased, while to the west is the tomb itself.

Tomb of Minh Mang

◎ 7 miles (12 km) S of Hue ◎ 7:30am–5:30pm daily

Located on the west side of the Perfume River, the mausoleum of Emperor Minh Mang, who died in 1841, is one of the most impressive royal tombs. The complex comprises picturesque lakes and gardens, as well as numerous pavilions and other structures with bright colors and lacquer finishes.

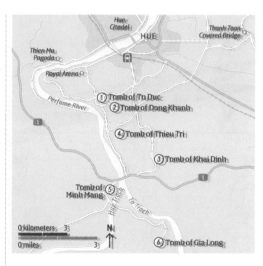

Tomb of Gia Long

◎ 10 miles (16 km) SE of Hue

The mausoleum of the first Nguyen emperor, Gia Long, can be reached by boat either from Hue or from the tiny village of Tuan, or by road via a bridge just south of the tomb

of Minh Mang. In a beautiful setting surrounded by mountains and hills, it is the most remote of all the tombs. Built during the 18th to 19th centuries, the site contains not only the tomb of Gia Long but these of the king's family and relatives. It suffered extensive damage during the Vietnam War but has been restored.

Boatmen on the
Perfume River
at sunset

A BOAT TOUR
PERFUME RIVER

Length 3–4 hours **Stopping-off points** Snacks available at Thien Mu and Minh Mang **Boat rentals** Take an organized tour or hire boats from the wharf at Le Loi Street

One of the main highlights of a visit to Hue is a boat ride along Song Huong or the Perfume River. Shown below are the sights you can typically see on a boat tour. Though not very long, the slow-winding river is extraordinarily beautiful. The effect is enhanced by the reflection of the Citadel, pagodas, towers, and the scenic countryside. Added to this is the picturesque river traffic – women sculling tiny, single-oared vessels, larger boats piled high with fish and fresh vegetables, and fishermen in narrow crafts.

CENTRAL VIETNAM

Perfume River boat tour

Locator Map
For more detail see p130

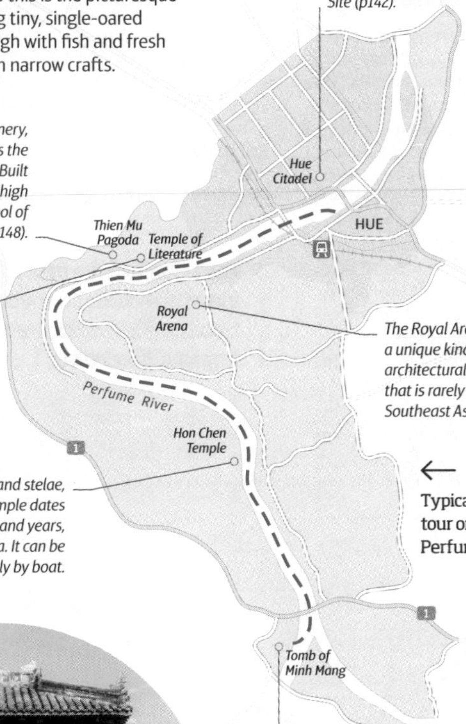

Once the royal seat of the Nguyen Emperors, the imposing Citadel is a UNESCO World Heritage Site (p142).

Hue Citadel

HUE

Set amidst verdant greenery, the Thien Mu Pagoda is the oldest pagoda in Hue. Built in 1601, the 69-ft (21-m) high tower is an official symbol of the city of Hue (p148).

Thien Mu Pagoda

Temple of Literature

The tiny Temple of Literature was built by Emperor Gia Long in 1808 to replace the venerable Temple of Literature in Hanoi.

Royal Arena

The Royal Arena is a unique kind of architectural structure that is rarely found in Southeast Asia (p149).

Perfume River

← Typical boat tour on the Perfume River

Hon Chen Temple

Full of altars, spirit houses, and stelae, the attractive Hon Chen Temple dates back more than a thousand years, to the ancient Champa. It can be approached only by boat.

Tomb of Minh Mang

The Tomb of Minh Mang is possibly the best preserved royal tomb in Hue. Graceful statuary, ponds, and landscaped gardens add to the mausoleum's grandeur (p151).

| 0 kilometers | 2 |
| 0 miles | 2 |

N ↑

← The Tomb of Minh Mang, one of the most impressive tombs of the Nguyen Emperors

EXPERIENCE MORE

Danang

🅐D4 🚗67 miles (108 km) S of Hue, 599 miles (964 km) N of HCMC ✈️🚌 From Hanoi, HCMC, and Nha Trang 🚆Reunification Express from Hanoi and HCMC 🚌 From Hanoi, Hue, HCMC, and Nha Trang 🅲32A Phan Dinh Phung; www.danang fantasticity.com

Situated almost halfway along the country's coastline, on the western bank of the Han River, Danang is one of the fastest-changing places in Vietnam. It is the fourth largest but third most important city. Now a major destination in its own right, Danang is also an excellent hub for exploring several nearby attractions, and is very well connected, with an air, road, and rail infrastructure linking it to points north and south. Three of Vietnam's World Heritage Sites – Hoi An (p132), My Son (p138), and Hue Citadel (p142) – as well as scenic beaches are within easy reach of the city.

Danang became prominent during the 19th century. After being captured by the French in 1859, it rapidly developed, replacing Hoi An as the main port for Central Vietnam. Further expansion took place during the Vietnam War (p50), when Danang became an important military base for the Americans. Vestiges of all three eras can still be seen in and around the city.

The **Museum of Cham Sculpture**, or Bao Tang Dieu Khac Cham, is one of the city's highlights. Founded in 1915 by École Française d'Extrême Orient, the museum show-cases the world's finest collection of Cham sculpture, including altars, sandstone pieces, busts of Hindu gods such as Vishnu, Shiva, and Brahma, and carvings of scenes from the *Ramayana* epic. All the sculptures were recovered from nearby Cham sites, including Tra Kieu, the first Champa capital, My Son, and Dong Duong among others, and date from the 7th to the 13th century. There are also contemporary artifacts focusing on Cham culture today

The pink-colored Danang Cathedral (known locally as Rooster Church) was built in

> The summit of the pass offers splendid views of mountains covered in thick clouds, with the blue waters of Danang Bay sparkling below.

→

The rose-pink facade of Danang's Cathedral, with its tall bell tower

1923 and has five tiers rising to a steeple crowned with a cockerel. Another interesting sight is the **Cao Dai Temple**, the largest after its main counterpart, Cao Dai Holy See *(p62)* in Tay Ninh. Also worth visiting are Phap Lam Pagoda, honoring the Thich Ca Buddha, and **Pho Da Pagoda**, which is pale cream, with orange tiles and green trimming. The central temple building, which houses the main altar, is flanked by two triple-roofed towers with flaring eaves. This lovely pagoda is also used as a Buddhist college for training monks and nuns.

Danang's most striking attraction is the spectacular Dragon Bridge, which is illuminated with LED lights at night, and spits water and breathes fire from its mouth from 9pm. The best place to

observe this is from the waterside cafés on the east bank just north of the bridge, or from a boat on the river.

Set on a hill a short distance from Danang's port and beach is a well-maintained cemetery containing the tombs of Spanish and French soldiers killed in the 1858 French attack on Danang.

About 18 miles (30 km) north of Danang, the Hai Von Pass on Truong Son Range has some of Vietnam's most breathtaking vistas. The summit of the pass offers splendid views of mountains covered in thick clouds, with the beautiful blue waters of Danang Bay sparkling below.

Museum of Cham Sculpture

🖈🖈🖈 📍 Bach Dang/Trung Nu Vuong sts 📞 (0236) 357 2935 ⏰ 8–11:30am, 2–4:30pm daily

Cao Dai Temple

📍 63 Hai Phong St 📞 (0236) 369 8710 ⏰ 6am–6pm daily

Pho Da Pagoda

📍 340 Phan Chu Trinh St 📞 (0236) 382 6094 ⏰ 5am–9pm daily

←

The magnificent Dragon Bridge spanning the wide Han River

EAT & DRINK

Fatfish

Contemporary international and Vietnamese dishes are served in stylish surroundings with romantic views across the river from the balcony. Famous for its pizzas, Fatfish's innovative local dishes, such as "cocky bird" chicken curry, are also worth trying, as are the many cocktails.

🅰 D4 📍 43,9 Tran Hung Dao, Danang 📞 (0236) 394 57 07

$$$

Market's

This solidly Vietnamese joint serves great local dishes. The barbeques and hot pots cooked at the table are superb, especially those featuring seafood.

🅰 D4 📍 29 Luu Quang Thuan, Danang 📞 (090) 500 1744

$$$

Marble Mountains

D4 2 Huyen Tran Cong Chua, Hoa Hai 09 0512 1997 Open 7am-5:30pm

Located on the road from Danang to Hoi An, this is, as the name suggests, a group of five peaks made of marble and riddled with caves and fissures, many of which contain Buddhist shrines, as well as a few Hindu grottoes. The Vietnamese name is Ngu Hanh Son, which means "five elements" and the individual hills are named Kim ("metal"), Thuy ("water"), Moc ("wood"), Hoa ("fire"), and Tho ("earth"). The main formation, the only one accessible to visitors, is Thuy Son, which can be ascended via steep steps and dark cave passages, stopping off at the various cave temples along the way.

Many of the caves contain beautiful shrines and statues carved out of the marble, such as the Buddhas in the Hoa Nghiem Grotto and the cathedral-like Huyen Khong Cave. The view from the top of the hill takes in the long stretches of beach on the coastline and the urban sprawl of Danang. It's best visited in the morning to avoid the heat and crowds, and also at around midday, to see the brilliant shafts of sunlight illuminating many of the cave interiors.

During the Vietnam War Huyen Khong Cave was used by the Viet Cong as a hospital, and as a handy hideout for raiding the nearby US airbase on the beach, and you can still see the odd bullet hole here and there from potshots taken from the US base.

Monkey Mountain

D4 15 miles (25 km) northeast of Danang

The best views in the area are from Nui Son Tra on the peninsula that juts out northeast from Danang. Also known as Monkey Mountain after the now dwindling troupes of red-faced monkeys that frequent it, Son Tra is easily visited by road, taking about 35 minutes to reach the 2,273-ft (693-m) peak from the city. The steep, winding road runs above jungle-covered cliffs through the national park, and offers fantastic views of the lovely coastline stretching away into the distance and Hi Van Mountain, Cham Island, and Danang City, which get better the higher you ascend. Halfway up you will find the 18th-century Linh Ung Pagoda, whose courtyard is dominated by the pristine-white, 220-ft- (67-m-) high statue of Lady Buddha Da

Nang, reportedly the tallest of all the goddess statues in Southeast Asia.

It's also possible to hike up to the top of Monkey Mountain from Bai Bac Beach (taking about four hours), on a well-marked path that passes by a 600-year-old banyan tree. You might see the rare red-shanked Douc langur monkey, with its red legs and white arms, and numerous species of birds. Be aware that at weekends and on religious holidays Monkey Mountain can be thronged with pilgrims.

↑ The dramatic Cau Vang Bridge, held up by giant stone hands

9

Ba Na Hill Station

🅰D4 🕒25 miles (40 km) W of Danang

A conveniently close getaway from Danang, this former French hill station provides a cool escape from the coast. Set on top of a mountain at an altitude of 4,593 ft (1,400 m), it is often shrouded in mist. Some of the 1920s French colonial villas here have been converted into guesthouses and hotels.

The chief attractions are a cable car, which has the world's longest non-stop single-track system, an amusement park, and hiking trails to waterfalls. A striking bridge, Cau Vang (Golden Bridge), opened in 2018, emerging from the trees in the Thien Thai gardens to loop round the mountain. The eight-span, ribbon-like bridge is held aloft by giant stone hands, and offers fantastic panoramic views over the Truong Son Mountains and Danang, with the South China Sea in the distance.

> ### Did You Know?
>
> During the Vietnam War the US airbase at China Beach was the busiest in the world.

10

China Beach

🅰D4 🕒3 miles (2 km) SE of Danang

The long stretch of beaches between Danang and the Marble Mountains is known to the Vietnamese as the My Khe, My An, and Non Nuoc beaches. However, these white sandy shores were known to US servicemen as China Beach and were later highlighted by an eponymous popular TV series. Though banned by the government, a number of developers have taken to using the designation China Beach in an attempt to encourage foreign visitors.

During the Vietnam War, the Americans – for whom Danang was among the most important and secure bases in South Vietnam – developed My Khe and My An beaches as a rest-and-recreation center for US forces taking a few days leave from the war. Today, nothing remains of the former R&R facilities, although several souvenir stalls and seafood restaurants have sprung up here. The area is a popular destination for surfing and swimming in summer.

←

Beautiful Huyen Khong Cave, with shrines and statues, on top of Thuy Son

Waterfall and stream
running through lush forest
in Bach Ma National Park

⓫

Bach Ma National Park

🗺️ D4 🚌 28 miles (45 km) SE of Hue 🚌 From Hue and Danang to Cau Hai from Danang, Hue, Hoi An, and Cau Hai 🕐 Daily 🌐 bachma park.com.vn

Located in the Hue-Danang provincial frontier, at an elevation of 4,757 ft (1,450 m), Bach Ma National Park was established as a hill station in the 1930s by the French. The Viet Minh did not like this imperialist occupation, and the area was subjected to many attacks during the First Indochina War (p50). By the end of the war, most of the French had abandoned their beautiful villas. In the 1960s, the Americans fortified Bach Ma and there were many bitter confrontations with the Vietcong in the hilly forests. After the Communist victory in 1975, however, the hill station lay forgotten for many years. Fortunately for Bach

---

Ma, in 1991, the authorities granted national park status to this 145 sq miles (375 sq km) of forested land.

Although sprayed with defoliants during the Vietnam War, the forest is showing signs of recovery due to dedicated conservation efforts. The park is home to more than 2,140 plant species, many of which are said to have medicinal properties. More than 130 species of mammals have been identified in the park; among them are the rare saola, the giant muntjac, and the recently discovered Truong Son muntjac. Primates living here include langurs, macaques, lorises, and the white-cheeked gibbon. It is even possible that leopards and tigers inhabit remote corners of the park, but this has not yet been confirmed. Bach Ma National Park is also a bird-watcher's paradise, with an astounding 363 species listed by the park authorities, among them the Edward's pheasant.

Little remains of the former French hill station – only a few ruins can be seen amid the foliage. A narrow path leads to an observation post at the park's highest point which, weather permitting, affords glorious views across the rugged Truong Son Range. Those who enjoy walking may like to wander along the Pheasant Trail, where the calls of gibbons can often be heard, or the Rhododendron Trail,

---

which leads to the 980-ft- (300-m-)tall Do Queyen waterfall.

Check that Bach Ma is open before visiting as road repairs can affect accessibility. Note also that the park can only be reached by public transportation.

⓬

Suoi Voi

🗺️ D4 🚌 40 miles (65 km) S of Hue; 9 miles (15 km) N of Lang Co on Hwy 1 🚌 from Hue 🕐 8am–5:30pm daily

A popular weekend destination for the inhabitants of Hue and Danang, Suoi Voi, also known as Elephant Springs, is named after a huge rock that resembles the animal. This is a wonderful bathing spot, not usually frequented by visitors.

On the way from Hue, look out for a large sign indicating a track leading off to the right toward the springs. About 1.5 miles (2.5 km) from here,

---

GREAT VIEW
Summit Trail

The short summit trail from the Bach Ma National Park car park is a gentle climb to a pavilion that offers stunning 360-degree views. Ba Be Lake, with its clear emerald water, is another beauty spot.

passing the old Thua Lau Church on the way, is the entrance gate and car park for Suoi Voi. From here, the walk to the main springs is about 1 mile (1.6 km). Several large boulders surround the tree-filled area. All this is set scenically against the thickly jungled peaks of the Truong Son Range. Facilities are minimal but there are usually food stands near the springs.

Lang Co Beach

A D4 **M** 47 miles (75 km) S of Hue; 22 miles (35 km) N of Danang on Hwy 1 **E** From Hue and Danang **T** From Hue or Danang

To appreciate the full beauty of the peninsula, catch a glimpse of it from the summit of the Hai Van Pass. Looking north from here, an idyllic picture in shimmering blue, white, and green appears. A narrow spit of pristine white sand runs south from the Loc Vinh commune, dividing a gleaming saltwater lagoon to its west from the choppy South China Sea to its east. Miles of palm-fringed, soft white sand contrast beautifully with the aqua-marine waters of the lagoon and the changing shades of the wave-flecked sea.

The beach is ideal for a leisurely swim, especially in the summer months before July, after which the area can get rather wet and dreary. There are several resorts for a longer stay, and an excellent seafood lunch can be enjoyed here in any season. The sleepy Lang Co village provides a glimpse into Vietnam's simple coastal way of living.

Just south of Lang Co, a bridge across the lagoon leads to the road tunnel that carries Highway 1 beneath the Hai Van Pass. This sheltered area provides a convenient harbor for local fishermen. A stroll here reveals brightly painted fishing boats as well as coracles (tiny circular boats, a little like wicker baskets).

Thuan An Beach

A D4 **M** 9 miles (15 km) NE of Hue on Hwy 49

One of the best beaches in the Hue region, Thuan An is located at

Sandy Thuan An Beach near Hue; colorful fishing boats *(inset)*

> Bach Ma National Park is a bird-watcher's paradise, with an astounding 363 species listed by the park authorities, among them the Edward's pheasant.

the northern end of a long, thin island that runs south from the mouth of the Perfume River, almost up to the little town of Phu Loc.

Thuan An shore features a pleasing strip of white sand flanked by tall, softly swaying coconut palms. It is washed by the calm blue waters of the Thanh Lam Lagoon to the southwest, while the stormy waves of the South China Sea lap its northeast shores. The sea is clear, and May to August are good months for swimming here.

Still relatively undeveloped, the village of Thuan An is sparsely settled by fishermen, whose boats are pulled up along the sandy shores. The manufacture of *nuoc mam* or fish sauce is an important industry here.

Thuan An is a convenient destination for a cycling day trip from Hue. Getting to the beach entails an enjoyable ride through several tranquil villages and rural scenery, dotted with several quaint pagodas along the way. The island and beach can be accessed via a small bridge over the Thanh Lam Lagoon.

Khe Sanh Combat Base

D4 **90 miles (145 km) NW of Hue on Hwy 9** **Minibus from Hue Museum: 1 mile (1.5 km) N of Khe Sanh town** **7am–5pm daily**

Situated close to the Laos border, the Khe Sanh Combat Base lies about 2 miles (3 km) away from Khe Sanh village, now known as Hoang Ho. It was initially developed as an airstrip by the Americans in 1962, and later enlarged and developed into a US Special Forces base charged with intercepting traffic on the Ho Chi Minh Trail (p163).

However, Khe Sanh is best known as the site of one of the most ferocious battles of the Vietnam War, and as the beginning of the end for the Americans in Vietnam. In 1968, US General William Westmoreland started a massive build-up at the base with a view to forcing the North Vietnamese Army into direct confrontation. Vietnam's General Vo Nguyen Giap took the bait, but in a masterful double-play, used the siege, which lasted from January to April 1968, to distract attention from the Tet Offensive. The heavy deployment of bombs and relentless gunfire caused a high number of casualties.

An estimated 207 US and 9,000 Vietnamese soldiers died, and several thousand civilians lost their lives.

Although this battle was not, as President Johnson feared, another Dien Bien Phu (p211), the Americans, though undefeated, were forced to withdraw from Khe Sanh. They took great pains to bury, remove, or destroy, rather than abandon their military equipment where it could be used as propagandist evidence of their "defeat."

Today, Khe Sanh is on the tourist map, with guided tours available. The drive along Highway 9, past statues and plaques, is part of the Central Vietnam experience. Though nothing had been left behind, American weaponry and vehicles were brought in from elsewhere in the south to fill the small museum here.

HISTORY OF THE DMZ

At the 1954 Geneva Conference, a decision was taken to establish the DMZ at the 17th Parallel as a "provisional demarcation line" between North and South Vietnam. The boundary stretched 3 miles (5 km) on either side of Ben Hai River, up to the Laos border. From the start, the North Vietnamese Army (NVA) managed to penetrate the DMZ with tunnels, trails, and guerilla tactics, while the Americans and South Vietnamese planted mines and built vast electrified fences along Highway 9. Ironically, the DMZ saw some of the heaviest fighting of the Vietnam War, particularly during the 1972 Easter Offensive.

Demilitarized Zone

C4 **53 miles (90 km) NE of Khe Sanh on Hwy 9** **Minibus and taxi from Hue** **7am–5pm daily**

Though it lost all strategic and political importance after reunification in 1975, the Demilitarized Zone (DMZ) has become a major tourist attraction and can be visited on a day trip from Hue or Dong Ha. Most tours start with the Hien Luong Bridge over the Ben Hai River, which once formed the frontier, and a visit to the well-constructed Vinh Moc Tunnels (p161). The Truong Son National Cemetery, based to the west of Highway 1, honors the many thousands of North Vietnamese soldiers and Vietcong fighters killed in the area.

From here, it is convenient to head inland from Dong Ha along Highway 9, passing former US bases en route. Camp Carroll, Khe Sanh, and Hamburger Hill (p49) have entered popular consciousness through Hollywood movies. While there is not much in the way of "sights," the DMZ provides a fascinating tour. It is especially popular with military historians and Americans.

←

Military hardware scattered around the Demilitarized Zone

Vinh Moc Tunnels

C4 **8 miles (13 km) E of Ho Xa on Hwy 1; 12 miles (20 km) NE of the DMZ** **Minibus from Hue and Dong Ha** **7:30am–5pm daily**

Some of the most resilient tunnels built in Vietnam were at Vinh Moc, a village along the South China Sea shore. Occupied by hundreds of people between 1968 and 1972, these tunnels were intended for long-term habitation. They are different from the better-known ones at Cu Chi (p76), which was more of a frontline fighting base.

Vinh Moc's troubles began because of its location. After the nation's partition in 1954, villages along the north of the Demilitarized Zone (p160), including Vinh Moc, found themselves under almost constant attack. Moreover, Vinh Moc faces Con Co Island, a North Vietnamese base used for transporting weapons and supplies to the south, making it a key target for strikes by the South Vietnamese Army. The United States Air Force (USAF) also contributed to the huge barrage of bombs, and Vinh Moc was very nearly razed to the ground. While some inhabitants fled, others decided to stay, even if they had to go underground. The villagers, aided by soldiers of the Vietcong, worked with nothing more sophisticated than spades, baskets, and their bare hands to excavate the complex tunnel network.

Created in about 18 months, the tunnel network stretches for 2 miles (3 km), with 13 entrance points. Family rooms, a hospital, and a meeting hall fill its three levels. Villagers and North Vietnamese soldiers lived here for more than four years – during which time, 17 children were born. From these tunnels, almost 12,000 tons of military supplies and equipment were sent to Con Co Island.

Today, the remarkable network of tunnels created by the villagers of Vinh Moc can be seen almost exactly as they were in 1972. Unlike Cu Chi, it is possible to negotiate these tunnels standing up straight, though taller visitors do have to stoop. The museum here also makes for a fascinating browse. An added advantage are the sunny beaches nearby.

↑ A guide leading the way through the Vinh Moc Tunnels, near the DMZ

18

Dong Hoi

C3 **101 miles (162 km) N of Hue on Hwy 1** **From Vinh, Dong Ha, and Hue** **Quang Binh Tourism, 58 Nguyen Huu Canh; www.quangbinh tourism.vn**

The capital of Quang Binh Province, Dong Hoi was once a charming little fishing village. Mirroring Vietnam's changing economic policies, it has evolved into a leading transit town. Though there are no major sights here, it is interesting to see how the town has recovered from the ravages of war. What was rubble a few decades ago is now wide avenues and well-maintained buildings. For the best part of 150 years, Dong Hoi marked the de facto frontier between the Trinh and Nguyen lords. Two major ramparts were built to keep the enemies apart, but all that remains of them is a crumbling gateway. There are some fine beaches nearby, including Nhat Le, 2 miles (3 km) north of town.

↑ Interior of Thien Duong
(Paradise Cave) within Phong
Nha-Ke Bang National Park

→ Trekker standing on the edge of the remarkable limestone fomations in Son Doong Cave

Phong Nha-Ke Bang National Park

 C3 Son Trach Village, 34 miles (55 km) NW of Dong Hoi From Dong Hoi 7am–5pm daily phongnhake bang.com

This national park thoroughly deserves its designation as a UNESCO World Heritage Site for its enormous caves. The most accessible of these is Phong Nha Cave. Packed with underground grottos, stalactites, stalagmites, and river systems, it extends back into the hills for many miles. The main cavern is some 5 miles (8 km) deep, with smaller but stunning caves clustered near it. So far speleologists have penetrated up to 22 miles (35 km) into the cave system.

Fleets of sampans wait at the visitors' center to ferry passengers upstream for about 3 miles (5 km), and into the huge cavern. About a mile (1.6 km) into the cave is an area once held sacred by the Cham, with an inscription carved by them centuries ago.

Also in the park are two spectacular caves: Thien Duong (Paradise Cave) and Son Doong (Mountain River Cave).

Son Doong Cave

C3 Phong Nha-Ke Bang National Park Jan–Aug oxalis.com.vn

Located within Phong Nha-Ke Bang National Park, Son Doong cave is the largest and one of the most beautiful caves in the world. Discovered in 1991 by a local hunter sheltering from a tropical downpour, it was explored by British-led caving expeditions in 2009 and 2010, which discovered its unique features, including the gargantuan main passage. Some 4 miles (6.5 km) long, 655 ft (200 m) high and 490 ft (150 m) wide, the cave is mostly lost in darkness except for two areas where the ceiling has fallen in and plant and animal life has thrived. With a lost-world feel, it is full of ferns, trees and creepers occupied by monkeys, flying foxes, and cave-dwelling creatures. There are gushing underground rivers, mirror-smooth lakes, some of the world's largest stalagmites and stalactites, and a 295-ft- (90-m-) high calcite wall, which can only be traversed by rope. Only one tour company, Oxalis Adventure Tours, organizes guided visits for just 700 visitors a year. Visitors must be of reasonable fitness and have some experience of mountain- and jungle-trekking.

Kim Lien

B3 9 miles (14 km) NW of Vinh Minibus from Vinh

A pilgrimage site of sorts, Kim Lien is celebrated as the birthplace and childhood home of Ho Chi Minh (p181), who was born in nearby Hoang Tru village in 1890. He lived there until he was five years old, and then moved to Hue. In 1901 he returned and stayed for five more years.

A man who always shunned the trappings of power, Ho Chi Minh vetoed a museum to his life at Kim Lien, arguing that the funds could be better used. Since his death in 1969, museums and shrines have been built. About 1 mile (2 km) away at Hoang Tru, is a reconstruction of the house where he was born. A small museum shows pictures and personal memorabilia of the leader's life. There is also a reconstruction of the house where he lived from 1901 to 1906. In keeping with his principles, entry to all these sites is free.

HO CHI MINH TRAIL

A complex network of hidden tracks and paths of about 12,427 miles (20,000 km), the Ho Chi Minh Trail, or Duong Truong Son, was used as a strategic connection between North and South Vietnam during the Vietnam War (1957–75). Built on simple tracks that had existed for centuries, the trail provided logistical support to Communist forces in the south, supplying them with weapons, food, and legions of North Vietnamese troops (NVA). The labyrinthine trail started in the north near Vinh. From there, it wound its way west through the Truong Suong Range, before snaking along the Vietnam/Laos border and crossing into Laos and Cambodia. It finally entered South Vietnam at various obscure points.

HANOI

The "City within the River's Bend," was founded by
Emperor Ly Thai To in AD 1010, near Co Loa, the
ancient capital of the first Viet state dating to the
3rd century BC. Ly Thai To structured this city, then
known as Thang Long, around a massive citadel.
To the east of this, a settlement of guilds was
established to serve the needs of the royal court.
By the 16th century, this area had developed into
Hanoi's celebrated Old Quarter *(p188)*. The arrival
of the French in the 19th century marked a period
of reconstruction, as they tore down parts of the
citadel and some ancient temples to make way for
the new European quarter. However, this cultural
vandalism was compensated for, to a large extent,
by the magnificent colonial architecture they
bequeathed the city. During the First Indochina
War *(p50)*, the city's central districts escaped
largely unharmed, and subsequently, in 1954,
Hanoi was proclaimed the capital of independent
Vietnam. Sadly, this was not the end of its violent
history as it was then plunged into the conflict-
ridden years against the US. Today, Hanoi has
emerged as an elegant, cultured, and affluent
city, where museums and galleries coexist with
chic shops and fashionable restaurants.

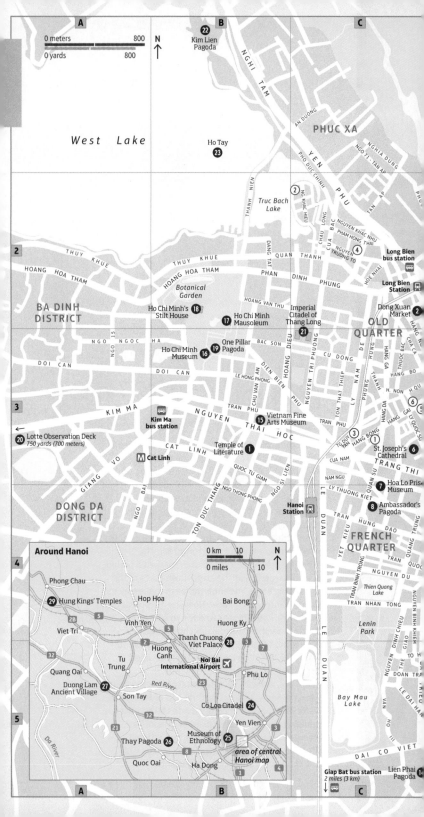

HANOI

Must See
1 Temple of Literature

Experience More
2 Dong Xuan Market
3 Bach Ma Temple
4 Thang Long Water Puppet Theatre
5 Hoan Kiem Lake
6 St Joseph's Cathedral
7 Hoa Lo Prison Museum
8 Ambassador's Pagoda
9 Vietnamese Women's Museum
10 Sofitel Legend Metropole Hotel
11 Opera House
12 Hai Ba Trung Temple
13 National Museum of Vietnamese History
14 Lien Phai Pagoda
15 Vietnam Fine Arts Museum
16 Ho Chi Minh Museum
17 Ho Chi Minh Mausoleum
18 Ho Chi Minh's Stilt House
19 One Pillar Pagoda
20 Lotte Observation Deck
21 Imperial Citadel of Thang Long
22 Kim Lien Pagoda
23 Ho Tay
24 Co Loa Citadel
25 Museum of Ethnology
26 Thay Pagoda
27 Duong Lam Ancient Village
28 Thanh Chuong Viet Palace
29 Hung Kings' Temples

Eat & Drink
1 Hanoi Social Club
2 Standing Bar
3 Nê

Shop
4 54 Traditions
5 Hanoi Moment
6 Kenly Silk

←

① The Huc bridge on Hoan Kiem Lake.

② Street food at Dong Xuan Market.

③ Flag Tower, Imperial Citadel of Thang Long.

④ Lotte Observation Deck.

Hanoi's attractions are conveniently clustered in the Old Quarter, the French Quarter, and Ba Dinh Square, making it easy to explore the city's temples, museums, and markets on foot.

2 DAYS
in Hanoi

Day 1

Morning Begin the day early with a trip to Hoan Kiem Lake *(p174)*. Cross the bright red The Huc bridge to Den Ngoc Son and watch locals lighting incense at the temple altars. Then stroll around the lake, past graceful Tai Chi practitioners, and admire the landmarks. Walk north to the bustling Old Quarter *(p188)*, where you will find the Memorial House Museum, the elegant Bach Ma Temple, and the imposing Quan Chuong Gate. Don't miss Dong Xuan Market *(p172)*, the oldest and largest market in the city, a great place to try Hanoi's famous street food for lunch.

Afternoon Head for the whitewashed walls and green shuttered windows of the grand Sofitel Legend Metropole Hotel *(p177)* before walking round the corner to see the imposing facade of the Opera House. Then pop into the informative National Museum of Vietnamese History *(p178)* nearby. After a couple of hours here, move on to the haunting Hoa Lo Prison Museum *(p176)*, and if there is still time, the Ambassador's Pagoda, only a short walk away and home to many Buddha statues.

Evening Some of the best dining options in the city can be found in the atmospheric French Quarter, just a couple of blocks south of the Old Quarter.

Day 2

Morning Pay respect to Vietnam's greatest hero at the Ho Chi Minh Mausoleum *(p180)* in Ba Dinh Square, followed by a visit to his Stilt House nearby, where he once lived. Next, make a short stopover at the lovely One Pillar Pagoda *(p182)*, which stands in a small lotus pond. Then explore the Imperial Citadel of Thang Long *(p183)*, which was the capital for almost 800 years.

Afternoon Enter the grounds of Hanoi's oldest and most popular attraction, the Temple of Literature *(p170)*, to admire its beautiful architecture. From here, take a cab to the Museum of Ethnology *(p186)* to learn about the country's various ethnic groups and then head for the huge Ho Tay lake *(p184)* to visit the temples and pagodas that decorate its shores.

Evening Watch the sunset by the lake, then hop in a cab and head to the Lotte Observation Deck *(p183)* to enjoy the cityscape vista along with a drink at the bar.

TEMPLE OF LITERATURE

B3 **Quoc Tu Giam St** **(04) 3845 2917**
7:30am-5:30pm Apr-Sep daily, 8am-5pm Oct-Mar daily

The oldest and possibly the finest architectural complex in Hanoi, Van Mieu, or the Temple of Literature, was established in 1070, during the Ly Dynasty (1009–1225). It is remarkably well preserved.

The temple was modeled on the original Temple of Confucius in the Chinese city of Qufu, and consists of five courtyards, the first two of which feature well-tended gardens. Each courtyard is separated by walls and ornamental gateways, and a central pathway through the complex divides it into two symmetrical halves. Founded in honor of the Chinese philosopher Confucius, the temple served as a center for higher learning. As the site of Vietnam's first university, established in 1076, it educated future mandarins for more than seven centuries. The university was destroyed by French bombs in 1947 but has been carefully reconstructed.

2313

The number of students who managed to pass the difficult exams between 1442 and 1779.

→
The Temple of Literature, modeled on the original in Qufu, China

Also known as the Constellation of Literature, the ornate Khue Van Cac gate was built in 1805 to reflect the brilliance of Van Mieu's literary legacy.

A square pool known as Thien Quang Tinh or the Well of Heavenly Clarity dominates the third courtyard. On either side of the pool are covered buildings that house 82 stone stelae, the most prized relics of the temple.

←
Khue Van Cac, a double-roofed gateway known as the Constellation of Literature

↑ Altar of Confucius with his statue dressed in rich robes of red and gold

↑ The Great Drum, standing to the east of the bell tower

During Tet, the fourth courtyard is the venue for human chess. The participants each represent a chess piece.

A magnificent bell tower was added to the fifth courtyard during restoration.

The counterpart of the bell tower is a giant drum. These two towers appear together in traditional Sinitic architecture.

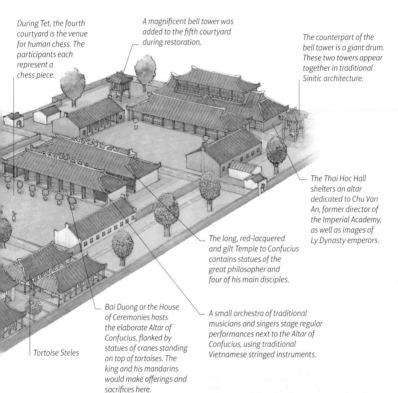

The Thai Hoc Hall shelters an altar dedicated to Chu Van An, former director of the Imperial Academy, as well as images of Ly Dynasty emperors.

The long, red-lacquered and gilt Temple to Confucius contains statues of the great philosopher and four of his main disciples.

Bai Duong or the House of Ceremonies hosts the elaborate Altar of Confucius, flanked by statues of cranes standing on top of tortoises. The king and his mandarins would make offerings and sacrifices here.

Tortoise Steles

A small orchestra of traditional musicians and singers stage regular performances next to the Altar of Confucius, using traditional Vietnamese stringed instruments.

TORTOISE STELES

Mounted on giant tortoise pedestals, these stone steles are inscribed with the names and brief personal details of scholars who passed Van Mieu's rigorous examinations. Dating from the 15th to the 18th centuries, only 82 out of the original 112 steles survive today.

EXPERIENCE MORE

Dong Xuan Market

📍 C2 🏛 Intersection of Dong Xuan and Hang Chieu sts, Old Quarter 📞 (024) 3792 5080 🕐 6am-6pm daily

As the oldest and largest covered market in Hanoi, Cho Dong Xuan holds a dominant position in the city. Near the end of the 19th century, the French tore down the old East Bridge Market that stood at this site, and replaced it with a covered building with five large halls. Dong Xuan is named after a hamlet that once stood on this site and is now a commercial center. However, in 1994, the market suffered a major setback when a massive fire burned down much of the building. Although it was rebuilt in 1996, all that remains of the original structure is the restored 1889 facade.

Today, this bustling three-story structure is packed with a wide range of clothing and household goods, fresh vegetables, meat and fish, and varieties of rice. Apart from local items, some low-cost, foreign goods are sold too. Located nearby is the historic Long Bien Bridge. Its strategic

> **Thang Long Water Puppet Theatre is possibly the best place in the country to see performances of the traditional art of _roi nuoc_.**

importance as the only bridge across Hanoi's Red River made it a prime target of the US Air Force during the Vietnam War. It survived the heavy bombing and is now used by trains, cyclists, and pedestrians.

Bach Ma Temple

📍 D3 🏛 76 Hang Buom St, Old Quarter 🕐 Sunrise-sunset daily

This small yet elegant temple is the oldest building in the Old Quarter (p188), dating in its original form from the founding of the capital city of Thang Long (p174), which became known as Hanoi in the 19th century. According to legend, when King Ly Thai To established the capital in 1010, the city walls kept falling down until a magical white horse appeared and indicated where

the new fortifications should be built. In an expression of gratitude, King Ly Thai To built the Bach Ma or White Horse Temple, and Bach Ma became the guardian spirit of the city.

The temple was restored in the 19th century, with contributions from the Hoa Chinese community settled on Hang Buom Street. Although a statue of the white horse still features prominently, the Hoa also introduced the veneration of Ma Vien, the Chinese general who re-established Chinese control over Vietnam in AD 43. An antique carved palanquin is also on display.

Thang Long Water Puppet Theatre

📍 D3 🏛 57 B Dinh Tien Hoang St, Hoan Kiem District 🕐 Performances at 3pm, 4:10pm, 5:20pm, 6:30pm & 8pm daily; also 9:30am Sun 🌐 thang longwaterpuppet.org

Thang Long Water Puppet Theatre is possibly the best place in the country to see performances of the traditional art of _roi nuoc_ or water puppetry. Master puppeteers make extensive use of dramatic music from the orchestra and startling special effects, such as smoke, firecrackers, and water-spraying dragon puppets to create a lively performance. At the end of the show, the bamboo curtain behind the stage rises to reveal the skilful puppeteers, standing waist deep in water. Seats by the stage promise great photos; note there is an additional charge for cameras.

←

Array of fruit and spices displayed on a stall in Dong Xuan Market

WATER PUPPET THEATER

Originating in the Red River Delta, *roi nuoc* or water puppetry is one of the most authentic expressions of Vietnamese culture. In times past, performances were held in villages, using rivers, lakes, or rice fields. Today, they are staged in water-filled tanks at theaters. Hiding behind the stage, the puppeteers stand waist deep in water, and manouver their wooden charges to the music of a traditional orchestra.

TRADITION

Special effects, including fire-breathing dragons, smoke, and fireworks add excitement to the show. The tales are told from the age-old perspective of a peasant culture and feature traditional themes and protagonists and villains such as warrior heroes, corrupt landlords, and cruel rulers. Mythical beasts in Viet culture, such as dragons, phoenixes, and unicorns, feature prominently, as do water buffalos and other domestic animals. Puppeteers emerge from behind the curtain at the end of a show. Their skill is acknowledged by claps and cheers.

Did You Know?

It is believed that water puppetry dates back almost a thousand years.

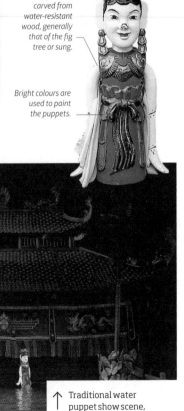

Puppets are carved from water-resistant wood, generally that of the fig tree or sung.

Bright colours are used to paint the puppets.

↑ Village folk in a boat shaped like a dragon, a mythical creature that is one of the most prominent characters

↑ Traditional water puppet show scene, with a fake palm adding a rural touch to the set

Visitors crossing
Sunbeam Bridge,
Hoan Kiem Lake

building is exquisitely preserved. Decorated with upswept eaves and elaborate carved dragons, the predominant colors are red, gold, yellow, and black. The temple was established by a mandarin named Nguyen Van Sieu. A stylized stone ink slab rests atop the temple's gate, while nearby, a tapering stone pillar depicts a traditional writing brush. The ideograms on the stele translate as "writing on a clear sky." A giant turtle that died in the lake in 1968 is preserved in a room at the back. Den Ngoc Son is dedicated to the spirits of the soil, medicine, and literature, as well as to Tran Hung Dao, who was the general who defeated the Mongols in the 13th century (p47).

To the east of the lake a large bronze Statue of Ly Thai To, the founder of the Ly Dynasty, honors the great founder of Thang Long. The statue, which has already become popular with pious Vietnamese, is venerated with incense and flowers.

Today, Hoan Kiem Lake is one of the city's most popular venues. It is generally filled

5 Hoan Kiem Lake

D3 ⬗ Hoan Kiem District
🕐 24 hours daily

Situated in the heart of Hanoi, Hoan Kiem Lake brims with mythology and lies close to the hearts of the Vietnamese people as a result. Legend has it that in the early 15th century, during the Ming Chinese occupation (p47), General Le Loi was presented with a magical sword by a divine golden turtle, which lived in the lake's waters. With the help of this sword, Le Loi expelled the Chinese from Thang Long, present-day Hanoi, and established himself as Emperor Le Thai To. Some time later, when the emperor was sailing on the lake, the divine turtle once again rose and reclaimed the sword. Since then, the lake has been known as Ho Hoan Kiem, or the Lake of the Restored Sword. In the mid-19th century, a small pagoda called Thap Rua or Turtle Tower was built to commemorate this super-natural event. Located on an islet in the

lake's center, the structure has become a city icon.

On an island at the northern end of Hoan Kiem Lake stands **Den Ngoc Son** or Jade Mountain Temple, one of the most beautiful and revered religious buildings in the capital. The temple can be accessed by an attractive red-painted, arched wooden bridge. This is the celebrated The Huc or Sunbeam Bridge. Dating from the Nguyen Dynasty in the early 1800s, the temple's

THE FOUNDING OF THANG LONG

In AD 968, Tien Hoang De, the first ruler of the Dinh Dynasty, moved his capital from Dai La, in the immediate vicinity of modern-day Hanoi, to Hoa Lu, 50 miles (80 km) to the south in Ninh Binh Province. Tien Hoang intended to relocate to a region that would be as far as possible from the Chinese frontier. However, this shift would not last long. Just 42 years later, Emperor Ly Thai To became unhappy with the isolation of Hoa Lu and determined to move the capital back to Dai La. In 1010, he returned to the former capital, defeated the Chinese in a violent battle, and established his kingdom here. According to legend, as he entered the city, a golden dragon took off from the top of the citadel and soared into the heavens. This event was taken by the emperor as an auspicious sign, and he renamed the city Thang Long or Ascending Dragon.

> Situated in the heart of Hanoi, Hoan Kiem Lake brims with mythology and lies close to the hearts of the Vietnamese people as a result.

with couples taking a stroll, people practicing Tai Chi, and old men playing chess. It is particularly enjoyable to visit on the weekend, when local traffic is banned.

Den Ngoc Son
🕐 7:30am–5:30pm daily

St Joseph's Cathedral

📍 C3 🏠 Nha Tho St, Hoan Kiem District 📞 (04) 3828 5967 🕐 5–11am & 2–7:30pm daily

Hanoi's most important church, St Joseph's Cathedral, also known as Nha Tho Lon, was inaugurated in 1886 and provides a focal point for the city's Catholics. Built in the late Neo-Gothic style, the building, with its majestic spires, is similar to a cathedral that might be found in any French provincial town. The interiors, which are more noteworthy, feature an ornate altar, French stained-glass windows, and a bas-relief painting of the Three Kings, complete with camels, on the cathedral's rear wall. St. Joseph's is usually packed to capacity on Sundays and on major holidays such as Easter and Christmas. However, on most days, its main doors are generally closed except during mass – though it is possible to gain entry via the side door.

Located to the east of the cathedral is **Chua Ba Da** or Stone Lady's Pagoda. Dating back to the 15th century, the pagoda was once known as Linh Quang or Holy Light. According to legend, the discovery of a woman's stone statue when the pagoda was being restored led to its more common local name. Entered by a narrow alley, Chua Ba Da is an oasis of tranquility in the heart of old Hanoi. The pagoda features several statues of the Thich Ca or Sakyamuni Buddha, and two large, antique bronze bells.

Chua Ba Da
🏠 2 Nha Tho St, Hoan Kiem District 🕐 Sunrise–sunset daily

EAT & DRINK

Hanoi Social Club
A popular hangout with hipsters who are attracted by its retro-chic decor, this café-bar has a menu of modern international dishes, including vegetarian options, and superb coffee and beer. It's a great spot for an evening tipple and regularly hosts live acoustic music.

📍 C3 🏠 6 Hoi Vu 📞 (04) 3938 2117

Standing Bar
Featuring a lovely view of Truc Bach Lake from its balcony, this expat-run bar has one of the most ample menus of local and international craft beers in the city, and live music or comedy almost nightly.

📍 C2 🏠 170 Tran Vu Street 📞 (024) 3266 8057

$$ $

Nê
Expert mixologists prepare innovative, tasty cocktails at this sophisticated bar that is popular with locals and has a relaxed atmosphere. There is also live jazz every night.

📍 C3 🏠 3B Tong Duy Tan 📞 (90) 488 6266

← Neo-Gothic St Joseph's Cathedral, set in a small square

7

Hoa Lo Prison Museum

📍C3 🏠1 Hoa Lo St, Hoan Kiem District 📞(04) 3824 6358 ⏰8am–5pm daily

The infamous Hoa Lo Prison was built by the French administration in 1896. Originally intended to hold around 450 prisoners, by the 1930s there were almost 2,000, the majority of them political prisoners. During the Vietnam War, Hoa Lo Prison achieved notoriety as a place of incarceration for downed US pilots, who ironically nicknamed it the Hanoi Hilton. Called Maison Centrale during French rule – the original sign still hangs over the entrance – most of the prison complex was demolished in 1997 in order to make way for the Hanoi Towers buildings. However, the architects preserved enough to create the Hoa Lo Prison Museum.

The majority of the exhibits here include a horrifying array of shackles, whips, and other instruments of torture, as well as solitary confinement cells, which date from the French colonial period, and the old, narrow sewer system through which more than 100 prisoners escaped in August 1945. A small section of the museum is devoted to the American period, contriving to show how well US prisoners (including US senator John McCain) supposedly fared in contrast to the brutality shown to the Vietnamese by the French. At the back of the museum is a guillotine.

8

Ambassador's Pagoda

📍C4 🏠73 Quan Su St, Hoan Kiem District 📞(04) 3825 2427 ⏰8–11am, 1–4pm daily

Established as a stopping point for visiting Buddhist dignitaries, Chua Quan Su or Ambassador's Pagoda is named after a guesthouse that stood here in the 15th century. The official center of Mahayana Buddhism in Hanoi, it is one of the most popular pagodas in the city, attracting hundreds of followers, especially during the important Buddhist holidays.

The present-day pagoda dates from 1942 and houses images of the past, present, and future incarnations of the Buddha – these are the A Di Da or Amitabha, Thich Ca or Sakyamuni, and Di Lac or Maitreya Buddhas. There are always many nuns and monks in attendance here. A small shop by the entrance sells Buddhist paraphernalia and ritualistic items.

9

Vietnamese Women's Museum

📍D4 🏠36 Ly Thuong Kiet ⏰8am–5pm daily 🌐womenmuseum.org.vn

This relatively little-known museum evocatively traces the role of women in historical and contemporary Vietnam. Visually arresting and well-organized, the museum comprises four floors of fascinating exhibits and photographs enhanced by informative captions in

↑ Colorful entrance to the Ambassador's Pagoda

Vietnamese, French, and English. There is also a pleasant courtyard café.

Women's roles, family life, history, and fashion are explored, giving the visitor an in-depth insight into the country's culture and history. Highlights include exhibits about the vital role played by women in the wars against the French and Americans, and the ceremonies and artifacts involved at each stage of a woman's life. There are heroic stories of many present-day outstanding Vietnamese women, as well as examples of the traditional female costume of all the 54 ethnic groups in Vietnam.

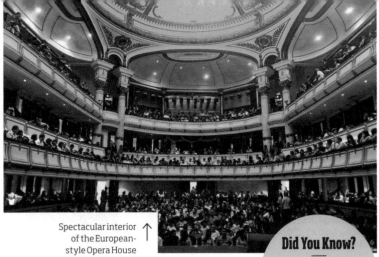

Spectacular interior of the European-style Opera House

Sofitel Legend Metropole Hotel

D3 **15 Ngo Quyen St, Hoan Kiem District** **24 hours daily** **sofitel-legend.com**

Hanoi's most prestigious and oldest hotel, the Metropole was constructed in French colonial style, with a wealth of wrought iron and Art Nouveau decorations. The grand hotel opened originally in 1901, and it was for many years the most favored accommodation in all of French Indochina. Notable guests, both past and present, include actors, writers, heads of state, and many other well-known public figures, among them writer W. Somerset Maugham, actor Charlie Chaplin, author Graham Greene, playwright Noël Coward, actor Michael Caine, musician Joan Baez, and Russian president Vladimir Putin.

During the Vietnam War guests used the hotel's large air raid shelter under the building. Although the hotel became deplorably rundown during the austere years of state socialism between 1954 and 1986, it has since been magnificently restored to its former glory and luxury.

The striking **Government Guest House**, just to the north of the Metropole, was built in 1919 as the palace of a French governor. Its colonial facade and multi-tiered portico in cast iron are attractive and well worth a second look.

Government Guest House

10 Ngo Quyen St, Hoan Kiem District **To the public**

Opera House

D4 **1 Trang Tien St, Hoan Kiem District** **During performances** **hanoioperahouse.org.vn**

Modeled on the Paris Opera designed by Charles Garnier, the Hanoi Opera House, also known as Nha Hat Lon or Big Song House, opened in 1911. It formed the centerpiece of French colonial architecture, not just in Hanoi, but in all of French Indochina.

Before World War II, the Opera House was at the center of the city's cultural life. At the end of French rule, however, it gradually fell into disrepair.

During the years prior to the nation's economic and cultural liberalization in the late 1980s, visiting Chinese or Russian artistes would appear. Performances such as the militant ballet *Red Detachment of Women* or a musical recital by an ensemble from Kiev, now in the Ukraine, were held here. By the mid-1980s, even these limited cultural exchanges had ceased, and the Opera House was all but abandoned.

In 1994, the authorities started a three-year restoration, which cost US$14 million. Today, the colonnaded building, with refurbished gilt mirrors and grand stairways, is a magnificent sight. The 600-seat theater, with state-of-the-art audio facilities, stages Vietnamese operetta, ballets, and recitals. Home to the Hanoi Symphony Orchestra, it hosts shows by visiting companies such as the US's Philadelphia Symphony Orchestra.

> **Hanoi's most prestigious and oldest hotel, the Metropole was constructed in French colonial style with a wealth of wrought iron and Art Nouveau decorations.**

Did You Know?

The Trung Sisters' army, which fought the Chinese in AD 40, had untrained forces and few supplies.

12

Hai Ba Trung Temple

📍 D5 🏛 Dong Nhan St, Hai Ba Trung District ⏱ Only during festivals

One of the most important temple complexes in Vietnam, the Hai Ba Trung Temple is dedicated to the popular cult of deified heroes. It honors the heroic Trung Sisters, who expelled the Chinese for a brief time in the first century AD. Founded by Emperor Ly Anh Ton in 1142, the temple enshrines the supposedly petrified remains of the sisters.

The temple stands on the bank of a small artificial lake called Huong Vien, and is entered through a broad gateway flanked by tall white columns. These bear auspicious Chinese symbols and characters for longevity topped by stylized lotus flowers.

The temple is generally not open to the public. However, during the annual festival (p34), it attracts hundreds of devotees when both statues are bathed in water from the nearby Red River and dressed in new red robes.

13

National Museum of Vietnamese History

📍 D4 🏛 1 Pham Ngu Lao St, Hoan Kiem District ⏱ 8am-noon, 1:30-5pm daily 🔒 First Mon of each month 🌐 baotanglichsu.vn

Originally known as the École Française d'Extrême-Orient, this museum was constructed

between 1925 and 1932. It was designed by Ernest Hébrard and it heralded a new hybrid style of architecture – called Indochinoise, it incorporated several elements of French, Khmer, and Vietnamese styles. The design is anchored by an octagonal pagoda and the building is painted ocher-yellow, and offset by dark green shutters. Although it is ornamented with fanciful colonnades, brackets, and balustrades, the overall effect remains Oriental.

Known in Vietnamese as Bao Tang Lich Su, the museum is one of the best in Vietnam, and offers tours (by prior arrangement only). It is spread over two floors and features a fine collection of artifacts from the prehistoric Dong Son culture of the Red River Delta, as well as the ancient Sa Huynh and Oc Eo civilizations of southern Vietnam. The museum also has sculptures dating from the Champa Empire. Some of the exhibits

THE TRUNG SISTERS

The 1st century AD was a period of resentment against Chinese rule. In AD 40, Trung Trac and her sister, Trung Nhi, established an army with the aid of the Vietnamese lords. Fighting fearlessly, the sisters expelled the Chinese, and established their own kingdom at Me Linh in the Red River Delta. In AD 43, however, the Chinese were able to quell the rebellion. To avoid capture, the sisters committed suicide by jumping into the Hat River. Centuries later, stone figures of two women washed up on a sandbank in the Red River. Believed to be the earthly remains of the Trung Sisters, petrified and turned into statues, they were taken to Dong Nhan village, now Hai Ba Trung District, and installed in a temple. Today, the sisters are honored as heroes of national independence.

↑ Handsome exterior of the National Museum of Vietnamese History

include wooden stakes from the 13th-century Battle of Bach Dang (p44). An annex to the museum lies across the street and this houses the former Museum of Vietnamese Revolution.

Lien Phai Pagoda

📍C5 🏠Ngo Chua Lien Phai St, Hai Ba Trung District ☎(04) 3590 6442 🕐7-11am, 1:30-5:30pm daily

Tucked away down bustling alleyways off the main road, offering a glimpse of everyday life in the city, Lien Phai Pagoda stands amid a pretty, peaceful garden. Also known as the Pagoda of the Lotus

Sect, Lien Phai is one of the few surviving relics of the Trinh lords (p184) in Hanoi.

According to the inscription on the central stele, Lord Trinh Thap had a palace in this area. One day his workers dug up a huge rock shaped like a lotus root in the gardens, and Trinh Thap took this as an indication from the Buddha that he should abandon his privileged life and become a monk. He ordered a temple to be built at the palace where the stone was discovered. The pagoda was built in 1726, and Trinh Thap spent the remainder of his life here as a monk. When he died, his ashes were interred in the pagoda, and some of his calligraphy hangs beside the main altar. The most

impressive structure here is the Dieu Quang or Miraculous Light Tower, which rises through ten levels. A bell tower was added in 1869, along with a wall. The Lotus Sect, founded by Trinh Thap, honors the A Di Da or Amitabha Buddha, and its followers believe that by chanting his name and ridding oneself of desire, one can be reborn in the Western Paradise of Sukhavati or Pure Land. This sect is very popular in China and Japan.

INSIDER TIP
Quang Ba Flower Market

Hanoi's largest flower market is open daily from 2am until after sunrise on Au Co Street. With its piles of beautiful blossoms, it is especially colorful during Tet Nguyen festivites (p43).

One of the most important temple complexes in Vietnam, the Hai Ba Trung Temple is dedicated to the popular cult of deified heroes.

↑ The Bodhisattva statue on display in the Vietnam Fine Arts Museum *(inset)*

15

Vietnam Fine Arts Museum

B3 66 Nguyen Thai Hoc St, Ba Dinh District 8:30am-5pm daily vnfam.vn

Housed in a fine old colonial building, the Bao Tang My Thuat or Fine Arts Museum has a varied and interesting selection of Vietnam's artifacts, architecture, paintings, sculpture, and many other works of art. The exhibits are displayed chronologically, starting with a fine collection of Stone and Bronze Age relics on the first floor. Several wood, stone, and lacquer sculptures feature as well, illustrating the versatile nature of Vietnamese art. One of the highlights here is an extraordinary Bodhisattva or Enlightened Being that supposedly has 1,000 eyes and 1,000 arms.

The exhibition rooms on the second floor contain some of the country's best lacquer paintings, and the third floor hosts many watercolor and oil works by Vietnamese artists. Other exhibits include carvings from the Central Highlands, woodblock paintings from the Dong Ho culture, and ethnic clothing. Replicas of antique pieces are for sale in the museum shop.

16

Ho Chi Minh Museum

B3 19 Ngoc Ha St, Ba Dinh District 8am-12pm Mon & Fri, 8am-4:30pm Tue-Thu & Sat-Sun; baotanghochiminh.vn

Established in 1990 – one century after Ho Chi Minh's birth – this interesting museum chronicles and celebrates the revolutionary leader's life and achievements in a series of displays. These include an eclectic mix of his personal memorabilia, as well as black-and-white photographs from his youth and the long period he spent abroad in Europe and China. Other displays include art installations that represent abstract concepts associated with Ho Chi Minh, such as freedom and social progress. Though unapologetically partisan, the museum is nevertheless informative, unusual, and well presented.

17

Ho Chi Minh Mausoleum

B2 Ba Dinh Sq, Ba Dinh District 8-11am Tue-Thu & Sat-Sun For about two months a year, usually in Oct & Nov, for embalming maintenance

On the west side of Ba Dinh Square, an imposing, heavy grey structure, built of stone quarried from the Marble Mountains near Danang *(p156)*, forms Ho Chi Minh's final resting place.

An unassuming man who prided himself on an austere, almost ascetic public image, Ho Chi Minh had allegedly requested that he be cremated and his ashes scattered in Northern, Central, and Southern Vietnam, symbolizing the national unity to which he had devoted his life. However, after Ho Chi Minh's death in 1969, the leading members of the Vietnamese politburo reportedly altered his final testament by deleting his request to be cremated. Instead, with the help of Soviet specialists, the leader was embalmed and installed deep inside the monumental marble Ho Chi Minh Mausoleum in 1975, which was inspired by Lenin's Mausoleum in Moscow.

The building's exterior is considered by many as both ponderous and unappealing. Astonishingly, the architects supposedly intended the structure to represent a lotus flower, though it is very difficult to see how this design was carried out. Inside, the mood is somber and decidedly respectful. Ho Chi Minh, dressed in the simple clothing favored by Chinese nationalist leader Sun Yat Sen, lies in a chilled, dim room, his crossed hands resting on dark cloth covers inside a glass sarcophagus.

The mausoleum is an important pilgrimage site for many Vietnamese, especially from the north, and should be approached with respect and reverence. Noisy behavior, loitering, inappropriate clothing (such as shorts and sleeveless tops), putting your hands in your pockets, crossing your arms, and photography are all strictly forbidden. Changing of the guard takes place periodically outside the mausoleum with much pomp.

HO CHI MINH

Acclaimed as the leader of Vietnam's struggle for independence, Ho Chi Minh was born in 1890 at Hoang Tru village, near Vinh. After studying in Hue, Ho Chi Minh, then known as Nguyen Tat Thanh, left Vietnam in 1911 to travel the world. Influenced by socialist ideologies during his stay in Europe, he founded Communist organizations in Paris, Moscow, and China.

VIETNAMESE INDEPENDENCE LEAGUE

He returned to Vietnam in 1941, where he took the name Ho Chi Minh (Bringer of Enlightenment) and formed the Vietnamese Independence League, or Viet Minh. In 1945, he became president of the Democratic Republic of Vietnam, leading long and bitter wars against France and the United States. Full-scale war broke out in 1946, and the Viet Minh, led by Ho Chi Minh, waged a battle that would last eight long years. Ho Chi Minh spent hours perfecting military strategies, which included employing underground resistance and guerilla tactics to expel the French. Though he died six years before reunification, Vietnam's independence is considered his greatest achievement.

→ Ho Chi Minh is featured in the form of statues and portraits throughout the country.

QUOC HOC SCHOOL

The prestigious Quoc Hoc School in Hue, the oldest in Vietnam, is where Ho Chi Minh studied, along with future general Vo Nguyen Giap and Pham Van Dong, the future prime minister of Vietnam.

↑ Personally a gentle and unassuming man, Ho was much loved by children and adults

→

A visitor enjoying the breathtaking Sky Walk at the Lotte Observation Deck

⑱ Ho Chi Minh's Stilt House

📍 B2 🏠 1 Bach Thao St, Presidential Palace, Ba Dinh District ⏰ 7:30–11am Mon; 7:30–11:30am, 2–4pm Tue–Thu & Sat–Sun

Believing that the Presidential Palace was too grand for him, Ho Chi Minh, on becoming president of the Democratic Republic of Vietnam in 1954, arranged for a modest wooden structure to be built in the palace's grounds. Modeled on a traditional stilt house, this simple two-story structure is known as Nha Bac Ho or Uncle Ho's House. Next to the stilts and surrounded by plants are the tables and chairs used by members of the politburo for meetings with Ho Chi Minh.

Wooden stairs at the back of the house lead to two rooms: a study and a bedroom, both kept just as they were when the great man was alive. The study has an antique typewriter and a bookcase. The bedroom is even more spartan, with a bed, electric clock, an old-fashioned telephone and a radio as the only concessions to comfort. Surrounding the house are carefully tended gardens with weeping willows, mango trees, and fragrant frangipani and jasmine. Ho Chi Minh lived here from 1958 to 1969.

Close to the presidential stilt house, the **Botanical Gardens** boast two lakes and abundant greenery, as well as an exhibition of sculpture.

Botanical Gardens

🌳 🏠 Hoang Hoa Tham St ⏰ 7:30am–10pm daily

Pagoda was constructed by Emperor Ly Thai Tong in AD 1049. Situated within the tiny Dien Huu Pagoda, also dating from the 11th century, this wooden pagoda is built, as the name suggests, on a single stone pillar, standing in an elegant lotus pond.

According to legend, the emperor, who had no son, had a dream in which he was visited by Quan Am, Goddess of Mercy. She was sitting on a lotus flower and presented him with a baby boy. Soon after, Ly Thai Tong married a new young queen who bore him a son. To show his gratitude for this happy outcome, the emperor then ordered the construction of a single-pillared pagoda representing a lotus flower. It symbolizes purity, just like a beautiful lotus flower blossoming in a muddy pond. The pillar is constructed of stone and measures 4 ft (1.25 m) in diameter.

Over the centuries, One Pillar Pagoda has been damaged and reconstructed on numerous occasions. The last time it was destroyed was by the French, who burned it in 1954. It was then rebuilt by the government.

Did You Know?

"Uncle Ho" had the toilet removed from his stilt house because it wasn't considered "traditional."

---

⑲ One Pillar Pagoda

📍 B3 🏠 8 Chua Mot St, Ba Dinh District ⏰ 8am–5pm daily

Rivaling Cot Co as one of Hanoi's most prominent icons, the Chua Mot Cot or One Pillar

Southeast Asia. The tower includes shops, offices, and a hotel. The Sky Walk, with its vertigo-inducing, crystal-clear glass floor, is worth the entrance fee. There are sublime views in all directions across Hanoi, allowing visitors to get a sense of the scale of the small Old Quarter among the rest of this sprawling modern city.

Lotte Observation Deck

📍 A3 🏛 54 Lieu Giai, Ba Dinh District 🕐 9am-11pm daily 🌐 lottecenter.com.vn

Without doubt, the best views of Hanoi are to be had from this 890-ft- (272-m-) high observation deck installed on the 65th floor of the Lotte Centre Hanoi. This is the only observation deck in the city, and the first to be built in

Imperial Citadel of Thang Long

📍 C3 🏛 9 Hoang Dieu, Ba Dinh District 🕐 8am-5pm Tue-Sun 🌐 hoang thanhthanglong.vn

Unfortunately, much of the site of the Imperial Citadel was destroyed by the French in the late 19th century. For centuries, the Citadel was only accessible to the country's rulers, but in 2010, it was recognized by UNESCO as a World Heritage Site and is now open to the public. The buildings that survived destruction are definitely worth a visit.

At the south end of this mammoth complex, adjacent to the Military History Museum, is the Cat Co, or the Flag Tower. North of here, the Doan Mon

Gate is probably the most impressive structure of the Citadel still remaining. The imposing walls containing five archways and supporting a double-roofed pavilion can be seen once the main entrance to the forbidden realm is entered. Beyond the gate are the excavations showing a sophisticated waterway, probably once used for irrigation. Nothing remains of the Kinh Tien Palace, which once functioned as the imperial residence, apart from the building's beautifully sculpted dragon balustrades.

In the heart of the complex is a squat colonial building named D67, which was a command center for northern forces during the Vietnam War. The conference table still has the reserved seats of luminaries such as General Giap (1911–2013), who was the mastermind behind many Vietnamese victories. There is also a bomb shelter deep below the ground.

North of the D67 building are two more structures of interest – Hau Lau and Cua Bac, the northern gate. On the west side of Hoang Dieu Street is a massive archaeological dig, consisting mostly of foundations of former palaces, giving an idea of the scale of the Citadel complex.

→ The magnificent Doan Mon Gate and the glass-covered excavations area

Located just off Hanoi Circus is Thong Nhat Park (also known as Lenin Park after its statue of Lenin). Popular with cyclists, skateboarders, and people playing soccer, it is a pleasant place to take a rest. The area is surrounded by trees and flowers and there is a lake offering the chance of a cool breeze. Swan-shaped boats can be hired if you want to take to the water.

㉒

Kim Lien Pagoda

 B1 🏠 Ho Tay, Tu Liem District ⏰ Sunrise-sunset daily

Situated on the northern shore of pretty Ho Tay lake, the stunningly attractive Kiem Lien Pagoda is somewhat out of the way, but well deserving of a visit nonetheless.

Legend has it that Princess Tu Hoa, the daughter of 12th-century Emperor Ly Than Tong, brought her ladies-in-waiting to the area so they could cultivate silkworms to produce cloth. Centuries later, in 1771, a pagoda was built on the foundations of her palace and named Kim Lien, which means Golden Lotus, in memory of the princess.

Now entered through a triple-arched gate, the pagoda comprises three elegant pavilions that are laid out in three lines, supposedly representing the Chinese character *san* or three. They each have sweeping eaves and stacked roofs.

㉓

Ho Tay

📍 **B1**

To the west of Hanoi are two beautiful lakes, separated from the Red River by the great dike to the north. The larger of the two is Ho Tay or West Lake (with a circumference of about 10.5 miles/17 km), which is home to Hanoi's sailing club. It is separated from Truc Bach or White Silk Lake to the east by an artificial causeway.

In times past, Ho Tay was associated with the Trinh lords, who built grand palaces and pavilions along its shores, as well as many Buddhist temples. The palaces are gone, but many temples remain, including the city's oldest, **Tran Quoc Pagoda**. According to legend, it was established alongside the banks of the Red River during the reign of Trinh lord, Ly Nam De (r.544–8), but was moved to its current location during the 17th century.

Also worth a visit is **Quan Thanh Temple**, reputed to have been patronized by Emperor Ly Thai To, founder of the Ly Dynasty *(p46)*. Rebuilt in 1893, it is dedicated to Tran Vo or Guardian of the North. An image of this Taoist divinity dominates the altar.

Today, the area around Ho Tay is becoming increasingly upscale, with lots of luxury hotels along its shore. It is also home to high-end restaurants, stylish bars, and chic boutiques.

Tran Quoc Pagoda

♻ 🏠 Kim Ngu Island, Thanh Nien Causeway ⏰ Sunrise-sunset daily

Quan Thanh Temple

🏠 Intersection of Thanh Nien Causeway and Quan Thanh sts ⏰ Sunrise-sunset daily

In times past, Ho Tay was associated with the Trinh lords who built grand palaces and pavilions along its shores, as well as many Buddhist temples.

↑ Tran Quoc Pagoda and
its garden reflected in
the tranquil waters of
Ho Tay at dusk

24

Co Loa Citadel

◉ B5 ⬥ 10 miles (16 km) N of Hanoi, Dong Anh District ⏱ 8am–5pm daily

This is the first known capital of an independent Vietnamese kingdom. The stories surrounding this ancient fortress rely on oral tradition long since written down but impossible to verify.

Stylized stone lions sit on guard outside the temple dedicated to King An Duong. A major festival takes place here each year in honor of the legendary king, and a statue of him is carried in a palanquin from the temple to the local *dinh* or communal house. To promote tourism and revive traditional culture, the festivities include games of human chess, cockfighting, singing, and dancing. On the last day, An Duong is carried from the *dinh* back to his temple.

25

Museum of Ethnology

◉ B5 ⬥ 60 Nguyen Van Huyen St, Cau Giay District ⏱ 8:30am–5:30pm Tue–Sun 🌐 vme.org.vn

Located west of the city center, the Bao Tang Dan Toc Hoc or Museum of Ethnology offers informative and well-documented displays on the country's many ethnic groups, from the dominant Kinh to the minorities in the highlands of the north and center.

Exhibits in the main building include elaborate and colorful hill-tribe costumes, weaving designs, musical instruments, fishing implements, and work tools. There are further displays in the extensive grounds, with examples of minority buildings from the Central Highlands, such as communal houses, steep pitched roofs, and elaborately carved tombs. A highlight is the re-creation of a Black Thai house.

The museum also serves as a research center for Vietnam's 54 recognized ethnic groups.

26

Thay Pagoda

◉ B5 ⬥ 20 miles (32 km) W of Hanoi, Ha Tay Province ⏱ Sunrise–sunset daily

Dedicated to the Thich Ca or the Sakyamuni Buddha, Chua Thay or Master's Pagoda is named for Tu Dao Hanh – a 12th-century monk and master water puppeteer. The temple is mainly renowned for being home to more than 100 religious statues, including two huge guardians, the largest in

> The Viet Palace complex sprawls over a shady, wooded hill, and it is easy to spend half a day here wandering the grounds and exploring their quirky nooks and crannies.

Vietnam. Made of clay and papier-mâché, these giants weigh more than 2,200 lb (1,000 kg) each.

Inside, to the left of the main altar stands a statue of the master, and to the right is a statue of Emperor Ly Nhan Tong (r.1072–1127), believed to be a reincarnation of Tu Dao Hanh, and under whose reign this attractive house of worship was established. The pagoda also hosts water puppet shows (*p173*) during its annual festival.

27

Duong Lam Ancient Village

◉ A5 ⬥ 37 miles (60 km) NW of Hanoi 🚌 70 from Dinh Thom in Northern Hanoi

No more than an hour away by road from Hanoi, this 1,200-year-old ancient village

← Thay Pagoda on a picturesque lake, and statue of the Red Guardian (inset)

gives visitors an insight into rural life in Vietnam without having to venture too far off the beaten trail.

Duong Lam features traditional houses, some up to 400 years old, with stone arches and courtyards, atmospheric narrow alleyways, and picturesque, cooling ponds. The village also has a well, a centuries-old French Catholic church, several pagodas, and a carved communal house, where villagers come together for a variety of cultural activities. There are also temples dedicated to two significant regional kings – Phung Hung (771–802) and Ngo Quyen (896–944) – both of whom were born in the village.

Many of the old rust-colored laterite buildings now house eateries and homestays, and the street stalls are a good place to pick up souvenirs. Duong Lam continues to be a working village, so visitors have the opportunity to see authentic Vietnamese rural life and traditional culture.

Surrounded by countryside, the village has some lovely vistas. An ideal way to enjoy the gorgeous views is to rent a bicycle and head out to the flooded, lush green rice paddies to take in the reflections of the far-off mountains in the water.

 28

Thanh Chuong Viet Palace

📍 B4 🚗 20 miles (32 km) N of Hanoi, Hien Ninh Commune, Soc Son District 🚌 7 or 58 to KCM Bac Thang Long, then bus 64 to Xom Nui 🕘 9am–5pm daily 🌐 thanhchuongviet palace.com

In 2001, Thanh Chuong, one of Vietnam's leading contemporary artists, chose this site as the perfect place in which to display his extensive art collection. Since then the complex has grown into what today would describe as an art installation in itself.

The Viet Palace comprises 15 heritage houses of varying architectural styles relocated here from around the country. The complex sprawls over a shady, wooded hill, and it is easy to spend half a day here wandering the grounds and exploring their quirky nooks and crannies. Here, pagodas loom from behind trees, stone patios surround ornamental lotus ponds, and a bewildering range of eclectic statuary is dotted around.

The collections inside the heritage buildings consist of about 2,000 historical and cultural artifacts, including plates, bowls, vases, statues, and works of art, spanning the entire history of Vietnam. There are ancient objects and contemporary works of art, and the range of items illustrates the varied nature of Vietnamese culture, art, and architecture.

The complex is situated just 6 miles (10 km) north of Na Bai International Airport in Hanoi, so it could make a wonderful final excursion before leaving the country.

→ Mountain God Tower in the gardens of Thanh Chuong Viet Palace

 29

Hung Kings' Temples

📍 A4 🚗 62 miles (100 km) NW of Hanoi, Phong Chau District, Phu Tho Province. Museum: 📞 (021) 386 0026 🕘 8–11:30am, 1–4pm daily

Believed by the Vietnamese to be the very earliest relics of their civilization, the temples of the Hung kings are located on Mount Nghia Linh. Built by rulers of the Vang Lang Kingdom, between the 7th and 3rd centuries BC, they are objects of great veneration. Stone stairs climb sharply up through the trees to the lowest temple, Den Ha, the middle temple, Den Hung, and the superior temple near the top of the hill, Den Thuong. The entire area is filled with pagodas, lotus ponds, and small shrines. The most important of these is Lang Hung – a tiny shrine with candle and incense holders, located a few feet down the slope from Den Thuong. It is evident that this tomb has undergone reconstructions.

The views from Mount Nghia Linh's summit sweep across the surrounding landscape. At the mountain's foot there is a small museum that displays various objects such as frog drums, pottery, and arrowheads, as well as other historical relics. The annual Hung Kings Festival in April is now a national holiday and attracts huge crowds.

A SHORT WALK
OLD QUARTER

Distance 0.6 mile (1 km) **Time** 15 minutes

Buzzing with noise and activity, the Old Quarter is the oldest and most lively commercial district in Hanoi. During the 13th century, several artisans settled along the Red River to cater to the needs of the palace. Later, the crafts became concentrated in this area, with each street specializing in a particular product.

Over the years, many distinct crafts guilds came into existence, and the area earned its nickname of 36 Streets. Today, you can admire the Old Quarter's historic charm as you wander the narrow alleys packed with hundreds of small shops, restaurants, and ancient tube houses.

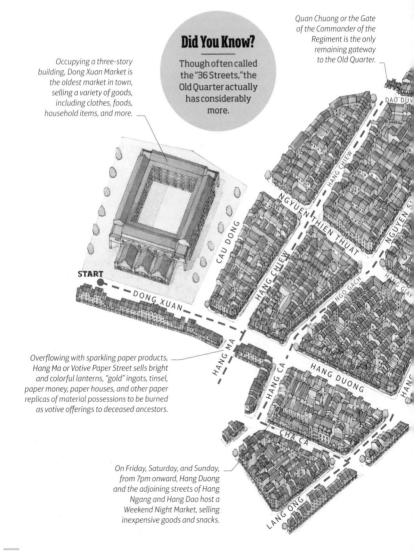

Occupying a three-story building, Dong Xuan Market is the oldest market in town, selling a variety of goods, including clothes, foods, household items, and more.

Did You Know?

Though often called the "36 Streets," the Old Quarter actually has considerably more.

Quan Chuong or the Gate of the Commander of the Regiment is the only remaining gateway to the Old Quarter.

START

Overflowing with sparkling paper products, Hang Ma or Votive Paper Street sells bright and colorful lanterns, "gold" ingots, tinsel, paper money, paper houses, and other paper replicas of material possessions to be burned as votive offerings to deceased ancestors.

On Friday, Saturday, and Sunday, from 7pm onward, Hang Duong and the adjoining streets of Hang Ngang and Hang Dao host a Weekend Night Market, selling inexpensive goods and snacks.

← Kitchen in the Memorial House Museum, inside a historic tube house

Locator Map
For more detail see p166

| 0 meters | 100 | N |
| 0 yards | 100 | |

Formerly the Sailmakers Street, Hang Buom now sells a remarkable selection of locally made sweetmeats and candies, many different varieties of fresh ground coffee, and imported alcohol, chiefly whiskies, brandies, and even wines.

Once the home of an affluent Chinese family, this beautifully restored tube house now contains the Memorial House Museum, which provides an excellent insight into the lives of merchants who lived in the Old Quarter centuries ago.

HANG CHINH

HANG BUOM

DAO DUY TU

LONG NGOC QUYEN

MA MAY

HANG MAM

HANG BE

● **FINISH**

The oldest religious building in the Old Quarter, the small Bach Ma Temple is dedicated to the city's guardian spirit, represented by a magical white horse.

Hang Mam Street or Pickled Fish Street is now lined with shops selling marble headstones, often engraved with an image of the deceased.

← Engraver at work at a shop on Hang Mam Street

NORTHERN VIETNAM

Vietnam's north has been inhabited for thousands of years, but little of its history was documented until the French occupation. The French established a hill station at Sapa in the 1920s but their dominion did not last long. Vietnam's independence movement secured the liberation of the northern provinces from French rule between 1945 and 1952. In the far west, close to the Laos border, the valley of Dien Bien Phu is of great historical importance as the site of the final Viet Minh victory over the French in 1954 – a triumphant chapter in Vietnam's history.

Relations between China and Vietnam deteriorated in the 1970s due to Vietnam's invasion of Cambodia, whose genocidal regime under Pol Pot was supported by China. In 1979 the Chinese sent 200,000 troops into Northern Vietnam, destroying hundreds of border towns – they were later driven out. Though much of the damage from the war has been repaired, unmarked minefields along the frontier remain. Most areas, and certainly those visited by tourists, are safe, but in more remote parts it's best to stick to official, well-trodden paths.

NORTHERN VIETNAM

Must Sees
1. Halong Bay
2. Perfume Pagoda

Experience More
3. Cuc Phuong National Park
4. Halong City
5. Bai Tu Long Bay
6. Cat Ba Island
7. Ninh Binh
8. Yen Tu Pilgrimage Sites
9. Haiphong
10. Hoa Binh
11. Mai Chau Valley
12. Moc Chau
13. Son La
14. Dien Bien Phu
15. Sapa
16. Bac Ha
17. Ba Be National Park
18. Cao Bang
19. Dong Van Karst Plateau Geopark

0 kilometers   50

0 miles   50

N

→

① Limestone karst shoreline at Ninh Binh.

② Buddha statue in Bai Dinh Temple.

③ A White Thai woman working in the rice fields of the Mai Chau Valley.

A tour of the North of Vietnam will take you off the beaten path to see beautiful places and meet culturally diverse peoples. It can be done independently or through one of the tour agencies run by indigenous peoples in Hanoi.

2 WEEKS
in Northern Vietnam

Day 1: Perfume Pagoda

Head off early from Hanoi to My Duc, from where local women ferry visitors on wooden boats upriver through the countryside to Fragrant Vestige Mountain. Walk up the mountain to Perfume Pagoda (p204). This complex of around 30 Buddhist shrines is one of the most spectacular in the country; some are located in pleasant grounds on the wooded slopes while others are set deep within the rock, the meager lighting inside reflecting off gilded statues through thick wreaths of incense smoke. You can easily spend most of the day here, with lunch at one of the vegetarian restaurants, before moving on south to Ninh Bin (p208) in time for dinner.

Day 2: Ninh Bin

Spend the morning taking a boat trip upriver to the flooded caves at Tan Coc, passing through the stunningly beautiful countryside, often called "Halong Bay on Land", where the karst outcrops jut majestically from a brilliant-green sea of rice paddies. Then, after lunch in Ninh Binh, hire a taxi to take you to the many interesting sights around the town such as Hoa Lu, the largely restored capital of the 10th-century Dinh Dynasty, whose impressive imperial buildings are set around a picturesque lake. From there, it's not too far to Vietnam's biggest temple complex, Bai Dinh Temple, which features an imposing pagoda and an amazing array of Buddha statues including an enormous 100-ton bronze Buddha.

Day 3: Cuc Phuong National Park

From Ninh Bin it's a short hop to the lush primary tropical forest at the Cuc Phuong National Park (p205), the oldest in the country thanks to its very diverse flora and fauna. You can spend the day wandering some of the shorter treks which take you through the raw jungle, past pretty waterfalls and to the botanical gardens and the Endangered Primate Rescue Centre where you can see langur, gibbons, loris, and other primates at close range. Stay overnight in a homestay in one of the Muong villages nearby.

Day 4: Mai Chau Valley

Another short journey will take you to the charming and fertile Mai Chau Valley (p210), where you can enjoy the warm hospitality of the White Thai people in a traditional stilt house. Spend a day wandering or cycling through the rice paddies, tea plantations, tiny hamlets, and jungle trails here. To venture farther off the beaten trail, trek in Pu Luong Nature Reserve before dining with your hosts, followed by watching a traditional music and dance show while sipping on potent *ruou can* homebrew. →

→

1 Tea fields in the Moc Chau Valley.

2 Memorial in Dien Bien Phu Military Cemetery.

3 A Black Hmong woman wearing traditional dress.

4 Beautiful beach at Co To Island, Bai Tu Long Bay.

Day 5: Moc Chau to Dien Bien Phu

After leaving Mai Chau, the long road northward to Dien Bien Phu offers a couple of rest stops along the way. Located among the tea fields, the market town of Moc Chau (p210) makes an excellent spot for lunch. You might want to spend a couple of hours exploring the picturesque hamlets and rice-terraced hills that surround it. Make a visit to the historically significant town of Son La (p210); the former prison and museum is a good place to learn about the horrors of French colonial rule and discover more about the local hill peoples who live in the area. Head back on the road to reach Dien Bien Phu (p211) by sunset. Situated near the Laos border, it was the site of the decisive battle of the First Indochina War in 1954, where French troops suffered a major defeat by the Communist Viet Minh forces.

Day 6: Dien Bien Phu

Spend the morning in the Dien Bien Phu Museum to learn about the history of the battle. Then head out to the valley to see monuments to the dead and the main battlefield, which is dotted with burned-out tanks and Viet Minh tunnels.

Days 7, 8, and 9: Sapa

Visit the famous mountain town of Sapa (p212), a delightful summer retreat due to its cool climate, fresh air, and stunning views. The best-developed tourist destination in the mountains, it also has pretty colonial architecture and is a melting pot of various hill peoples. Around Sapa are a multitude of trekking routes. Take a gentle hike to Ham Rong hill, where you can see traditional dance performances. For a more challenging hike, walk up to the summit of the 10,300-ft (3,140-m) Mount Falisan, the highest peak in Vietnam (the less energetic can take the cable car to the top). Walk or cycle through verdant valleys to the traditional Hmong villages of Cat Cat and Sin Chai, or the Red Dao village of Ta Phin. It's also worth checking out Thac Bac, a magnificent 328-ft (100-m-) high waterfall that is accessible by road northwest of the town.

4

Day 10: Hanoi to Uong Bi

Catch the morning bus from Sapa to Hanoi (5 hours), and a connecting bus to the town of Uong Bi (3 hours), a convenient stopover for visiting the holy mountain of Yen Tu *(p208)*. Have a quick wander and dinner in this typical town. If you have a few hours, visit the grand Chua Va Bang temple just to the north of town.

Day 11: Yen Tu Pilgrimage Site

Make an early start to the pilgrimage sites on nearby Yen Tu mountain, which form one of the oldest and most significant in the country. A holy place for around 2,000 years, Yen Tu has over 800 religious structures, the majority built from the 13th century onwards, nestled among the mountain's verdant slopes. Either walk up thousands of steps, or take a cable car to the Hoa Yen Pagoda about halfway up, followed by another to visit the beautiful Bronze Pagoda, dating to the 15th century, at the mountain's 3,478-ft (1,060-m) peak.

Days 12, 13, and 14: Bai Tu Long Bay

For stunning natural beauty, take a bus (3–4 hours) from Nam Mau to Cai Rong, the jumping-off point to explore the little-visited Bai Tu Long National Park in Bai Tu Long Bay *(p206)*. From Cai Rong, a two-hour ferry ride to Co To Island will take you through the marine national park, with its crystal-clear waters, golden beaches, and karst limestone islands. At Co To stay next to the beach in the main town, or at one of the more remote resorts. Spend a couple of days cycling around this tiny island, stopping at the many delightful coves and beautiful beaches that decorate its coast. Enjoy lovely vistas from its many hills, one of which boasts a lighthouse. If lazing on the beach doesn't appeal, explore the relatively intact red and green coral reefs that surround the island for a snorkeling or scuba diving adventure.

◁ Annamese Silver Pheasant

Identifiable by its red face and legs, which offset its beautiful silver plumage, this fowl is found mainly in the Truong Son and Hoang Lien Son mountains. It's a large bird, and flies only short distances, making it easy to spot. The birds thrive well in captivity and make exotic pets.

Orchids ▷

Vietnam is home to a multitude of orchid species, many unique to the country. Botanists and amateur lovers of the "Queen of Flowers" discover new species regularly. The north seems to be their favored habitat and Mount Fansipan, the country's highest mountain, always has one species or another in bloom. Closer to Sapa town, Ham Rong Mountain has an excellent garden with many potted specimens. Hanoi hosts an annual Orchid Fair in the spring.

NORTHERN VIETNAM'S
FLORA
AND FAUNA

It is in the northern part of Vietnam that the tropical ecosystems of Southeast Asia meet the temperate ecosystems of mainland Asia, resulting in fantastically diverse plant and animal life. The abundant karst limestone formations here provide habitats to thousands of types of flora and fauna.

◁ Indochinese Tiger

While this majestic creature once roamed throughout the region, symbolizing power, and sometimes terrorizing villagers, it is now highly endangered. Populations continue to decline, largely due to its continued use in traditional medicine – the bones and particularly the penis are considered aphrodisiacs. Today the Indochinese tiger population in Vietnam is estimated to be around 50 animals, and they are confined to the evergreen Annamite forests.

△ Red-Shanked Douc langur

This rare primate has orange-red rear legs and white forearms that so resemble clothing that it is sometimes called "the costumed ape." Its distinctive appearance is completed by a yellow face framed by a white ruff. A long white tail aids its agility. Like most simians, it is highly social, and travels among the tree-tops in groups of up to 50. If you're fortunate enough to spot one, it will be in the Van Long Wetland Nature Reserve, south of Hanoi.

ENDANGERED SPECIES

The International Union for Conservation of Nature (www.iucn.org) lists over 40 critically endangered species in Vietnam. Habitat encroachment and poaching are the main problems. The government is taking steps to conserve the country's plant and animal resources through the establishment of national parks, signing the Convention on International Trade in Endangered Species agreement, and initiating campaigns to raise public awareness of the long-term value of wildlife. Visitors can help by not buying any ivory, tortoiseshell, animal horn, or coral souvenirs and not eating in restaurants serving wildlife.

◁ Butterflies

During the spring and summer months, the forests come alive with large numbers and varieties of butterflies, of which there are over 500 subspecies. Cuc Phuong and Ba Be national parks are perfect places to view them. Cuc Phuong even has a butterfly festival in April, when large colonies are in residence.

△ Cave Swiftlets

These birds live in limestone caves throughout the north. To see them, just be present at a cave entrance at sunset when they return to their nests after a day's work catching insects. At the same time, nocturnal bats will be exiting the cave in similarly large numbers, creating quite a spectacle.

Floating village among the towering limestone pillars in Halong Bay ↑

 1

HALONG BAY

🅐**D2** 🅐 **102 miles (164 km) E of Hanoi; 37 miles (60 km) NE of Haiphong** 🚌**From Hanoi to Halong City** 🚢**From Tuan Chan Tourist Wharf, 5 miles (8 km) west of Halong City**

A UNESCO World Heritage Site, Halong Bay is a magnificent seascape of myriad outcrops, caves, and sandy coves. Sailing past the evocatively shaped islets and dramatic caves is a magical experience.

According to local legend, the bay was formed when a gigantic dragon – *ha long* means descending dragon – plunged into the Gulf of Tonkin, and created the many islets and rock formations by lashing its tail to form a barrier against invaders. Spread across a 580-sq-mile (1,500-sq-km) area, the bay has more than 2,000 pinnacle-shaped limestone and dolomite outcrops scattered across it, the highest concentration found anywhere in the world. The spectacular karst topography is the product of selective erosion over the millennia.

At least an entire day can be spent exploring the islands and grottos, many of which house religious shrines. Many of the caves have floodlights to illuminate the stalagmites and stalactites. Plenty of tour operators in Hanoi organize excursions to Halong Bay, lasting between one and several days. Most of the best-known sites lie in the western part and these are often crowded. It is possible to charter a private boat from Cat Ba Island *(p207)*, hire a knowledgeable guide, and sail around the less visited but equally beautiful areas of the shimmering bay, making for a quieter experience.

①

Hang Dau Go

Named Grotte des Merveilles or Cave of Marvels by the French in the 19th century, Hang Dau Go is full of strangely formed stalactites and stalagmites, enchantingly lit with green and blue colored floodlights. One of the most famous and beautiful caves in Halong Bay, Hang Dau Go or Hidden Timber Cave is located on Dau Go Island, on the way to Cat Ba Island. The huge cave has three chambers reached via 90 steps. Its name dates from the 13th century when General Tran Hung Dao used it to hide his lethally sharpened metal stakes in the battles against the Mongolians. The weapons were later planted in the shallow waters near the shore to destroy enemy Mongol fleets.

Hang Thien Cung

Also on Dau Go Island, Hang Thien Cung or the Celestial Palace Grotto is part of the same cave system as Hang Dau Go. It was discovered only in the mid-1990s. Floodlights in pink, green, and blue softly illuminate the sparkling stalactites that hang from the high ceiling.

FORMATION OF KARST

Across much of the Gulf of Tonkin, both offshore in Halong Bay and on land at Tam Coc, weathered limestone pinnacles rise almost vertically from the surrounding plain, creating truly breathtaking scenery. These karst outcrops are made of sediment that settled on the seafloor in prehistoric times and subsequently rose to the surface through geological upheaval and erosion. On exposure to warm, acidic rainfall, these striking alkaline limestone formations are worn into strange, almost spectacular shapes, providing a remarkable sight.

INSIDER TIP
Cruises

Most boat tours include stopping off at an island, several caves, and a visit to one of Halong Bay's numerous floating fishing villages. The best time to visit is November, which brings sunshine and fewer crowds than in May to August, the peak season.

faintly with an eerie percussive sound when a strong wind blows past its stalactites and stalagmites.

Dao Tuan Chau

A large island to the southwest of Bai Chay, Tuan Chau is the starting point for many tours of the bay and is reached by a short road from the mainland. It has a sprawling recreation complex, a marina, two white sandy beaches, and several restored French colonial villas.

Dao Titop

The main attraction of this island is its isolated beach, which is very popular with swimmers. Visitors can enjoy watersports facilities at the small beach, including swimming, parasailing, and kayaking among the tranquil waters. It is also worth climbing up about 400 steps to the top of the island, where there is the most spectacular view of Halong Bay.

↑ Floodlit stalactites in Hang Sung Sot

Hang Sung Sot

Aptly known as the Cave of Awe, Hang Sung Sot is located on Bo Hon Island, which the French knew as the Isle de la Surprise, and is the most visited cave in Halong Bay.

The first cavern in the three-chambered Sung Sot features a large, phallus-shaped rock, lit in lurid pink, which is regarded as a fertility symbol. Other formations include a Buddha and a tortoise. Those in the inner chamber, named the Serene Castle, are particularly fascinating, seeming to come alive when the reflections of the water outside play upon them – they are said to resemble a group of sentries conversing. The top of the cave leads to a vantage point with great views of the junks and sampans below.

Nearby, Hang Bo Nau or Pelican Cave, a favorite among photographers, draws visitors for the fantastic views it offers across the bay.

Dong Tam Cung

A massive karst fissure discovered only in the mid-1990s, Dong Tam Cung or Three Palaces consists of three chambers, each of which is packed with stalactites and stalagmites. All three grottos of Dong Tam Cung are illuminated by strategically placed spotlights, which emphasize the strange, massed, carrot-shaped array of stalactites. Opinion is divided, but some consider Dong Tam Cung to be even more impressive than Hang Dau Go.

Hang Trong

A short distance southeast of Hang Bo Nau, the small Hang Trong or Drum Cave echoes

All three grottos of Dong Tam Cung are illuminated by strategically placed spotlights, which emphasize the strange, massed, carrot-shaped array of stalactites.

Cruising Halong Bay in a junk, a great way to admire its natural beauty

❷ ⊗ ⊗ ⊡ 🏛

PERFUME PAGODA

🅰C2 🏠40 miles (65 km) SW of Hanoi along Hwy 21, My Duc township
🚌From downtown Hanoi and Ninh Binh to My Duc, where rowboats ferry passengers along to Perfume Pagoda 🕐Daily

Nestled in forested limestone cliffs on Nui Huong Tich or Fragrant Vestige Mountain, and overlooking the Suoi Yen River, Perfume Pagoda is one of Vietnam's most spectacular sights.

The pagoda is actually a complex of around 30 Buddhist shrines. Each year, during the Perfume Pagoda Festival (p43), thousands of Buddhists embark on a pilgrimage up the mountain, praying for absolution, good health, and, in the case of childless couples, a baby.

Highlights

Den Trinh Pagoda is the first stop on the mountain, where all pilgrims are required to "register" or pray and ask for acceptance of their journey up to Huong Tich Pagoda, the most fascinating shrine set deep in a cavern in the mountainside. The steep walk up to Huong Tich takes at least an hour. The phrase "Most Beautiful Cavern under the Southern Sky" is carved near its entrance, where 120 steps lead down into the cave. Dedicated to Quan Am, the incense-filled Huong Tich has several gilded figurines of the Buddha and Quan Am.

Also known as the Heavenly Kitchen Pagoda, the 18th-century Thien Tru rises through three levels on the mountainside. An elegant triple-roofed bell pavilion stands in front of the temple and a statue of Quan Am dominates the main altar inside. Giai Oan, or the Undoing Injustice Pagoda, is popular with pilgrims seeking purification and justice, while one of the holiest shrines, Tien Son Pagoda, is set in a cave and contains four ruby statues.

EXPERIENCE MORE

3 🔧 🎿 🍴 🖥 🛍

Cuc Phuong National Park

🅰 B2 📍 Nho Quan District, 28 miles (45 km) W of Ninh Binh; 87 miles (140 km) SW of Hanoi 🚌 Minibus from Ninh Binh 🕐 8am–5:30pm by arrangement with park authorities 🌐 cucphuong tourism.com

Established as Vietnam's first national park in 1962, Cuc Phuong covers 86 sq miles (223 sq km) of largely primary tropical forest, and is home to over 100 species of mammals and reptiles, and more than 300 types of birds. The park is also famous for its range of flora, which includes soaring 1,000-year-old trees as well as medicinal plants.

One of the main highlights at the park is the **Endangered Primate Rescue Center**, which cares for animals that have been rescued from hunters. It also promotes breeding and conservation programs, and rehabilitates endangered primates for release into the wild. The center is home to a wide variety of primates, including langur, gibbon, loris, and others, making it a great place to see these animals at close range.

Cuc Phuong has excellent trekking opportunities and other attractions such as waterfalls and a botanical garden. There are also Muong villages nearby that offer visitors overnight stays.

Endangered Primate Rescue Center
🕐 Daily 🌐 eprc.asia

↑ Perfume Pagoda, built into the karst cliffs of Nui Huong Tich mountain

Ben Hieu waterfalls in Cuc Phuong National Park and a red-shanked douc langur *(inset)* ↓

BOAT TRIP TO PERFUME PAGODA

A fleet of boats, rowed by women, ferries tourists from the township of My Duc up the breathtaking Suoi Yen River between limestone cliffs to the magnificent Perfume Pagoda. The 90-minute journey is a tranquil glide through verdant rice paddies, the profound silence broken only by the slap of the oars. The path to the top of the mountain is steep in places. Allow at least two hours to climb to the top on foot and return. Alternately, take the cable car (for a fee).

④

Halong City

C2 **⌂** 102 miles (164 km) E of Hanoi on Hwy 18; 37 miles (60 km) NE of Haiphong on Hwy 10 🚌 From Haiphong and Hanoi 🚢 From Haiphong 🚇 **ℹ** Halong Bay Tourism, (086) 831 1283

Formed in 1994 with the official amalgamation of the towns of Bai Chay and Hon Gai, Halong City is bisected by the Cua Luc straits, which are linked by a suspension bridge.

Located to the west of the straits, Bai Chay is an affluent tourist town, home to several tour operators, hotels, and restaurants. For most visitors this area holds little appeal except as a convenient place to stay and eat. East of the bridge, the town of Hon Gai is the more historic part of Halong City. Although there are a few hotels and restaurants here, the area's wealth comes from industry, particularly the huge opencast coal mines that dominate the coast east of Cua Luc.

Beyond the docks is Nui Bai Tho or Poem Mountain, one of the main attractions of Halong City. The limestone mountain has earned its name from the weathered inscriptions on its sides, written in praise of the beauty of Halong Bay. The earliest of these is said to have

been composed by King Le Thanh Tong in 1468. On the northern lee of the mountain stands Long Tien Pagoda, Halong City's most colorful and interesting religious site.

---

⑤

Bai Tu Long Bay

D2 **⌂** 37 miles (60 km) E of Halong City 🚌 From Halong City 🚢 From Halong City and Cai Rong

An island-peppered stretch of shallow coastal waters, Bai Tu Long Bay may not be quite as celebrated as Halong Bay, but it is just as spectacular. With hundreds of karst outcrops, tiny islets, a few large islands and lovely beaches, it is less crowded and more pristine than Halong Bay.

The area offers few tourist facilities, and as a result, most visitors prefer to join a tour from Hanoi, spending the night on board a boat and exploring the bay. Another option is to drive from Hon Gai to Bai Tu Long Bay, passing through Cam Pha and Cua Ong. The huge, opencast coal mines on the way are quite a sight. From here, boats may be chartered to explore the outlying reaches of the bay.

The largest, most developed island in the bay is Van Don, accessible by road and sea

from the industrial port of Cua Ong. Gorgeous beaches and dense mangrove swamps line the southeast coast of the island, making it a popular destination. Most of the accommodations in the Bai Tu Long area are concentrated in Van Don's main town, the colorful fishing port-town of Cai Rong. The outermost of the three islands south of

←
Halong City and bay seen from Nui Bai Tho (Poem Mountain)

A ship in Bai Tu Long Bay cruising among the rocky islets ↑

Van Don is Quan Lan. The main attraction here is Bai Bien, a lovely white-sand beach, and one of the few places past Cai Rong with facilities for an overnight stay.

Co To is the farthest island off Cai Rong. The ferry journey takes about five hours each way. With a small beach and simple accommodations at Co To village, it is a quiet spot.

About 12 miles (20 km) from Cai Rong is Bai Tu Long National Park. Spread across Ba Mun Island and its surrounds, this park has fascinating marine ecosystems and rare animals and plants.

 6

Cat Ba Island

🅰 C2 **🅰** 28 miles (45 km) E of Haiphong; 14 miles (22 km) S of Halong City **🚇🚢** Hydrofoil from Haiphong, charter boats from Halong City and Bai Chay **Ⓦ** catbavietnam.com

The largest island in a scenic archipelago of more than 350 islets and islands, Cat Ba's main appeal is its relative isolation and its waterfalls,

freshwater lakes, mangrove swamps, hills, and coral reefs. Unfortunately Cat Ba Town is becoming increasingly polluted and crowded. Most boats dock here as it is possible to stay overnight and eat in some comfort. There is little to recommend it except as a gateway to **Cat Ba National Park**, the island's main attraction.

In 1986, in order to safeguard the island's varied habitats, nearly half of Cat Ba was given the status of a national park. Famous for its rugged landscape, with craggy limestone outcrops, lakes, caves, grottos, and thick mangroves, it has an astonishing range of flora. More than 800 species have been cataloged. The forests sustain fauna, such as wild boars, deer, macaques, and a large number of bird and reptile species. The park is renowned for its community of endangered

Cat Ba langurs. Today, their number are estimated at a dismal 50 animals.

The park also offers treks and camping for the adventurous. Facilities are limited, and visitors need to bring their own equipment and supplies. The shortest and most popular trek climbs to the 656-ft (200-m) summit of Ngu Lam peak, from where there are panoramic views. A longer hike (4–6 hours) leads through the tree-canopied interior, past Ech Lake, to the hamlet of Viet Hai. From here, boats can be chartered back to Cat Ba Town. Boats may be chartered from Cat Ba to explore Halong Bay or the smaller but picturesque Lan Ha Bay, to its northeast, which has tiny, exclusive beaches that can be visited for a small fee.

Cat Ba National Park

Ⓐ Ⓖ **🅰** 12 miles (20 km) NW of Cat Ba Town **Ⓞ** Sunrise-sunset daily

> **Famous for its rugged landscape, with craggy limestone outcrops, lakes, caves, grottos, and thick mangroves, Cat Ba has an astonishing range of flora.**

Ninh Binh

🅰C2 🕐59 miles (95 km)
S of Hanoi on Hwy 1
🚆Reunification Express
between Hanoi and HCMC
🚌Hanoi 🛈Dinh Tien Hoang
Rd; www.dulichninhbinh.
com.vn

An ideal base from which to
explore the southern part of
the Red River Delta, Ninh
Binh is a popular tourist
destination. While the town
itself is unremarkable, it
features several interesting
attractions in its vicinity.

The historic site of Hoa Lu,
7 miles (12 km) northwest of
Ninh Binh, was established as
a royal capital in AD 968 by
Emperor Tien Hoang De, the
founder of the Dinh Dynasty
(r.968–980). A massive palace
and citadel constructed by
him is now mostly in ruins, but
is still impressive. A second
royal temple in the vicinity
is dedicated to Le Dai Hanh,
founder of the Early Le
Dynasty (r.980–1009), which
succeeded the Dinh Dynasty.
The early Le are credited with
replacing Chinese currency
with Vietnamese coinage.

Just 7 miles (12 km)
northwest of Hoa Lu is
Vietnam's biggest temple
complex, Bai Dinh Temple.
It opened in 2010 and
features statues of 500 *arhats*
(enlightened Buddha) and a
100-ton bronze Buddha. To
the southwest of Hoa Lu in
Thanh Hoa Province is the
Ho Citadel, a World Heritage
Site recognized by UNESCO
in 2011. Established by the
Ho Dynasty in the early 15th
century, all that remains are
four walls of massive stones
and four arched gateways.

Tam Coc or Three Caves,
lying 6 miles (10 km) southwest of Ninh Binh town, is

often promoted as Vietnam's
"Halong Bay on Land."
Here karst outcrops rise
majestically from a sea of
green rice fields. It takes
about three hours to visit Tam
Coc by rowboat along the
watery landscape and
through three long caves.
Trang An, 4 miles (7 km) west
of Ninh Binh, offers a similar
experience to Tam Coc, and is
also explored by boat. It was
listed as a UNESCO World
Heritage Site in 2014 for its
cultural and natural heritage.

Located 13 miles (21 km)
northwest of Ninh Binh, the
idyllic fishing village of Kenh
Ga is also worth a visit.
Centered on a small island
and surrounded by stark karst
formations, it features fish
farms, herds of ducks, and all
things aquatic. It takes three
hours to tour Kenh Ga by boat,
and it is very relaxing to chug
slowly along to Van Trinh
Grotto observing tranquil
rural scenery en route. Kenh
Ga is accessed via the town
of Tran Me, as are the reed-
filled marshes of **Van Long
Nature Reserve**, where a
small community of the
rare Delacour's langur lives,
safe among the inaccessible
limestone outcrops.

Around 19 miles (30 km)
southeast of Ninh Binh, Phat
Diem town is home to **Phat
Diem Cathedral**, one of the
most well-known churches
in Vietnam. Alexandre de
Rhodes, a French Jesuit priest
who developed the nation's
Romanized writing system,
preached here in 1627, but

Did You Know?

Ninh Binh's dramatic
scenery provided the
backdrop for the
Kong: Skull Island
(2017) movie.

it was Tran Luc, a Vietnamese
priest, who organized the
construction of this unique
cathedral. It was completed in
1898, and combines European
Gothic church architecture
with Sino-Vietnamese
temple tradition.

Van Long Nature Reserve
♻♿ 🅰Gia Vien Dist, Ninh
Binh Province 🕐Daily by
arrangement

Phat Diem Cathedral
📞(0229) 386 2058 🕐Daily

**Yen Tu Pilgrimage
Sites**

🅰C2 🕐81 miles (130 km)
NE of Hanoi; 9 miles (14 km)
N of Uong Bi 🚌From Hanoi,
Halong City, and Haiphong
to Uong Bi 🚕

The Holy Mountain, Yen Tu, at
3,477 ft (1,060 m), is the highest peak in the range of the

Bai Dinh Temple
complex nestling
in the greenery

same name. It is named for Yen Ky Sinh, a monk who attained nirvana at the peak about 2,000 years ago. During the 13th century, Emperor Tran Nhan Tong (r.1278–93) retired here to become a monk. Some of the 800 religious structures claimed to have been built by the emperor and his successors are still here.

For centuries, thousands of pilgrims have made the arduous ascent to the summit of Yen Tu by foot, although now a cable car whisks sightseers to Hoa Yen Pagoda, just over halfway up the mountain. From here, another cable car goes up to the important Chua Dong or Bronze Pagoda, built during the 15th century and the spiritual home of the Truc Lam or Bamboo Forest sect of Mahayana Buddhism. It has been beautifully refurbished, with 70 tons of bronze used to form a 215-sq-ft (20-sq-m) temple intended to symbolize a lotus.

Situated on the western slopes of the Yen Tu range, about 3 miles (5 km) north of Sao Dao on Highway 18, are two of the country's most important pilgrimage sites.

GREAT VIEW
Yen Tu

The best view from Yen Tu is from just above the Chua Dong Pagoda, near its peak. If you arrive very early, you should be able to see the pagodas and temples through the mystic ocean of clouds.

Chua Con Son, one of the attractive pagodas in the north, is dedicated to Nguyen Van Trai, the poet-warrior who aided Emperor Le Loi in expelling the Chinese from Vietnam in the 15th century. The popular pagoda is always active, with monks and nuns chanting prayers continually.

Nearby is the small Den Kiep Bac temple, which is dedicated to Tran Hung Dao, a general of the Tran Dynasty in the late 13th century and a deified national hero. An annual festival is held in his honor.

9

Haiphong

🅰C2 🏛62 miles (100) km E of Hanoi on Hwy 5 ✈From HCMC and Danang 🚆From Hanoi 🚌From Hanoi and Halong City ⛴From Cat Ba Island 🅘18 Minh Khai St; www.haiphongtourism. gov.vn

The third-largest city in the country after Ho Chi Minh City and Hanoi, Haiphong is the north's most important port. Its strategic location has made it the target of foreign invaders. It also faced heavy bombing during the First Indochina War, and in the war against the US. Having survived its violent past, Haiphong is a leading industrial metropolis, specializing in cement manufacture, oil refining, and coal transportation.

Haiphong draws few tourists, even though the atmosphere is relaxed, and

the food and accommodations good. The most attractive and noteworthy sights are the beautiful French colonial buildings. These include a 19th-century cathedral by Tam Bac River, the Opera House on Quang Trung Street, and **Haiphong Museum**, the Gothic facade of which is more remarkable than the exhibits inside. The 17th-century Du Hang Pagoda, on Chua Hang Street, is known for its elaborate architecture, while Dinh Hang Kenh, on Nguyen Cong Tru Street, is a fine old communal house.

Haiphong Museum
♿ 🏛 11 Dien Tien Hoang St 🕐8–11:30am Tue & Thu, 7:30–9:30pm Wed & Sun

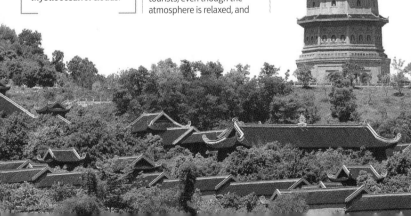

Hoa Binh

🅰C2 ⏱46 miles (74 km)
SW of Hanoi 🚌Hanoi
ℹ395 An Duong Vuong St;
(0218) 385 4374

A pleasant little town, Hoa Binh's name means "peace." Ironically, its strategic location next to the Song Da or Black River Valley made it the site of many battles during the First Indochina War. Relics from these turbulent times are displayed in the **Hoa Binh Museum**. A French landing craft and a destroyed French tank are in its grounds.

Traditionally home to the Muong community, the town has shaded avenues and some good eateries, making it a convenient stop on a tour from Hanoi to Moc Chau and around Mai Chau Valley.

A few miles northwest of Hoa Binh is Song Da Reservoir. Boat trips to local villages and the reservoir can be arranged through tour operators.

Hoa Binh Museum

♿ 🅰6 An Duong Vuong St
📞 (0218) 385 2177 🕐7–11am,
1:30–4:30pm daily

11

Mai Chau Valley

🅰B2 ⏱87 miles (140 km)
SW of Hanoi; 43 miles
(70 km) SE of Moc Chau on
Hwy 6 🚌From Hanoi and
Son La

Surrounded by the foothills of the Truong Son Range, this charming and fertile valley is dotted with green rice paddies and small, quaint stilt-house villages. Most of the inhabitants here are White Thai. Well known for their hospitality, families here offer homestay facilities in stilt huts – an authentic and comfortable way of experiencing life on the hills, though the area can get crowded at weekends. Some of the larger homestays

Did You Know?

The White and Black Thai people are the biggest ethnic group in the Mai Chau region.

put on traditional Thai music and dancing. At night, visitors can enjoy the local alcohol *ruou can*, which is drunk communally from large jars through long bamboo straws.

There are excellent trekking opportunities here, provided by the valley's delightful trails, fields, and villages.

12

Moc Chau

🅰B2 ⏱124 miles (200 km)
SW of Hanoi; 75 miles
(121 km) SE of Son La on
Hwy 6 🚌From Hanoi
and Son La

The semirural market town of Moc Chau, surrounded by a plateau of the same name, is renowned for its tea plantations and burgeoning dairy industry. The generous yield of fresh cow's milk, as well as the creamy yogurt and rich sweets made here are transported to Hanoi daily. Since Moc Chau is not as convenient as Mai Chau for longer stays,

most people stop here only for refreshments on the drive from Hanoi to Son La. The Hmong *(p215)* and Thai occupy the neighboring hamlets, which are definitely worth a visit.

13

Son La

🅰B1 ⏱199 miles (320 km)
NW of Hanoi on Hwy 6;
93 miles (150 km) E of Dien
Bien Phu on Hwy 6 🚌From
Hanoi and Dien Bien Phu

Bisected by the narrow Nam La River, the busy little town of Son La was once known as "Vietnam's Siberia." The infamous French-era **Son La Prison** stands menacingly on a wooded hill. Son La's isolation and cold weather were considered ideal conditions for the incarceration of Vietnamese nationalists and revolutionaries. Recalcitrant prisoners were shackled and confined in windowless cells, and the prison guillotine saw regular use. However, the prison also served as a revolutionary academy of sorts. Some of the political prisoners included luminaries such as Truong Chinh and Le Duan, both of whom later became

←
Tea plantations covering the Moc Chau hills near the village

Surrounded by new buildings, the main battlefield on the east bank of the Nam La River still has a few old, rusty French tanks. Nearby stands a poignant memorial to the French dead. Chronicling the great battle, **Dien Bien Phu Museum** has weapons, maps, pictures, dioramas, and soldiers' possessions. Opposite is the Dien Bien Phu Martyrs' Cemetery, where the Viet Minh fallen are buried. To the north is Hill A1, where there is a French general's subterranean bunker, covered with a rusting, corrugated-iron roof and reinforced with concrete.

On the hilltop is a monument to martyred Vietnamese heroes, and a tunnel entrance used by the Viet Minh to reach a French camp, which they blew up. Farther north is the 120-ton victory monument in bronze, which commemorates the battle's 50th anniversary. It is one of Vietnam's largest monuments.

Dien Bien Phu Museum
⊛ ⌂ 1 Muong Thanh
⊙ 7:30–11am, 1:30–5pm daily

General Secretaries of the Vietnamese Communist Party. The prison museum displays remnants of French brutality such as cramped underground cells and leg irons. Somewhat incongruously, hill tribe artifacts and clothing are also on display here.

A major attraction in town is the market on the east bank of the Nam La. Fresh fruit and vegetables, as well as handicrafts and cloth hand-woven by the White and Black Thai, are on sale, along with ducks, chickens, and pot-bellied pigs, while small food stalls serve Son La's specialty, goat meat or *thitde*. The more adventurous can sample *tiet canh*, congealed goat's blood served with chopped peanuts and shallots.

Located 4 miles (7 km) north of town is the Black Thai village of Ban Hin, where traditional stilt houses are surrounded by fruit orchards and coffee bushes. The scenery around Son La is very attractive and the drive to Dien Bien Phu leads past picturesque fields, hills, and interesting minority villages.

Son La Prison
⊛ ⌂ Dai Khao Ca ☎ (0212) 385 2859 ⊙ 7:30–11am, 1:30–4:30pm daily

 14
Dien Bien Phu

🅰 A1 🕒 292 miles (470 km) NW of Hanoi; 93 miles (150 km) W of Son La 🚏 Hanoi 🚌 From Hanoi, Son La, and Lai Chau

Situated in a fertile valley near the Laos border, this historic town is famous for the decisive battle of Dien Bien Phu. In 1954, following French infiltration of the area, Viet Minh troops systematically broke down the French position. In the end, General de Castries, commander of the French army, and his troops were captured. Today, the town is developing fast. Dien Bien Phu was once part of Lai Chau Province, a section of which has now been submerged by the waters of the Son La Dam. As a result, the province of Dien Bien Phu was created, leading to a boom in construction.

→
Waving the flag for victory – the Dien Bien Phu Victory Monument

15

Sapa

🅐 B1 🚗 236 miles (380 km) NW of Hanoi 🚆 From Hanoi to Lao Cai 🚌 Lao Cai
🛈 2 Fansipan St; www.sapa-tourism.com

With cascading rice terraces and lush vegetation, Sapa is perched at an elevation of 5,250 ft (1,600 m) on the eastern slopes of the Hoang Lien Mountains, also known as the Tonkinese Alps. Jesuit priests first arrived here in 1918 and sent word of the idyllic views and pleasant climate back to Hanoi. By 1922, Sapa was established as a hill station where the French built villas, hotels, and tennis courts, transforming the town into a summer retreat.

In this scenic setting, French colonists or *colons* would flirt, gossip, eat strawberries, and drink lots of wine. These idyllic conditions lasted until World War II and the Japanese invasion of 1941. Many villas and hotels were destroyed or abandoned in the next four decades during wars with the French and the US. However, worse was to come – still more destructive was the Sino-Vietnamese War during 1979, when the town itself suffered damage.

Fortunately, following the introduction of Vietnam's economic reforms or *doi moi* in the 1990s and the subsequent gradual opening of the country to tourism, Sapa gained a fresh lease on life. Revived by local entrepreneurs and rediscovered by foreign visitors, the town slowly regained the distinction it enjoyed in colonial times.

Set on several levels joined by small sloping streets and steep flights of steps, Sapa is home to diverse hill peoples, as well as ethnic Kinh and a growing army of visitors who come for the stunning views and fresh mountain air. A major section of hill people here are the Black Hmong, whose costumes are a deep indigo, followed by the Red Dao with their red-patterned turbans. Young women wander the streets wearing exquisitely embroidered skirts and jackets, elaborate headdresses, and heavy silver jewelry.

The small and simple Sapa church, which was built in 1930 and set in a square, forms the center of town, where the locals gather to celebrate on feast days. Sapa market, once the town's main attraction, draws less interest since it was moved out of the center to near the bus station. However, it is still a bustling place selling fresh produce. Above the market are two shops selling Black Hmong and Red Dao crafts.

→ Stunning terraced rice paddies in the Sapa highlands

Trekking is a popular activity, and it is easy to walk to nearby villages. Southeast of the town is Ham Rong or Dragon Jaw's Hill. A gentle climb leads up through rockeries and grottos to a summit. From here, there are magnificent views of the tree-filled valleys below, dotted with colorful villas. Traditional dance performances are staged at the top of the hill.

The "Gateway to Sapa," Lao Cai lies at a distance of about 25 miles (40 km) northeast of Sapa. It holds little of interest except as a stopping-off point for crossing to China or passing through to visit Sapa and Bac Ha. It has some useful hotels and restaurants.

About 5 miles (8 km) from Sapa, Mount Fansipan is the country's highest peak. It is around 10,300 ft (3,140 m) tall and is covered in lush sub-tropical vegetation to a height of about 660 ft (200 m), and then by temperate forest. Although the terrain can be difficult and the weather bad, the climb to the peak has always been popular with trekkers. The construction of a cable car connecting Sapa with the top of Fansipan, while allowing access to the peak for all, has also drawn complaints from environmentalists angered by the scale of the building project in previously unspoiled terrain.

The lovely Black Hmong village of Cat Cat is just 2 miles (3 km) south of Sapa. Visitors normally walk down the steep trail, but take a motorcycle taxi for the uphill ride back to town. The Hmong live in houses of mud, wattle, bamboo, and thatch, surrounded by vats of indigo-colored liquid, which is used to dye their clothing. Around 2.5 miles (4 km) beyond Cat Cat is another Hmong village, Sin Chai, while the Red Dao village of Ta Phin is only about 6 miles (10 km) from Sapa. The route to Ta Phin passes through a low-slung valley that is carved with curved rice terracing, glinting brightly in the sun. Just before Ta Phin is an abandoned, semi-destroyed French seminary, which was built in 1942. Around 9 miles (15 km) northwest of Sapa, on the road to the Tram Ton Pass, is the Thac Bac or Silver Waterfall. This powerful 330-ft- (100-m-) high cascade is a magnificent sight, attracting many visitors. Here, women from the Kinh, Black Dao, and Red Hmong set up stalls selling delicious fruit.

16

Bac Ha

🅐 B1 🕐 205 miles (330 km) NW Hanoi, 43 miles (69 km) E of Lao Cai 🚌 From Lao Cai and Sapa 🛈 009, 20-9 St; www.bacha tourist.com

A small town set 2,950 ft (900 m) above sea level in the Chay River massif, Bac Ha has a deserted air for much of the week. However, on Sunday mornings, it attracts hill peoples, such as the Dao, Tay, Thai, Nung, and the colorful Flower Hmong among many others from all over the surrounding mountains. They head for Bac Ha's dusty town center and market, leading ponies stacked high with firewood, and carrying baskets loaded with merchandise.

Items sold and exchanged at the market include bush meat, vegetables, fruits, spices, and exquisitely

↑ A gathering of Flower Hmong women in colorful dress in Bac Ma

embroidered goods. Most hill people also use this occasion to stock up on necessities as well as luxuries that are not available in the hills. Toiletries, religious paraphernalia, and incense sticks, as well as needles, thread, and cloth for embroidery are a few of the products in demand here.

Many visitors to Bac Ha also head farther north in order to combine a visit to the Sunday market with a trip to the small settlement of Can Cau. Located roughly 12 miles (20 km) from Bac Ha town, this charming village hosts a Saturday market that is very popular with locals and visitors alike, especially for being delightfully vibrant and extremely colorful.

Bac Ha district is also known for its potent maize alcohol, which is distilled at the small village of Ban Pho, a Flower Hmong settlement around 2.5 miles (4 km) to the west of Bac Ha town.

 INSIDER TIP
Bac Ha Market

For the best experience of the busy, colorful Bac Ha Sunday market, avoid the main crowds and get there very early by leaving Sapa by 5am or Lao Cai by 6:30am.

Ba Be National Park

🅐C1 **📍149 miles (240 km)**
N of Hanoi; 37 miles (60 km)
N of Bac Kan Town
📞(0209) 387 1180

Set in a remote upland region, this lush park is centered on three linked lakes – Ba Be means Three Bays – that together form the country's largest freshwater lake area. Covering about 40 sq miles (100 sq km), the park is dominated by dramatic limestone peaks, waterfalls, and grottos. The region's tropical forests are also home to an abundance of wildlife, including the François langur and the endangered Tonkin snub-nosed monkey.

The main attractions here include the Dau Dang Falls, a spectacular series of cascades found at the northwest end of the lake, and the Hang Puong, a fascinating grotto that passes through the mountains. At around 7 miles (12 km) up the Nang River, this narrow cave can be navigated in a small boat – the trip takes up most of a day. To the south of the lake lies Pac Ngoi, a charming village inhabited by the Tay people. Many villagers have set up their houses as homestays.

18

Cao Bang

🅐C1 **📍168 miles (270 km)**
N of Hanoi on Hwy 3
🚌Hanoi and Lang Son

Off the beaten track in the high mountains along the Chinese frontier, the thickly forested area around the small town of Cao Bang is home to several ethnic groups, including the Tay, Dao, and Nung. While the town itself is unremarkable, its surroundings are spectacular, and trekking opportunities abound. The Vietnamese regard it as a place of historical significance for its links to the 16th-century Mac Dynasty, and years later, because Ho Chi Minh (p181) made it his first base on returning to Vietnam.

Around 37 miles (60 km) northwest of town, Hang Pac Bo or Water Wheel Cave is where Ho Chi Minh stayed on his return in 1941 from self-imposed exile, and this is seen as the birthplace of the Viet Minh struggle. There is a small but interesting museum here. About 56 miles (90 km) northeast of Cao Bang, Thac Ban Gioc is the largest waterfall in Vietnam. It straddles the China-Vietnamese border and a pass from Cao Bang's police station is required to visit the area.

↑ Jade-green pools under the beautiful Thac Ban Gioc waterfall

19

Dong Van Karst Plateau Geopark

🅐B1 **📍212 miles (342 km)**
N of Hanoi **🚌Ha Giang**

Vietnam's northernmost province of Ha Giang contains unforgettable landscapes in the Dong Van Karst Plateau Geopark, recognized in 2010 by UNESCO as the first global geopark in Vietnam.

These limestone peaks rise to an average of 4,920 ft (1,500 m). Visitors need a permit, available at all hotels, and a 4WD or a motorbike to navigate the rough mountain roads.

The spectacular views begin at Heaven's Gate, above the town of Tam Son, where a lush valley is bordered by rugged karst outcrops. From here the route passes through Yen Minh to Dong Van, the northern-most town of Vietnam, and then to Meo Vac via the Ma Phi Leng Pass, offering breath-taking views of the Nho Que River in the canyon below. It is possible to head south to Cao Bang or Ba Be Lake via the small town of Bao Loc.

HMONG OF NORTHERN VIETNAM

One of the largest ethnic minority groups in Vietnam, the Hmong or Meo were a nomadic group who emigrated from China to Vietnam in the early 19th century, and settled in the northern highlands. Known for their independent spirit – *hmong* means free in their language – the group has remained fiercely loyal to its indigenous customs, resisting assimilation with the Viet majority.

HMONG VILLAGES

Known as *giao*, Hmong village are small communities featuring wooden huts with thatched roofs. Unlike other hill communities, their homes are not built on stilts. They are usually constructed according to ancient customs, stipulating that houses must be built on land blessed by ancestors.

TEXTILES AND EMBROIDERY

Hmong textile stalls are a staple of the weekly markets of the Northern Highlands. The Hmong have been relatively successful in selling their handicrafts to visitors. Their appliqué work and embroidered fabrics are now very popular.

HMONG GROUPS

Flower Hmong

Flower Hmong wear very bright, patterned, bead-encrusted costumes. They flock to Bac Ha Market once a week to sell fresh produce, and stock up on necessities.

Black Hmong

The Black Hmong are distinguished by their black-dyed clothing. The men dress in baggy trousers, short tunics, and skullcaps, while women wear trousers or skirts and leggings, often piling their hair into an open hat.

Red Hmong

Known for their giant bouffant hairdos, Hmong women painstakingly collect all of the hair they shed naturally, and weave it around a headpiece along with their living tresses *(right)*.

↑ Wooden huts in a Hmong village nestled among paddy fields

Appliqué bags and aprons are indicators of marital status

Gui (woven baskets), into which babies are tucked, are carried on the backs of mothers

Indigo is often used by the Black Hmong to dye their outfits

Bright strips of cloth, embroidered in vibrant patterns, decorate the blouses of the women

Hmong women selling ↑ incense at the Bac Ha Sunday market

EXCURSION TO ANGKOR

The ancient capital of the great Khmer Empire, Angkor is, beyond doubt, one of the most magnificent wonders of the world and a site of immense archaeological significance. Located in dense jungle on the hot and torpid plains of western Cambodia, its awe-inspiring temples transport visitors into an enchanting and mysterious world of brooding grandeur and past glory. For six centuries, between AD 802 and 1432, it was the political and religious center of the Khmer Empire, which once extended from the South China Sea almost to the Bay of Bengal. The remains of the metropolis of Angkor now occupy 77 sq miles (200 sq km) of northwest Cambodia and, although its old wooden houses and palaces decayed centuries ago, the stunning array of stone temples erected by a succession of self-styled god-kings still stand. Set between two baray or reservoirs, Angkor today contains around 70 temples, tombs, and other ancient ruins. Among them is the spectacular Angkor Wat, the world's single largest religious complex.

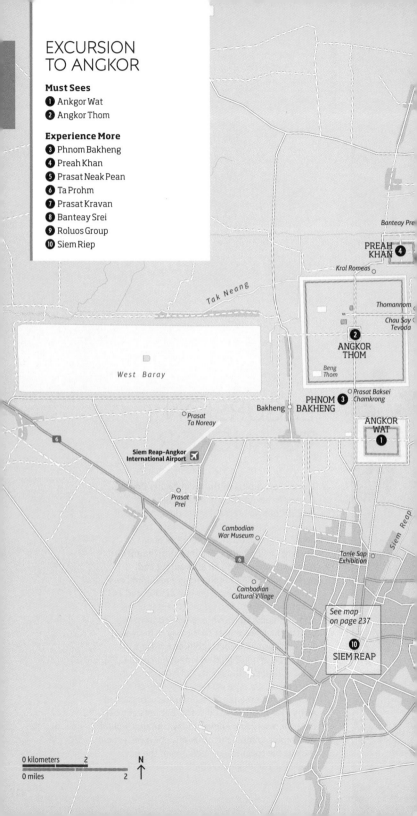

EXCURSION TO ANGKOR

Must Sees
① Ankgor Wat
② Angkor Thom

Experience More
③ Phnom Bakheng
④ Preah Khan
⑤ Prasat Neak Pean
⑥ Ta Prohm
⑦ Prasat Kravan
⑧ Banteay Srei
⑨ Roluos Group
⑩ Siem Riep

Banteay Prei

PREAH **④**
KHAN

Krol Romeas ○

Tak Neang

Thomannnom

Chau Say ○
Tevoda

②

ANGKOR
THOM

Beng
Thom

West Baray

○ *Prasat Baksei*
Chamkrong

PHNOM **③**

Bakheng ○ **BAKHENG**

ANGKOR
WAT

①

○ *Prasat*
Ta Noreay

Siem Reap–Angkor
International Airport ✈

○ *Prasat*
Prei

Cambodian
War Museum ○

Tonle Sap
Exhibition

○ *Cambodian*
Cultural Village

See map
on page 237

⑩
SIEM REAP

0 kilometers   2
0 miles   2   N ↑

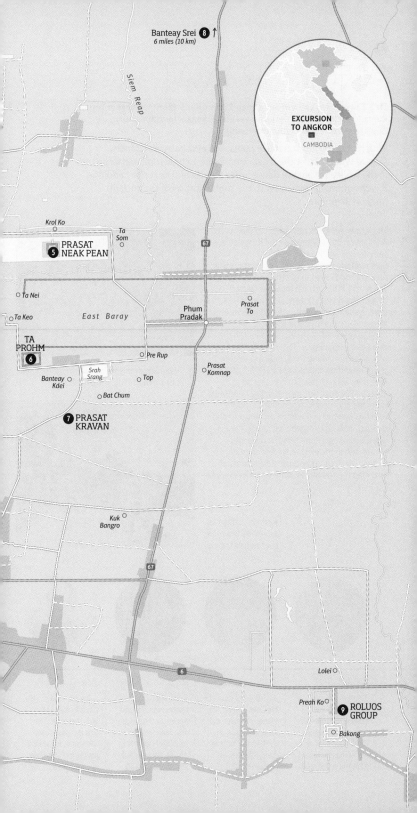

❶ ⬩

ANGKOR WAT

📍 C3 🏠 4 miles (6 km) N of Siem Reap 🚌 Siem Reap 🛈 Khmer Angkor Tour Guide Association, Siem Reap; www.khmerangkortourguide.com
🕐 5:30am–6pm (ticket office from 5am)

With its tall towers, reflective pools, and epic bas-relief panels, Angkor Wat is one of the most remarkable architectural masterpieces in the world. Set among dense green forests and neat rice paddies, it is the ultimate testament to the sophistication of the ancient Angkorian empire.

The largest religious monument in the world, Angkor Wat literally means the City which is a Temple. Built during the 12th century by King Suryavarman II, this spectacular complex was originally dedicated to the Hindu god, Vishnu. The layout is based on a mandala (sacred design of the Hindu cosmos). A five-towered temple shaped like a lotus bud, representing Mount Meru, the mythical abode of the gods and the center of the universe, stands in the middle of the complex. The intricate carvings on the walls marking the temple's perimeter are outstanding and include a 1,970-ft (600-m) long panel of bas-reliefs, and carvings of apsaras (celestial dancing girls). The outermost walls and the moat surrounding the entire complex symbolize the edge of the world and the cosmic ocean, respectively. Angkor Wat, unusual among Khmer temples, faces the setting sun in the west, a symbol of death. Some believe this is because Suryavarman II intended the temple as a funerary monument.

↑ Bas-reliefs representing warriors in combat during the Battle of Kurukshetra

→ Monks crossing the causeway towards the main entrance

Timeline

1130–50
▲ Suryavarman II presides over the building of Angkor Wat, then probably known as Varah Vishnu-lok, with work coming to an end shortly after his death.

1181–1218
▲ After being sacked by the Chams in 1117, the temple is restored and its focus shifts from Hinduism to Buddhism during the reign of Jayavarman VII.

1431
▲ The capital shifts to Phnom Penh and most Angkorian temples are abandoned, though a handful of monks keep Angkor Wat itself active until the Colonial era.

1860
▲ French explorer Henri Mouhot visits Angkor Wat. Though not the first European to see the temple, his account popularizes knowledge of it worldwide.

PICTURE PERFECT
Angkor Wat

To get a good picture of Angkor Wat reflected in the giant pool, head to the temple shortly before it closes at 6pm, when the five towers are bathed in golden light. Crouch down by the pool to the left of the causeway and start snapping away.

The five towers of Angkor Wat reflected in one of the giant pools in front of the temple ↑

Exploring the Temple

Angkor Wat is a sublime combination of grand impression and minute detail. Although its astonishing overall form is best viewed from afar, particularly from the approaching causeway, up close the staggering complexity and craftsmanship of the bas-reliefs and statuary becomes apparent. The temple's sacred splendor reveals itself as you pass through each of the concentric enclosing walls.

The third enclosing wall is the place to pause for an anticlockwise circuit of the long, shady galleries lined with intricate bas-relief panels depicting the Hindu epic *Mahabharata*.

Beyond this, visitors pass through a shady, cloister-like section spanning the second enclosure to reach the innermost parts of the temple where the walls are crowded with exquisite *apsara* carvings.

Towering over the complex, the Central Sanctuary is a steep climb, intended to symbolize the difficulty of ascending to the kingdom of the gods. Its four entrances feature images of Buddha, reflecting how Buddhism eventually went on to displace Hinduism at Angkor Wat.

↑ Bas-relief depictions of *apsaras* lining the walls of the second enclosure

Central Sanctuary

The carvings of hundreds of sensual apsaras line the walls of the temple.

The library provides views of the upper levels of Angkor Wat.

→ Illustration of the three central enclosures of Angkor Wat

↑ Visitors making the steep climb to the Central Sanctuary of Angkor Wat

GETTING AROUND THE TEMPLES

There are various ways to get around the temples of Angkor. Though many people visit on organized tours by minibus, traveling independently gives you a lot more freedom. A popular option is to charter a motorbike taxi or tuk-tuk for the day – with many drivers also doubling as informal guides. If you'd prefer to travel under your own steam, it's possible to walk between the major temples, though you'll need to get transport out from Siem Reap at the start. Alternatively, bicycles are available to rent in Siem Reap, and the area around the temples is mercifully flat.

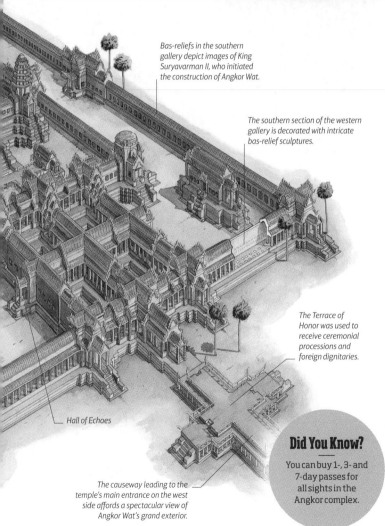

Bas-reliefs in the southern gallery depict images of King Suryavarman II, who initiated the construction of Angkor Wat.

The southern section of the western gallery is decorated with intricate bas-relief sculptures.

The Terrace of Honor was used to receive ceremonial processions and foreign dignitaries.

Hall of Echoes

The causeway leading to the temple's main entrance on the west side affords a spectacular view of Angkor Wat's grand exterior.

Did You Know?

You can buy 1-, 3- and 7-day passes for all sights in the Angkor complex.

ANGKOR THOM

📍 C6 🚗 1 mile (2 km) N of Angkor Wat; 5 miles (8 km) N of Siem Reap ℹ️ Khmer Angkor Tour Guide Association; (063)-964-347 🕐 5am–6pm daily

Remarkable in scale and architectural ingenuity, the ancient city of Angkor Thom, which means Great City in Khmer, was founded by King Jayavarman VII in the late 12th century. The largest city in the Khmer Empire at one time, it is protected by a 26-ft- (8-m-) high wall, and surrounded by a wide moat. Within the city are several ruins, the most famous of which is the atmospheric Bayon temple (p228).

① South Gate

This is the best preserved of the five gateways into Angkor Thom. Its approach is via a causeway flanked by 154 stone statues – gods on the left side, demons on the right – each carrying a giant serpent.

Surrounded by statues of the three-headed elephant Erawan (the fabled mount of the Hindu god, Indra), the gate is a massive 75-ft-(23-m-) high structure surmounted by a triple tower with four giant stone faces pointing towards the cardinal directions.

② Baphuon

Following over 50 years of restoration, Baphuon opened to the public in 2011. Believed to be one of Angkor's greatest temples, it was built by King Udayadityavarman II in the 11th century. Its striking pyramidal mountain form represents Mount Meru, the mythical abode of the Hindu gods. A central tower with

↑ Exterior of the Baphuon temple, opened to the public in 2011

BAFFLING BAPHUON

French architects began restoring Baphuon in 1959. They dismantled the temple so they could reinforce the structure and put it back together again, a technique called "anastylosis". However, plans identifying the 300,000 pieces were destroyed by the Khymer Rouge in the Civil War. When restoration work began again in 1996, it took over 16 years to complete what architect Pascal Royere called the "largest 3D jigsaw puzzle in the world".

←
Gods lining the causeway leading up to the South Gate

four entrances once stood at its summit, but has long since collapsed.

The temple is approached via a 656-ft- (200-m-) long raised causeway and has four gateways decorated with bas-relief scenes from Hindu epics such as the Mahabharata and Ramayana (Reamker in Khmer). Inside, spanning the western length of Baphuon, is a huge Reclining Buddha. Since the temple was dedicated to Hinduism, this image was probably added later, in the 15th century.

The temple is approached via a 656-ft- (200-m-) long raised causeway and has four gateways decorated with bas-relief scenes from Hindu epics.

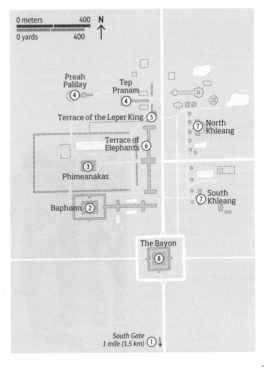

Phimeanakas

This royal temple-palace was built during the 10th century by King Rajendravarman II, and added to later by Jayavarman VII. Dedicated to Hinduism, it is also known as the Celestial Palace, and is associated with the legend of a golden tower that once stood here, where a nine-headed serpent resided. This magical creature would appear to the king as a woman, and the king would sleep with her before going to his other wives and concubines. It was believed that if the king failed to sleep with the serpent-woman, he would die, but by sleeping with her, the royal lineage was saved.

The pyramid-shaped palace is rectangular at the base, and surrounded by a 16-ft- (5-m-) high wall of laterite enclosing an area of around 37 acres (15 ha). It has five entrance-ways, and the stairs, which are flanked by guardian lions, rise up on all four sides. There are corresponding elephant figures at each of the four corners of the pyramid. The upper terrace offers great views of the Baphuon to the south.

④

Preah Palilay and Tep Pranam

Two of the lesser, yet still impressive, structures at Angkor Thom, Preah Palilay and Tep Pranam are located a short distance to the northwest of the Terrace of the Leper King.

Preah Palilay dates from the 13th or 14th century and is a small Buddhist sanctuary set within a 164-ft (50-m) square laterite wall. The sanctuary,

→

Huge sandstone elephants lining the Terrace of Elephants

which is partially collapsed, is entered via a single gateway, and rises to a tapering stone tower. A 108-ft- (33-m-) long causeway leads to a terrace to the east of the sanctuary, which is distinguished by fine *naga* (serpent) balustrades.

Nearby, to the east, lies Tep Pranam, a Buddhist sanctuary built in the 16th century. This was probably originally dedicated to the Mahayana school. Used as a place of Theravada worship now, it features a big sandstone Buddha image, seated in the "calling the earth to witness" mudra (posture).

⑤

Terrace of the Leper King

This small platform dates from the late 12th century. Standing on top of this structure is a headless statue known as the Leper King. Once believed to be an image of King Jayavarman VII, who, according to legend, had leprosy, it is in fact a representation of Yama, the God of Death. This statue is, however, a replica – the original was taken to Phnom Penh's National Museum.

The terrace is marked by two walls, both beautifully restored and decorated with exquisite bas-reliefs. Of the two, the inner one is more remarkable, and is covered with figures of underworld deities, kings, celestial females, multiple-headed nagas, devadas, apsaras, warriors, and strange marine creatures.

The exact function of this terrace, which appears to be

↑ The remarkable gateway of the Preah Palilay

an extension of the Terrace of Elephants, is not clear. It was probably used either for royal receptions or cremations.

Terrace of Elephants

Built by King Jayavarman VII, this structure is more than 950 ft (300 m) long, stretching from the Baphuon to the connecting Terrace of the Leper King. It has three main platforms and two smaller ones. The terrace was primarily used by the king to view military and other parades. It is decorated with almost life-sized images of sandstone elephants in a procession, accompanied by mahouts. There are also images of tigers, serpents, and Garuda – mythical beasts mounted by Vishnu. For an spectacular unobstructed view

of the whole complex, head to very the top of the terrace's middle stairway.

North and South Khleang

These two similar buildings are located to the east of the main road running past the Terrace of Elephants. The North Khleang was constructed by King Jayavarman toward the end of the 10th century, and the South Khleang was built by King Suryavarman I during the early 11th century. The main architectural features of the Khleangs are their stone lintels and elegant balustered windows. Unfortunately, the original function of the buildings is unknown. Khleang, which means storehouse, is a modern designation, and is considered misleading.

ASPARA DANCE PERFORMANCES

There is a remarkable continuity between the images of divine *aspara* dancers that decorate many of the temples of Angkor, and contemporary entertainment laid on for travelers. Though the *aspara* tradition declined during the Colonial era, and then suffered Khmer Rouge hostility, it has since been revived. Dancers are trained at the Royal University of Fine Arts in Phnom Penh. The Aspara Theater in Siem Reap (www. angkorvillageresort. asia/apsara-theatre) has nightly shows.

↑ Buddhist monks and visitors exploring the Bayon temple

⑧ ✎

THE BAYON

◉ C2 ⌂ Angkor Thom ⊙ 5am–6pm daily

Located in the heart of Angkor Thom, the Bayon is one of the city's most extraordinary structures, epitomizing the "lost civilization" of Angkor. Shaped like a pyramid, this symbolic temple-mountain rises on three levels, and features 54 towers bearing more than 200 huge, yet enigmatic stone faces.

The central sanctuary of the Bayon, with its forest of towers, is ringed by an outer enclosing wall, stretching between eight, evenly spaced cruciform bastions. This wall was once a shaded gallery, like that of Angkor Wat. The roof has long since collapsed, but the bas-reliefs remain, and while it is the huge faces on the inner towers that get most of the attention, these carvings are where much of the Bayon's unique interest lies. Unlike the reliefs at Angkor Wat, which are dominated by religious narratives, these teem with scenes from Angkorian daily life, as well as tales from local folklore.

Beyond this epic in carved stone, more bas-relief friezes ring the inner enclosing wall before the innermost sanctum with its looming mass of towers. Each tower bears the all-seeing face of Avalokiteśvara. The central structure – a craggy depiction of the mythical Mount Meru – rises from a circular base 141 ft (43 m) above the ground. A large statue of Buddha once occupied the sanctuary but was destroyed when the Bayon became a Hindu temple. It has since been restored and is now on display in a small pavilion at Angkor.

> **The central structure – a craggy depiction of the mythical Mount Meru – rises from a circular base.**

↑ Stone faces depicting Avalokiteśvara on the towers of the Bayon

THE BODHISATTVA OF COMPASSION

Most archeologists now believe that the enigmatically smiling faces of the Bayon represent Avalokiteśvara, the bodhisattva who embodies compassion and who often appears outside Cambodia as a striking, thousand-armed figure. The fact that they also resemble the king who commissioned the temple, Jayavarman VII *(p226)*, is probably no coincidence, as Southeast Asian concepts of kingship often rested on the identification of a living ruler with a deity.

Timeline

12th century
△ Construction of the Bayon begins. It is to be the centerpiece of Angkor Thom, King Jayavarman VII's vast and ambitious new capital city.

13th century
△ Jayavarman VIII, a Hindu king, takes the throne. The temple is altered to reflect the new religion and the Buddha icon in the sanctuary is destroyed.

15th century
△ Angkor Thom is sacked at the hands of the mighty Ayutthaya Kingdom, led by King Borommarachathirat II, and the Bayon is abandoned to the jungle.

20th century
△ The École Française d'Extrême Orient starts restoring the temple in the early 20th century. Conservation continues in the 1990s, led by the Japanese government.

History of the Bayon

The Bayon was the last great state temple built at Angkor, before the empire began its slow, centuries-long decline. It is unique among Angkor's vast array of religious edifices as the only temple originally built to honor Mahayana Buddhism. King Jayavarman VII was one of the most successful of all Angkorian rulers, seeing off regional rivals and consolidating the empire. He also broke with the religious traditions of his Hindu predecessors, and ruled as a Buddhist monarch, dedicated to the Mahayana school. When it came time to command his own mighty contribution to the Angkor cityscape, he ordered the construction of a Mahayana temple, the Bayan. After Jayavarman's death, the Bayon was retooled for a resurgent Hinduism, with many sculptures adapted. Later, its focus shifted again as Theravada Buddhism came to dominate. But there was no way to erase the vast and essentially Mahayana faces of Avalokiteśvara.

Bas-relief showing a female *devata*, a Hindu deity ↑

 INSIDER TIP
Visit at Sunrise

To dodge the crowds, the best time to visit is first thing in the morning, while the rest of the early risers are snapping the sunrise at Angkor Wat, and before the tour buses turn up.

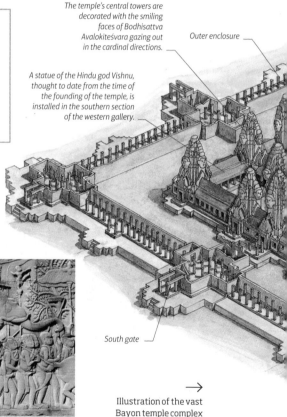

The temple's central towers are decorated with the smiling faces of Bodhisattva Avalokiteśvara gazing out in the cardinal directions.

A statue of the Hindu god Vishnu, thought to date from the time of the founding of the temple, is installed in the southern section of the western gallery.

Outer enclosure

South gate

→
Illustration of the vast Bayon temple complex

↑ Bas-relief showing a Khmer king on his elephant, marching his soldiers to battle

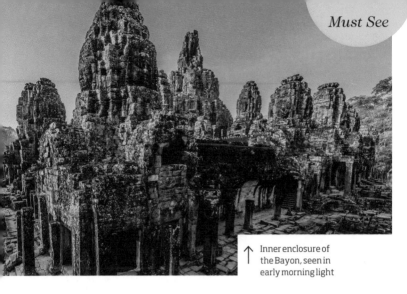

↑ Inner enclosure of the Bayon, seen in early morning light

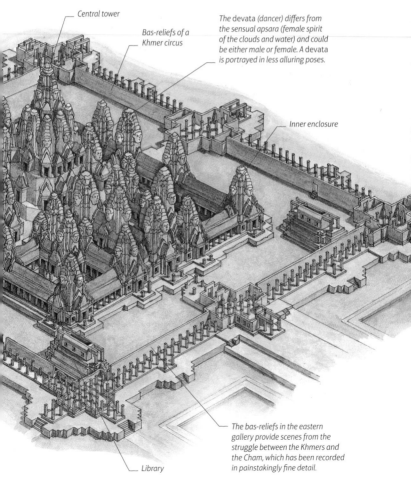

Central tower

Bas-reliefs of a Khmer circus

The devata *(dancer) differs from the sensual* apsara *(female spirit of the clouds and water) and could be either male or female. A* devata *is portrayed in less alluring poses.*

Inner enclosure

The bas-reliefs in the eastern gallery provide scenes from the struggle between the Khmers and the Cham, which has been recorded in painstakingly fine detail.

Library

ARCHITECTURE OF ANGKOR

Angkor-period architecture generally dates from Jayavarman II's construction of the Khmer capital near Roluos in the early 9th century AD. From then until the 15th century, art historians identify five main architectural styles. The earliest, Preah Ko, is rooted in the pre-Angkorian traditions of Sambor Prei Kuk, to Angkor's east, and the 8th-century temple style of Kompong Preah, relics of which are found at Prasat Ak Yum by the West Baray. Khmer architecture reached its zenith during the construction of Angkor Wat.

The oldest temple in the Rolous Group, Preah Ko was built in 879. Its distinctive towers and elegant carvings influenced the design of other, later temples in the area.

Unlike the later temples which were typically built entirely of stone, Preah Ko features a combination of sandstone and brick. The towers were originally entirely covered with plaster, a few traces of which still remain.

Completed in 907, Phnom Bakheng impressively exemplifies the Bakheng style. It was built onto a natural hill, with the terraces and stairways cut into the bedrock. The five towers at the top are arranged in the standard quincunx pattern.

Preah Ko
(AD 875–90)

▲ The Preah Ko style was characterized by a simple temple layout, with one or more square brick towers rising from a single laterite base. The Roluos Group (p236) saw the first use of concentric enclosures entered via the *gopura* (gateway tower). Another innovation was the introduction of a library annex, possibly used to protect the sacred texts from fire.

Bakheng to Pre Rup
(AD 890–965)

▲ The temple-mountain style, based on Mount Meru, evolved during the Bakheng period. Phnom Bakheng (p234), Phnom Krom, and Phnom Bok all feature the classic layout of five towers arranged in a quincunx - a tower on each corner, with a fifth at the center. The Pre Rup style developed during the reign of Rajendravarman II (r.944-68). It continues the Bakheng style, but the towers are higher and steeper, with more tiers.

↑ An aerial view of Angkor Wat, showing the symbolic layout of the complex

Did You Know?

The central quincunx of towers at Angkor represent the five peaks of the sacred Mount Meru.

The central tower of Angkor Wat marked the physical and spiritual culmination of the complex – and of the Khmer Empire too.

The towers of the Bayon are decorated with faces representing the Bodhisattva Avoalokitescara, who bears a striking resemblance to Jayavarman VII.

Banteay Srei, built between AD 967 and 1000, is known for its fine craftsmanship, evident in the detail of the stone lintels.

Banteay Srei to Baphuon (AD 965–1080)

▲ Represented by the delicate and refined Banteay Srei (see p236), this eponymous style is characterized by ornate carvings of sensuous apsaras and *devadas* (dancers). By the mid-11th century, when Khmer architecture was reaching its majestic apogee, this style had evolved into the Baphuon style, which is distinguished by vast proportions and vaulted galleries.

Angkor Wat (AD 1080–1175)

▲ Art historians generally agree that the style of Angkor Wat (p220) represents the apex of Khmer architectural and sculptural genius. The largest and greatest of all temple-mountains, it also boasts the finest bas-relief narratives, particularly in the gallery of the third enclosure. The art of lintel carving also reached its zenith during this magnificent period of construction.

Bayon (AD 1175–1240)

▲ Considered a synthesis of previous styles, Bayon - the last great Angkor architectural style - is characterized by a detectable decline in quality. There is more use of laterite and less of sandstone, as well as more Buddhist imagery and fewer Hindu themes. This is the style that was adopted in Angkor Thom (p224), King Jayavarman VII's ambitious capital.

EXPERIENCE MORE

3

Phnom Bakheng

F7 ⬛ Just S of Angkor Thom ⬛ Sunrise-sunset daily

The ancient temple complex of Phnom Bakheng (*phnom* means mountain) sits on a steep hill that rises 220 ft (67 m) above the plain.

Built by King Yasovarman I (r.889–910) and honoring the Hindu god Shiva, the Bakheng complex features one of the region's first temple-mountains (*p232*) – a style of temple architecture that has become a mainstay of Khmer-style religious buildings. The central sanctuary was surrounded by 108 towers, though most are now missing. However, the well-crafted statues of lions, flanking each of the five terraced tiers of the temple, can be seen even today.

The central sanctuary, one of five in all, is adorned with several decorative posts and statues of *apsaras* or celestial

← Carving of a beautiful *apsara*, or mystical dancing girl, Phnom Bakheng

dancing girls, and *makaras* or mythical sea creatures. Visitors can climb the hill, a relatively easy walk taking 20 minutes. Here, there are spectacular views over Angkor and the Western Baray. At dusk, thousands of tourists jostle for position, so it is better to head there in the morning.

4

Preah Khan

F7 ⬛ 1.3 miles (2 km) NE of Angkor Thom ⬛ Sunrise-sunset daily

Named for the sacred sword owned by the 9th-century ruler Jayavarman II, Preah Khan temple complex was established by Jayavarman VII (r.1181–1218), and functioned as a monastery and religious college. It is also believed to have been a temporary capital for Jayavarman VII during the restoration of Angkor Thom after the city's sacking by the Kingdom of Champa in 1177. An inscribed stone stele found here indicates that the temple was based at the center of an ancient city, Nagarajayacri. The central sanctuary was dedicated to the Buddha, but the Hindu rulers succeeding Jayavarman VII replaced several Buddha images on the walls with Hindu deities.

Today, the complex extends over a sprawling 141 acres (57 ha), and is surrounded by a 2-mile- (3-km-) long laterite

wall. The premises also have a massive reservoir or *baray*. Access to the central sanctuary, built on a cross-shaped layout, is through four gates, set at the cardinal points of the compass.

One of the main highlights at Preah Khan is the Hall of Dancers, named for the exquisite *apsara* bas-reliefs that line the walls. The shrine of the White Lady, a wife of Jayavarman VII, is still venerated by locals who leave offerings of flowers and incense. The most notable temple here is the Temple of Four Faces, named for the carvings on its central tower. Like Ta Prohm, Preah Khan is studded with great trees whose creeping roots cover and pierce the laterite and sandstone structures on which they grow. Yet, unlike Ta Prohm, the complex has undergone extensive restoration. Many of the giant trees have been felled, and the walls are being rebuilt.

5

Prasat Neak Pean

F7 ⬛ 2.5 miles (4 km) NE of Angkor Thom ⬛ 5am-6pm daily

One of the most unusual temples at Angkor, Prasat Neak Pean or Temple of Coiled Serpents dates from the late 12th century. Like much else at Angkor, it was founded by King Jayavarman VII and dedicated to Buddhism. It is located in the middle of a now dry lake, North Baray.

The temple is built around an artificial pond surrounded by four smaller square ponds. In the center is a circular island with a shrine dedicated to Bodhisattva Avalokitesvara. Two intertwined serpents circle its base, giving the temple its name. To the east of the island is the sculpted figure of the horse Balaha, a manifestation of Avalokitesvara, who, according to Buddhist mythology,

> Like Ta Prohm, Preah Khan is studded with great trees whose creeping roots cover and pierce the laterite and sandstone structures on which they grow.

Did You Know?

The face of Prajnaparamita looking over Ta Prohm is based on that of the king's mother.

transformed himself into a horse to rescue shipwrecked sailors from a sea ogress.

The pond represents a mythical lake, Anavatapta, believed to be the source of the four great rivers of the world, symbolized by four gargoyle-like heads with spouts. When the temple was functioning, Buddhist devotees would seek the advice of resident monks, and then bathe in the holy waters.

6

Ta Prohm

F7 **0.6 miles (1 km) E of Angkor Thom** **5am–6pm daily**

Perhaps the most evocative of all the temple structures at Angkor, Ta Prohm, which means Ancestor of Brahma, was originally a Buddhist monastery, built in King Jayavarman VII's reign. A stone stele at the complex describes how powerful the monastery was. At its peak, it owned more than 3,000 villages, and

was maintained by 80,000 attendants, including 18 high priests and over 600 temple dancers. The wealth of the temple, and of its founder, Jayavarman VII, is also listed; it includes 40,000 pearls.

The French began archaeological restoration during the colonial period, deliberately attempting to preserve Ta Prohm in its existing state, cutting down as little of the dense jungle as possible. As a result, the temple buildings remain smothered with the roots of giant banyan trees, just as 19th-century explorers must have experienced them.

The temple sits on the peak of a hill and has a complex of stone buildings, surrounded by a rectangular laterite wall. The narrow passageways of the structure, along with huge kapok trees, provide relief from the tropical sun, and wooden walkways link a series of musty, darkened galleries. The main entrance is filled with images of the Buddha recovered from the ruins. Beyond the gate is the fascinating Hall of Dancers. This must-see sandstone building is decorated with false doorways and rows of intricate

↑ Atmospheric ruins of Ta Prohm covered with the roots of Banyan trees

apsara (celestial dancing girl) bas-reliefs. To the west is the main sanctuary, a simple stone structure distinguished by its jungle setting.

7

Prasat Kravan

F7 **2 miles (3 km) E of Angkor Wat** **5am–6pm daily**

Dating from the early 10th century, Prasat Kravan was founded by Harshavarman I (r.915–23). Comprising five brick towers, it is one of the smaller temples in the complex, and was dedicated to the Hindu god Vishnu.

The temple, whose name means Cardamom Sanctuary, is chiefly remarkable for its brickwork and bas-reliefs. These represent Vishnu, his consort Lakshmi, Garuda his eagle mount, *naga* the serpent, and a number of other divine attendants. The doorway of the southern-most tower has fine image of Vishnu.

↑ Banteay Srei temple complex, seen from across the mote and detail of an exquisite stone carving *(inset)*

sanctuary. The goddesses, with their long hair tied in buns or plaits, are dressed in loosely draped skirts, and are laden with heavy jewelry.

8

Banteay Srei

⚑F6 🚗19 miles (30 km) NE of Siem Reap ⏰5am–5pm daily

The remote temple complex of Banteay Srei (also known as Srey) or the Citadel of Women is famed for its finely detailed carving. The complex of pink sandstone was founded in the second half of the 10th century by Hindu priests. Unlike other monuments in Angkor, it is not a royal temple.

Rectangular and enclosed by three walls and the remains of a moat, the central sanctuary contains ornate shrines dedicated to Shiva, the Hindu God of Destruction, and scenes from the Hindu epic *Ramayana*. Also exceptional are the carved figures of gods and goddesses in the niches of the towers in the central

9

Roluos Group

⚑F7 🚗7 miles (12 km) SE of Siem Reap ⏰5am–6pm daily

The oldest monuments in the Angkor area, these temples mark the site of Hariharalaya, the very first Khmer capital, established by Indravarman I (r.877–89). Three main complexes can be found here.

Lolei temple, founded by King Yasovarman I (r.889–910), stands on an artificial mound on a small reservoir. The four central brick towers have well-preserved inscriptions. To the south of Lolei stands Preah Ko or the Sacred Bull. Built by Indravarman I, this Hindu temple was dedicated to Shiva.

It was intended to honor the king's parents, as well as Jayavarman II. The main sanctuary consists of six brick towers resting on a raised laterite platform. Close by are three statues of the sacred bull Nandi, for whom the temple was named. The motifs on the false doors, lintels, and columns include *kala*, mythical creatures with a grinning mouth and large, bulging eyes, *makara*, sea creatures with snouts, and Garuda, the eagle mount of the god Vishnu.

Beyond Preah Ko, the huge mass of Bakong cannot be missed. This temple is also dedicated to Shiva, and was founded by Indravarman I in the 9th century. A pathway protected by a seven-headed *naga* leads to it. In the center of the complex is an artificial mound representing Mount Meru, the center of the Hindu world and abode of the gods. The mount rises in five stages, the first three of which are enhanced by stone elephants. At the summit rests the central sanctuary, with four levels and a lotus-shaped tower rising from the middle. The mound is surrounded by eight brick towers with finely carved sandstone decorations.

STAY

Raffles Grand Hotel d'Angkor

Housed in a landmark colonial building and exuding class, this is one of the best hotels in Cambodia. Rooms are lavishly furnished and service is par excellence.

🅰F7 🏠1 Vithei Charles de Gaulle Ⓦraffles.com

Ⓢ⑤⑤

Heritage Suites Hotel

This modern, chic hotel with Khmer-inspired decor in a colonial-style building is tucked away in a peaceful location. The rooms come with hardwood floors and high ceilings, and service is impeccable.

🅰F7 🏠Slokram Village Ⓦheritage suites hotel.com

⑤⑤Ⓢ

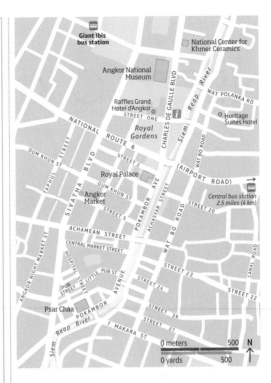

🔟

Siem Riep

🅰F7 🏠155 miles (250 km) NW of Phnom Penh 🛈Khmer Angkor Tour Guide Association; www. tourism cambodia.com

Located in northwest Cambodia, Siem Riep is the capital of the Siem Reap Province and has achieved prominence as the main base for people visiting the temples of Angkor. It is the ideal place to unwind after a day exploring the ancient sites

The small Royal Palace, which is occasionally visited by the reigning King Sihamoni, is close to the splendidly restored Raffles Grand Hotel d'Angkor. South of a statue of Vishnu marking the center of town, Pokambor Avenue runs down the right bank of the Siem Reap River to Psar Chaa. This old market is a great place to shop for souvenirs. Nearby, the renovated old French Quarter is home to some of the most atmospheric restaurants in the Angkor area. For those who wish to explore the area, the banks of the Siem Reap River offer a pleasant stroll. Several blue-painted stilt houses and creaky bamboo waterwheels can be seen here. The modern, air-conditioned **Angkor National Museum** is filled with information on, and artifacts from, Angkor Wat.

Farther south, situated some 6 miles (10 km) away, is the ferry landing on the Tonle Sap. The largest freshwater lake in Southeast Asia, it is also a biosphere reserve.

The main monuments at Angkor, the ticket office, and conservatory are all about 4 miles (6 km) north of town. About halfway, at Wat Thmei, is a *stupa* displaying the skulls of local Khmer Rouge victims.

Angkor National Museum

🏠968 Charles De Gaulle Ⓒ8:30am–6pm daily Ⓦangkornational museum.com

↑ Smiling face carved in stone at the temple of Angkor Thom

NEED TO KNOW

Woman riding a bicycle

Vietnam

Angkor

BEFORE YOU GO
VIETNAM

Forward planning is essential to any successful trip. Be prepared for all eventualities by considering the following points before you travel.

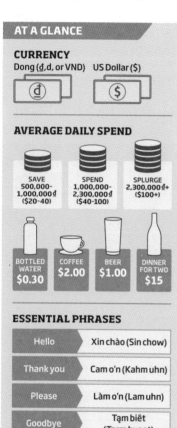

AT A GLANCE

CURRENCY
Dong (đ,d, or VND)   US Dollar ($)

AVERAGE DAILY SPEND

SAVE
500,000-
1,000,000đ
($20-40)

SPEND
1,000,000-
2,300,000đ
($40-100)

SPLURGE
2,300,000đ+
($100+)

BOTTLED WATER
$0.30

COFFEE
$2.00

BEER
$1.00

DINNER FOR TWO
$15

ESSENTIAL PHRASES

Hello	Xin chào (Sin chow)
Thank you	Cam o'n (Kahm uhn)
Please	Làm o'n (Lam uhn)
Goodbye	Tạm biêt (Tarm byeet)
Do you speak English?	Bạn nói tiêng Anh duoc không?
I don't understand	Tôi không hiêu (Toy kohng hugh)

ELECTRICITY SUPPLY
Most power sockets are type C, fitting two round pins. Standard voltage is 220V (occasionally 110V in remote areas).

Passports and Visas

Visitors from the UK and many EU countries do not need to apply for a visa for stays of up to 15 days. For stays of more than 15 days a visa is required. Those from the US , Australia, and New Zealand will need to apply for a visa to enter the country for any length of time. Visa requirements change regularly, however, and it's strongly advised to check the latest regulations online or with your nearest Vietnamese embassy.

If you are arriving by air into one of the six international airports in Vietnam, you can obtain a visa online from **Vietnam Visa Center** or **Vietnam Visa Choice**. It takes three working days, after which you'll be e-mailed a visa confirmation letter. Those not arriving by air must apply for a visa from their Vietnamese embassy.
Vietnam Visa Center
w vietnamvisacenter.org
Vietnam Visa Choice
w vietnamvisachoice.com

Travel Safety Advice

Visitors can get up-to-date travel safety information from the UK Foreign and Commonwealth Office, the US State Department, and the Australian Department of Foreign Affairs and Trade.
AUS
w smartraveller.gov.au
UK
w gov.uk/foreign-travel-advice
US
w travel.state.gov

Customs Information

On entering Vietnam, you'll need to fill in a yellow customs declaration, and the duty free allowances are as follows:
Tobacco products 400 cigarettes or 100 cigars or 500g of tobacco.
Alcohol 1.5 liters of spirits over 22% volume or 2 liters of fortified wines or liqueurs under 22% volume or 3 liters of other alcoholic drinks.
Cash US$ 5,000 or more must be declared.

Insurance

A general travel insurance policy is greatly advisable. Make sure that, in addition to illness, injury, and theft, it covers medical evacuation in case of an emergency.

Vaccinations

The only official vaccination required is yellow fever if you're arriving in Vietnam from an area where the disease is present. However, it is a good idea to be inoculated against typhoid, hepatitis A, tetanus, and polio. Consider rabies and hepatitis B vaccines if you're traveling to remote areas. Check the latest vaccination requirements with your doctor 4–6 weeks before traveling. Ask your doctor about malaria and Dengue fever prevention as some remote areas of Vietnam carry a risk of these diseases.

Money

The official currency is Vietnamese dong, but US dollars are also widely accepted across Vietnam. Most establishments catering to tourists accept major credit, debit, and pre-paid currency cards. Cash is needed for smaller purchases and can be withdrawn from ATMs, which are prevalent even in small towns. Foreign currency can be exchanged at banks for a better rate than at private bureaux de change.

Booking Accommodations

Most accommodations can be booked online, and this is especially advised during the high season in July–August and during Tet Nguyen Dan (p42) and other festivals when prices can also increase by up to 50 percent. When checking into a hotel or private accommodations, you'll have to hand over your passport so that the hotel can register your presence with the local police.

Travelers with Specific Needs

Facilities for disabled access are quite rare in Vietnam. Elevators are not very common, toilets for the disabled are virtually unheard of, and regular bathroom doors are often less than 23 inches (60 cm) wide. Nonetheless, many high-end hotels and resorts are now well-equipped to accommodate those with special needs, while travel agents can hire an assistant for those who require one. Neither trains nor buses are fully accessible, so hiring a car/van and driver is the best option. With planning and advice from specialist agencies such as **Disability Travel Advice**, **Accessible Journeys**, and **Disability Horizons**, inconveniences can be minimized.

Disability Travel Advice
ⓦ disabledtraveladvice.co.uk
Accessible Journeys
ⓦ disabilitytravel.com
Disability Horizons
ⓦ disabilityhorizons.com

Language

The official language is Vietnamese but in cities and tourist areas English is widely spoken, especially by younger people, while French may be spoken by the elderly.

Closures

Public holidays Most offices and businesses close for public holidays. The major national holiday is Tet Nguyen Dan, when much of the country closes for 3–7 days.

Opening times Basic business hours are 7:30–11:30am and 1:30–4:30pm Mon–Fri. Banks and offices are usually closed over the weekend, though banks can be open longer in tourist areas. Shops and markets generally open seven days a week and often until late, though it's common for private shopkeepers to take an afternoon nap.

Museums Most museums shut for public holidays, and one day a week, usually Monday.

PUBLIC HOLIDAYS 2019	
1 Jan	New Year's Day
5–9 Feb	Tet Nguyen Dan
14 Apr	Hung Kings' Temple Festival
30 Apr	Liberation Day
1 May	International Workers' Day
2 Sep	National Day

GETTING AROUND
VIETNAM

Whether you are visiting for a short city break or trekking in the mountains, discover how best to reach your destination.

TRANSPORTATION COSTS
Typical transportation costs from Hanoi to HCMC (prices given are US dollars) by:

TRAIN
$54–125
One way

LUXURY BUS
$40–50
One way

PLANE
$49–150
One way

TAXI
$900
One way

SPEED LIMITS

HIGHWAYS AND RURAL ROADS

37 miles/h (60km/h)

URBAN AREAS

25 miles/h (40km/h)

Arriving by Air

Hanoi's Noi Bai and and HCMC's Tan Son Nhat are the main airports for long-haul flights into Vietnam, although Danang Airport is expanding rapidly as an international hub. Domestic flights are relatively inexpensive and can cut travel times considerably, with **Vietnam Airlines** and the budget **Jetstar** and **VietJet Air** the main operators. For information on getting to and from the main airports, see the table opposite.

Vietnam Airlines
w vietnamairlines.com
Jetstar
w jetstar.com/vn/en/home
VietJet Air
w vietjetair.com

Train Travel

Domestic Train Travel
Vietnam Railways' network stretches from the Chinese border crossings in the north at Lao Cai and Dong Dang to Hanoi. From Hanoi there are branch lines to Halong and Haiphong, while the Reunification Line runs down the entire east coast to HCMC. Seat types are hard seat, soft seat, hard berth (6ppl) and soft berth (4ppl), and all have aircon except the hard seat. You should book tickets at least two days in advance at stations, through travel agencies (for a fee), or online either through the official **Vietnam Railways** booking site or **Baolau**, which is easier to use. Luxury carriages are attached to many scheduled trains by independent companies and can be booked through **Vietnam Impressive**.

Vietnam Railways
w dsvn.vn
Baolau
w baolau.com
Vietnam Impressive
w vietnamimpressive.com

International Train Travel
Vietnam's only international train journeys are those to China from Hanoi, with one daily 13-hour train to Nanning, and one twice-weekly 38-hour route to Beijing, via Nanning and Guilin.

GETTING TO AND FROM THE AIRPORT

Airport	Distance to city	Taxi fare	Transportation	Journey time
Can Tho (Can Tho)	10 km (6 miles)	220,000 d	bus	25 mins
Dalat (Lien Khuong)	30 km (19 miles)	430,000 d	bus	45 mins
Danang (Da Nang)	2 km (1 mile)	60,000 d	None	10 mins
Hai Phong (Cat Bi)	6 km (4 miles)	150,000 d	bus	20 mins
Hanoi (Noi Bai)	45 km (28 miles)	320,000 d	bus	45 mins
HCMC (Tan Son Nhat)	6 km (4 miles)	160,000 d	bus	20 mins
Hue (Phu Bai)	15 km (9 miles)	250,000 d	bus	20 mins
Nha Trang (Cam Ranh)	30 km (19 miles)	400,000 d	bus	35 mins
Phu Quoc (Phu Quoc)	10 km (6 miles)	50,000 d	bus	10 mins
Vinh (Vinh)	7 km (4 miles)	60,000 d	None	20 mins

ROAD JOURNEY PLANNER

This map shows the approximate road travel times between the main tourist destinations in Vietnam by car.

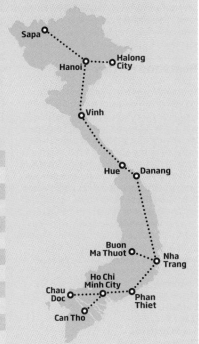

Hanoi to Sapa	5 hrs
Hanoi to HCMC	32 hrs
Hanoi to Halong City	3.5 hrs
Hanoi to Vinh	6 hrs
Vinh to Hue	7 hrs
Hue to Danang	2 hrs
Danang to Nha Trang	10 hrs
Nha Trang to Buon Ma Thuot	4.5 hrs
Nha Trang to Phan Thiet	4 hrs
Phan Thiet to HCMC	4.5 hrs
HCMC to Can Tho	3.5 hrs
HCMC to Chau Doc	5.5 hrs

Long-Distance Bus Travel

Private Buses

Most visitors utilize privately run buses which serve the main tourist routes. These are the most comfortable bus option and many have "sleeper" buses with berths. "Open tour" tickets can be bought for multiple stop-offs on the longer routes, such as Hanoi to HCMC. Private buses run from their company offices, though some also do pickups from hotels. Tickets can be bought directly from bus organizations' websites such as **Mai Linh Express**, through transportation sites such as Baolau (p242), or via travel agencies, such as **The Sinh Tourist**.

Mai Linh Express
ⓦ mailinhexpress.vn/en

The Sinh Tourist
ⓦ thesinhtourist.vn

National Bus Service and State Buses

Running from town and city bus stations, these once rickety buses are slowly being upgraded to more comfortable vehicles and, although cheaper, are slower than private buses as they make more frequent stops. You'll probably only use these if traveling off the main tourist trails.

Minibuses

Private minibuses often ply the same routes as state buses, leaving from or near bus stations. Although usually uncomfortably full, they make for an interesting way to experience the real Vietnam. Fares are negotiable, so ask locally as to how much a particular journey should cost.

Boats and Ferries

Scheduled ferries run to Vietnam's offshore islands such as Phu Quoc (from Ha Tien), Bai Tu Long (from Cai Rong), Cat Ba (from Haiphong) and Con Dao (slow boat from Vung Tau or speed-boat from Soc Trang). All can be booked most easily online through Baolau (p242). Offshore ferries can be cancelled due to weather conditions.

There are also a few long-distance slow river boats and fast hydrofoil services in the Mekong Delta. **Greenlines** runs from HCMC to Vung Tau via Can Gio, and from there to My Tho and Ben Tre, while **Lan Anh Cruise** runs fast boats from HCMC to Chau Doc, via Can Tho, and then upriver to Phnom Penh in Cambodia. HCMC has a **Saigon Waterbus** service, which is especially useful during rush hour.

Greenlines
ⓦ greenlines-dp.com

Lan Anh Cruise
ⓦ lananhcruise.com

Saigon Waterbus
ⓦ saigonwaterbus.vn

Local Transportation

Public transportation in cities is currently limited to buses, taxis, motorbike taxis, and the odd waterbus. Rush-hour congestion is a big problem in the bigger towns and cities and you should factor this in when trying to get to transportation hubs or appointments. If traffic is really bad, and you don't have much luggage, consider walking or taking a motorbike taxi. One of the easiest ways of getting around towns and cities is by bicycle, which can be rented locally for a few US dollars a day.

Local Buses and Minibuses

Although inexpensive, city buses in Vietnam are often quite uncomfortable and crowded, although they are improving rapidly – most cities now run more modern, air-conditioned buses. Minibuses are available for hire for groups/families at affordable rates, and can be arranged by most hotels and travel agencies.

Taxis

Taxis are widely available in all urban areas and are metered. **Mai Linh** is a nationwide taxi company which also runs motorbike taxis and an inter-city bus service. The dominant ride-hailing app in Vietnam for both cars and motorbikes is **Grab**, though its prices increased considerably after they took over Uber in the region. Consider also downloading one of the free local apps such as TaxiGo, Vivu, T.net, Xelo, or Vato, which offer a less expensive service.

Mai Linh
ⓦ mailinh.vn

Grab
ⓦ grab.com/vn/en

Organized Tours

There are numerous companies in both Hanoi and HCMC offering organized tours. Check with a few tour companies such as **Queen Travel** in Hanoi or **Kim Tran Travel** in HCMC for the best deal available. For touring hill tribe areas, it's best to pick an ethical agency run by locals, such as **Sapa Chau**, who have an office in Hanoi.

Queen Travel
ⓦ queentravel.vn

Kim Tran Travel
ⓦ thekimtourist.com

Sapa Chau
ⓦ sapaochau.org

Metro

Both Hanoi's and HCMC's metro systems were still under construction at the time of going to press. Beset by delays, they will open some time between 2019 and 2021. Check online for the latest information once the metro systems have their websites up and running.

Driving

Driving Licences

To drive in Vietnam you need to hold a current Vietnamese driving licence. You can convert your home country or international driving licence to a Vietnamese one, but this takes at least five days and a considerable amount of bureaucratic hassle (and you will need to have at least three months on your visa).

Car Rental

Since self-driving is not really an option for the majority of foreign visitors, most rent a car, jeep, or minibus with a driver. This can prove particularly economical if traveling in a group and can be arranged via car-hire companies, travel agencies, or local accommodations. Clarify who pays for the driver's accommodations and meals, fuel, tolls, and parking charges, and especially repairs and major breakdowns.

Motorbikes

To legally ride a motorbike of more than 50cc in Vietnam, you will need to hold a Vietnamese driving licence, though hiring and driving a 50cc scooter or moped is permitted without a licence. Make sure that your insurance will cover this under "high-risk activities" and remember your policy won't pay out if you're driving illegally, i.e. without a helmet, third-party insurance, a licence where one is required, or with two people on the bike. Despite the generally low road speeds, driving a motorbike on Vietnam's chaotic roads is a risky business, and it's the highest cause of injury and death for foreigners visiting the country.

Road Safety

If you are self-driving a motorbike, observe and familiarize yourself with the general flow and movement of traffic, usually erratic, for a few days first. Keep an eye out for livestock on the road.

For the average tourist, the main consideration is how to cross the street. There are few traffic lights, and those that do exist are often considered to convey an advisory rather than a compulsory message. Watch the locals step out into traffic and follow their lead, first waiting for four-wheeled vehicles to pass, and then walking slowly and steadily through a sea of two-wheelers. Don't hesitate or stop suddenly as drivers will not be able to predict your movement and you will risk a collision.

Cycling

The best way to get a feel of the real Vietnam is on a bicycle. The route between Hanoi and HCMC has become the Holy Grail for many cyclists. Highway 1 is congested and is also susceptible to flooding, so the preferred route is Highway 14. The Mekong Delta region offers easy riding on flat roads. Views here are superb, especially at rice harvest time (Feb/Mar, Aug/Sep, and Dec/Jan). In the Central Highlands, mountain cycling is taking off, though there are few dedicated trails at present. The condition of the roads along the southern route can vary; however, the many rivers and bridges on the way provide scenic stopovers. **Veloasia** organizes customized cycling tours to remote parts of the country, as does Bangkok-based **SpiceRoads**. However, try to avoid long-distance tours in the northern mountains in December and January as the roads can be slippery and quite dangerous. For cycling in Dalat and the South Central Highlands, try **Phat Tire Ventures**.

Cyclists planning to travel independently should bring their own repair kit – rented bikes can be unreliable. You will also have to be vigilant against theft of your possessions.

Veloasia
🌐 veloasia.com
SpiceRoads
🌐 spiceroads.com
Phat Tire Ventures
🌐 ptv-vietnam.com

OTHER VEHICLES

Here are a few other ways of getting around in cities and rural areas:

Motorbike Taxis
Known locally as *xe on*, these are the cheapest option for traveling short distances, though they are less safe than car taxis. You must agree a price before getting on. Prices start at around 15,000–20,000 d for up to a mile.

Easy Rider
For traveling off the beaten path, these English-speaking motorbike-taxis-cum-tour-guides can translate for you and organize accommodations and food in rural areas. Prices start at around US$60–80 per day, though you should confirm that accommodations and food costs are included, as well as who will pay for petrol and repairs. They should also provide you with a good helmet.

Cyclo
These three-wheel bicycle rickshaws are mostly found in tourist areas in main cities, and are a pleasant way to travel short distances. Agree a price in advance, which should be around 12,000–25,000 d for a short hop. Beware that drivers have a reputation for overcharging foreign visitors.

PRACTICAL INFORMATION
VIETNAM

A little local know-how goes a long way in Vietnam. Here you will find all the essential advice and information you will need during your stay.

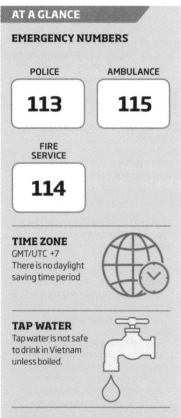

AT A GLANCE

EMERGENCY NUMBERS

POLICE	AMBULANCE
113	**115**

FIRE SERVICE

114

TIME ZONE
GMT/UTC +7
There is no daylight saving time period

TAP WATER
Tap water is not safe to drink in Vietnam unless boiled.

TIPPING
Tipping is not part of Vietnamese culture, so anything you do tip will be appreciated but not expected, especially outside of tourist areas. "Keep the change" or a few thousand dong should be sufficient in most situations for outstanding service, though this is more for a personal guide or driver.

Personal Security

Though traveling in Vietnam is generally quite safe, there are some basic precautions that should be followed. Since petty crimes such as bag-snatching and pickpocketing are prevalent in larger cities, avoid carrying large sums of money or wearing much jewelry. Keep part of your cash and a copy of your passport in a hidden money belt, and leave your passport and valuables in your hotel's safe. Watch out for motorbike-mounted snatch thieves.

Undetonated Explosives

Leftover or unexploded bombs, mines, and artillery shells are still a matter of some concern in areas such as the DMZ (p160), though all major tourist areas have been cleared of these dangers. Should you venture off the beaten path and see anything that looks suspicious, walk away carefully and inform the authorities.

Health

Local hospitals can treat minor ailments, but for serious medical problems head to HCMC and Hanoi. Doctors and hospitals expect immediate payment in cash; you will then need to get reimbursement from your insurance company.

Pharmacies in major towns can help with minor ailments and stock a wide variety of drugs, but check the expiry date before buying. Remember to bring medicines that you're likely to need with you; however, some medicines may be prohibited to bring through customs, so check before you go, and carry your prescription.

Disease-carrying mosquitos are more active at dusk or dawn; to avoid getting bitten, apply a repellent and sleep under a mosquito net. Take a prophylaxis for malaria if visiting jungle areas or the Mekong Delta, but seek advice from a doctor first. Stick to bottled water, or well-boiled water, tea, and coffee. Avoid eating salads in restaurants, which may have been washed in tap water. Bird flu has been recorded in Vietnam, so avoid contact with live birds, such as in markets and around temples.

Smoking, Alcohol, and Drugs

Smoking is officially prohibited in most indoor public areas, although many people ignore this. Vietnam has a strict limit of 0.25mg/l of alcohol when driving. Possession of illegal drugs, even in small quantities, risks a long prison sentence or even the death penalty.

ID

By law you must carry photo identification at all times. A photocopy of your passport photo page and visa page is acceptable and means you can leave your passport in your hotel's safe.

Local Customs

Although Vietnam is a fairly liberal country, especially in the cities, there are a few local values to bear in mind. Women should dress modestly in rural areas, do not touch people's heads (even children), and avoid pointing your feet at people or religious icons when seated. Taking photos of political demonstrations or near military installations can get you into trouble, as can criticizing the government.

LGBT

Homosexuality is legal in Vietnam and increasingly accepted, particularly by the young and in cosmopolitan cities such as Hanoi and HCMC. However, smaller towns and rural areas are often traditional in their views, and overt displays of affection may receive a negative response from locals. Visit www.utopia-asia.com for more information.

Visiting Sacred Sights

Act and take photos respectfully, and dress modestly. Shorts and sleeveless shirts are not appropriate in pagodas, temples, and other religious sites. Remove your shoes before entering if you see footwear left by the entrance.

Mobile Phones and Wi-Fi

Using a local SIM card, locally called a "chip" or "simkaa," is a great way to save money. Viettel is the largest of the four mobile operators and has the best overall coverage, although it can still be sketchy in the countryside. All mobile operators sell tourist SIMs (100,000–500,000 d). Take your passport when you purchase. Wi-Fi is available in virtually all accommodations, as well as many cafés, restaurants, and malls.

Post

Packages can be sent abroad from most post offices, which are open seven days a week. The quickest, most reliable, and most expensive of the three postal options is the Express Mail Service, which typically costs 200,000 d/500g and takes two to four days to most Western nations. DHL, Federal Express, and UPS are all available in large towns and cities.

Taxes and Refunds

Foreign travelers can receive an 85 percent refund on the 10 percent VAT for larger purchases when departing from the six international airports. When buying goods worth at least 2,000,000 d (US $100) in a store licenced to implement a VAT refund (only one per day), present your original passport and you'll receive an invoice and VAT refund declaration. Take these documents and the goods in question to the VAT Refund Goods Customs Inspection Counter at the airport before checking in your luggage, where they'll issue a "checked" stamp. Take this to the VAT Refund Counter along with your boarding pass and you'll receive your refund in Vietnamese dong.

> ### WEBSITES AND APPS
>
> **National Administration of Tourism**
> Check out Vietnam's official tourism website at www.vietnamtourism.com
>
> **Happy Cow**
> A useful website for finding vegetarian restaurants is www.happycow.net. It is also available as an app.
>
> **Homestay**
> Choose from over 250 homestays in Vietnam at www.homestay.com
>
> **Zalo°**
> Download the most popular chatting app in Vietnam.

BEFORE YOU GO
ANGKOR

Forward planning is essential to any successful trip. Be prepared for all eventualities by considering the following points before you travel.

AT A GLANCE

CURRENCY

Riel (KHR)　　　US Dollar ($)

AVERAGE DAILY SPEND

SAVE
$30

SPEND
$60

SPLURGE
$100+

BOTTLED WATER
$0.50

COFFEE
$1

BEER
$1.50

DINNER FOR TWO
$20

ESSENTIAL PHRASES

Hello	Joom reapsooa
Goodbye	Joom reapleah
Please	Soom
Thank you	Awkoon
Do you speak English	Taw neak niyiay Phiasaa Awngkles
I don't understand	Khnyom min yul tee

ELECTRICITY SUPPLY

Power sockets are mainly type C, fitting two round pins. Standard voltage is 220v.

Passports and Visas

Most travelers, including citizens of the UK, US, Canada, Australia, New Zealand, and the EU, can obtain a 30-day tourist visa on arrival at Cambodian airports and land borders for a fee of US $30. A passport photo is required. Alternatively, apply in advance for an **e-visa**. Citizens from other ASEAN countries don't need a visa to visit as a tourist.

e-visa
Ⓦ evisa.gov.kh

Travel Safety Advice

Visitors can get up-to-date travel safety information from the UK Foreign and Commonwealth Office, the US State Department, and the Australian Department of Foreign Affairs and Trade.

AUS
Ⓦ smartraveller.gov.au
UK
Ⓦ gov.uk/foreign-travel-advice
US
Ⓦ travel.state.gov

Customs Information

Enforcement of Cambodian customs rules is generally fairly relaxed – though strict regulations are applied to the export of antiques (see www.customs.gov.kh for details). An individual is permitted to carry the following within Cambodia for personal use:

Tobacco products 400 cigarettes, 100 cigars, or 400 grams of tobacco

Alcohol 2 liters of wine or one bottle of spirits

Cash $10,000 or more must be declared on both arrival and departure.

Vaccinations

Discuss vaccination requirements with your doctor at least eight weeks before traveling to Cambodia. Vaccinations against hepatitis, tetanus, and typhoid are typically recommended. Proof of yellow fever vaccination is required when arriving in Cambodia directly from an infected area. Malaria is present throughout Cambodia, beyond the immediate vicinities of Phnom Penh and Siem Reap. Seek current advice from a doctor about suitable prophylaxis.

Money

Two currencies are in everyday use in Cambodia – the Cambodian riel and the US dollar. Generally, dollars are used to pay for hotel accommodations, high-end purchases, and tourist services, while riel are more useful for minor purchases. However, the currencies are used interchangeably – change may be given in riel for purchases made in dollars at local shops. Generally it's best to obtain dollars in advance for travel to Cambodia; riel can be obtained from local moneychangers for everyday purchases.

Credit cards can be used in higher-end hotels, restaurants, and shops, and ATMs are widely available.

Booking Accommodations

It is possible to book online for virtually all accommodations in Siem Reap and other large towns – either through the property's own website, or via booking websites.

The cooler, drier months from November to March are peak season for Cambodia, when accommodations costs rise and advanced booking is advisable. During the rainy season, from April to October, good online deals are often available, especially in Siem Reap.

High-end hotels sometimes fail to include a 10 percent tax in their published room prices, with the amount only added to the final bill.

Travelers with Specific Needs

Cambodia has limited facilities for disabled visitors. Few temples or other attractions, or public buildings, have proper wheelchair access, and smaller hotels seldom have elevators. However, a number of tour operators do make specialist arrangements, including **About Asia** and **Accessible Holidays**.

About Asia
w aboutasiatravel.com

Accessible Holidays
w disabledholidays.com

Getting to Angkor

The two main international gateways for Cambodia are Phnom Penh International Airport and Siem Reap-Angkor International Airport, with regular flights to regional hubs such as Bangkok, Kuala Lumpur, and Singapore, and onward connections worldwide.

There are excellent long-haul bus connections between Phnom Penh and HCMC in Vietnam, and between Siem Reap and Bangkok in Thailand. These are served by modern, air-conditioned coaches running along decent highways.

Arriving by Air
Vietnam Airlines and Cambodia Angkor Air fly up to six times a day to Siem Riep-Angkor International airport from HCMC, about four times a day from Hanoi, and once a day from Danang. There are also several flights a week from Phu Quoc Island to Siem Riep. Regional budget airlines, such as AirAsia, also serve Siem Riep, making a visit as part of a wider exploration of Southeast Asia straightforward.

Siem Riep-Angkor International airport is situated 4 miles (6 km) from the city center and the taxi fare to the city costs an average of US $10, with a journey time of about 20 minutes. Alternatively, you can take a tuk-tuk. Tuk-tuks are fixed at the same price as taxis within the airport grounds, but if you walk just outside the airport gates you will find tuk-tuk drivers prepared to offer a reduced fare.

Arriving by Land
Regular services run from Phnom Ngo Lao in HCMC to Cambodia's capital, Phnom Penh, throughout the day (taking about 6 hours). You will then have to connect to another bus at Phnom Penh to carry on to Siem Riep (taking about another 6 hours). The entire journey from HCMC to Siem Riep can take between 12 and 20 hours depending on the length of the stopover at Phnom Penh.

There are numerous minor border crossings in Cambodia, including that with Laos at Trapeang Kriel. These usually have to be traversed using a combination of local transportation on either side of the frontier.

Long-distance bus tickets can be booked in advance online at Baolau *(p242)*.

PRACTICAL INFORMATION
ANGKOR

A little local know-how goes a long way in Cambodia. Here you will find all the essential advice and information you will need during your stay.

AT A GLANCE

EMERGENCY NUMBERS

AMBULANCE
119

POLICE
117

FIRE SERVICE
118

TIME ZONE
GMT +7, as in Thailand and Vietnam; no daylight saving.

TAP WATER
Tap water is not safe to drink in Cambodia; use bottled water or refill from dispensers available in hotels and restaurants.

TIPPING

Waiter	5–10%
Hotel Porter	$1
Tour guide	10%
Taxi driver	Not expected

Personal Security

Although violent crime is rare, bag-snatchings occur, especially in Phnom Penh. Be very careful with your belongings, especially when riding a tuk-tuk or moto. Pickpocketing is also an issue in busy markets. Report any theft to the English-speaking tourist police if you wish to make an insurance claim.

Scams are common, and most work by appealing to travelers' consciences. There are a number of fake orphanages, set up to elicit donations, while requests for help to buy rice and baby formula are usually profit-sharing scams run in collaboration with shopkeepers. Be very careful about straying from clearly marked trails when exploring the countryside – unexploded ordnance is still a significant problem in Cambodia.

Health

Healthcare provision is generally poor in Cambodia, though there are good – if expensive – private clinics in Phnom Penh, including the International **SOS Medical Center** (international-sos.com). Pharmacies are often able to provide advice for minor ailments.

Minor stomach upsets, caused by unfamiliar food and climate, and poor hygiene, are the commonest issue. Rest and rehydration are the main treatments; seek advice from a pharmacy or clinic if there is no improvement after a couple of days.

Mosquitoes are a nuisance in Cambodia, particularly toward the end of the monsoon. Cover up in the evenings, and use repellent.
SOS Medical Center
W international-sos.com

Smoking, Alcohol, and Drugs

Smoking is officially banned in public places such as bars and restaurants, though this rule is often ignored. Alcohol is widely available, and socially acceptable – though homebrew liquor is sometimes dangerously tainted and so best avoided.

It's not unusual for tourists to receive unsolicited offers of illegal drugs on the streets, especially in Phnom Penh. Possession can result in lengthy prison sentences, or extortion by corrupt officials.

ID

Tourists are not legally required to carry ID, though it is advisable to carry at least a photocopy of some form of official identification, particularly when traveling outside of towns.

Local Customs

The *sompeyar* (a slight bow with palms pressed together) is the traditional greeting, although handshakes are becoming more common.

Despite the apparent anything-goes atmosphere around some tourist areas, Cambodia is a conservative society. Public displays of affection are inappropriate. Neat, relatively modest dress (covered shoulders and below-the-knee shorts for both men and women) will make a good impression. Noisy or aggressive behavior is considered highly improper.

LGBT Safety

Compared to some other countries in the region, Cambodia is a relatively gay-friendly place, with no legal restrictions on same-sex relationships, and a reasonable degree of social acceptance in urban areas. There are lively gay scenes accessible to foreigners in Phnom Penh and Sihanoukville, and a number of gay-friendly hotels and bars around the country (see www.cambodia-gay.com). Public displays of affection are not appropriate for couples of any orientation, however, and attitudes in rural areas are much more conservative, though more likely to result in bemusement than overt hostility.

Visiting Temples

Cambodian temples are open to non-Buddhists, but respectful behavior is essential. Shoulders and legs should be covered for both men and women, and shoes should be removed before entering any buildings within a temple complex. Be aware that monks are forbidden to touch women – a rule which includes handshakes or contact while posing for photos.

Mobile Phones and Wi-Fi

Wi-Fi is ubiquitous in bigger towns, with virtually every hotel, restaurant, and café providing a free connection. Connection speeds are not particularly fast, but usually adequate for browsing or using social media.

International GSM mobile phones usually have coverage in Cambodia – though check with your provider before traveling. Pre-paid local SIM cards are also readily available from any phone shop. It is necessary to show proof of ID to buy a card, and vendors will generally set it up for you if you have an unlocked phone. Top-up credit is available from any phone shop.

Post

Post offices are available in all but the smallest towns. Letters and postcards can take up to two weeks to reach destinations outside of Asia, though postage is very cheap. Courier companies such as DHL and UPS, which have agents in Siem Reap and Phnom Penh, are faster and more reliable for sending parcels.

Taxes and Refunds

A 10 percent sales tax is usually included in the marked price of retail goods, though some hotels and high-end restaurants do not include it in posted prices and add it to the bill at the end. No tax refunds are available for departing visitors, and duty free items on sale at airports are sold at dramatically marked-up prices.

WEBSITES AND APPS

tourismcambodia.org
The official government tourism website has some decent information on destinations and events.

phnompenhpost.com
The website of Cambodia's main English-language newspaper is a great place to keep abreast of the latest happenings.

Audio Khmer
This is a free app that works well for basic communications using English and Khmer.

INDEX

Page numbers in bold refer to main entries

PHRASE BOOK

Vietnamese belongs to the Mon-Khmer group in the Austroasiatic family of languages. Besides Standard Vietnamese, which is spoken in the Hanoi area, there are several other dialects, the most important being those of the central and southern regions. These differ mainly in phonetics (for example, they have fewer tones than standard Vietnamese) and lexicology, but not grammar.

For centuries, Chinese (*chu han*) was the official language for administration and education as there was no written form of Vietnamese. Later, a special script called *chu nom* was developed to record the native language. By the 17th century, a romanized script, *quoc ngu*, was devised by Roman Catholic missionaries in southeast Asia as a simple way of transcribing Vietnamese. With the arrival of the French, *quoc ngu* was officially introduced. Despite early opposition to the new script, perceived to be an instrument of colonial rule, the fact that it was relatively easy to learn gradually won over its critics.

THE SIX TONES

Vietnamese is a complex tonal language, which means that words are pronounced at varying levels of pitch. Standard Vietnamese has six tones, which are marked by special diacritics usually positioned above the vowel.

Tone can affect the meaning of words dramatically. For example, *ma* has six meanings depending on the pitch at which it is delivered. Accents indicate the tone of each syllable in the following chart:

Ma (ghost)	High, level tone
Mà (but)	ow (falling), level tone
Mã (horse)	Rising broken tone with a glottal stop
Mả (grave)	Falling-rising tone
Má (Cheek)	Rising tone
Mạ (rice seedling)	Sharp falling tone, heavy glottal stop

KINSHIP TERMS

Words denoting family relationships, known as "kinship terms," are used when people address each other. The choice of expression depends on gender, age, social status, and the relationship and degree of intimacy between the speakers. The most common terms are:

Anh (older brother) to address a young male.
Chị (older sister), female equivalent of **anh**.

Em (younger sibling) to address someone younger than you.
Ông (grandfather) to address an older man, formal and respectful, similar to Sir in English.
Bà (grandmother) to address an older woman, formal and respectful.
Cô similar to Madam in English.

GUIDELINES FOR PRONUNCIATION

Most of the consonants are pronounced as in English, except the following:

d	as in Zoo (in the north); as in You (in the south)
đ	as in Down
gi	as in Zoo (in the north); as in You (in the south)
kh	aspirated K
ng	nasal n, as in learniNG
ngh	nasal n, as in learniNG
nh	as in KeNYa
r	as in Zebra
t	as in Top
th	as in Top
tr	as in CHop
x	as in See

VOWELS ARE PRONOUNCED AS FOLLOWS:

a	as in bAsk
â	as **ơ** but shorter
ă	as in hUt
e	as in End
ê	as in hEllo
i	as in Ink
o	as in lOng
ô	as in bAll
ơ	as in liOn
u	as in pUt
ư	as in mountAIn

COMMUNICATION ESSENTIALS

Hello!	**Xin chào!**
Goodbye!	**Tạm biệt!**
Yes/no	**Vâng/không**
I understand	**Tôi hiểu**
I don't understand	**Tôi không hiểu**
I don't know	**Tôi không biết**
Thank you	**Cám ơn!**
Do you speak English?	**Anh/chị có biết tiếng Anh không?**
I can't speak Vietnamese	**Tôi không biết tiếng Việt**
Sorry/Excuse me!	**Xin lỗi!**
Not at all	**Không dám**

Come in please!	**Mời anh/chị vào!**
emergency	**Cấp cứu**
police	**Công an**
ambulance	**Xe cấp cứu**
fire brigade	**Cứu hỏa**

USEFUL PHRASES

My name is ...	**Tên tôi là ...**
What is your name?	**Tên anh/chị là gì?**
How do you do/ pleased to meet you	**Rất hân hạnh được gặp anh/chị**
How are you?	**Anh/chị có khỏe không?**
What work do you do?	**Anh/chị làm nghề gì?**
How old are you?	**Anh/chị bao nhiêu tuổi?**
What nationality are you?	**Anh/chị là người nước nào?**
What is this?	**Đây là cái gì?**
Is there ... here?	**Ở đây có... không?**
Where is .... ?	**.... ở đâu?**
How much is it?	**Cái này giá bao nhiêu?**
What time is it?	**Bây giờ là mấy giờ?**
Congratulations	**Chúc mừng**
Where is the restroom/toilet?	**Phòng vệ sinh ở đâu?**
Where is the British Embassy?	**Đại sứ quán Anh ở đâu?**

USEFUL WORDS

I	**tôi**
man	**đàn ông**
woman	**đàn bà**
family	**gia đình**
parents	**bố mẹ/cha mẹ/ ba má**
father	**bố/cha/ba**
mother	**mẹ/má/mạ**
younger brother	**em trai**
older brother	**anh trai**
younger sister	**em gái**
older sister	**chị**
big/small	**to/nhỏ**
high/low	**cao/thấp**
hot/cold	**nóng/lạnh**
good/bad	**Tốt/xấu**
young/old	**trẻ/già**
old/new	**cũ/mới**
expensive/cheap	**đắt/rẻ**
here	**đây**
there	**kia**
What?	**gì?**
Who?	**ai?**

Where?	**(ở) đâu?**
Why?	**(tại) sao?**
How? What is it like?	**thế nào?**

MONEY

I want to change US $100 into Vietnamese currency.	**Tôi muốn đổi 100 đô la Mỹ ra tiền Việt.**
exchange rate	**tỷ giá hối đoái**
I'd like to cash these travelers' checks.	**Tôi muốn đổi séc du lịch này ra tiền mặt.**
bank	**ngân hàng**
money/cash	**tiền/tiền mặt**
credit card	**thẻ tín dụng**
dollars	**đô la**
pounds (sterling)	**bảng**
Vietnamese dong	**đồng (Việt Nam)**

KEEPING IN TOUCH

I'd like to make a telephone call.	**Tôi muốn gọi điện thoại.**
I'd like to make an international phone call.	**Tôi muốn gọi điện thoại quốc tế.**
mobile phone	**máy điện thoại di động**
telephone enquiries	**chỉ dẫn điện thoại**
public phone box	**trạm điện thoại công cộng**
area code	**mã (vùng)**
post office	**bưu điện**
stamp	**tem**
letter	**thư**
registered letter	**thư bảo đảm**
address	**địa chỉ**
street	**phố**
town	**thành phố**
village	**làng**

SHOPPING

Where can I buy...?	**Tôi có thể mua ... ở đâu?**
How much does this cost?	**Cái này giá bao nhiêu?**
May I try this on?	**Tôi mặc thử có được không?**
How much?	**Bao nhiêu?**
How many?	**Mấy?**
expensive/cheap	**đắt/rẻ**
to bargain	**mặc cả**
size	**số, cỡ**
color	**màu**
black	**đen**
white	**trắng**
blue	**xanh da trời**

green	xanh lá cây
red	đỏ
brown	nâu
yellow	vàng
grey	xám
bookstore	hiệu sách
department store	cửa hàng bách hóa
market	chợ
pharmacy	hiệu thuốc
supermarket	siêu thị
souvenir shop	cửa hàng lưu niệm
souvenirs	đồ lưu niệm
lacquer painting	tranh sơn mài
painting on silk	tranh lụa
wooden statue	bức tượng gỗ
silk scarf	khăn lụa
tablecloth	khăn trải bàn
tray	khay
vase	lọ hoa

SIGHTSEEING

travel agency	công ty du lịch
Where is the international ticket office? (plane)	Phòng bán vé máy bay quốc tế ở đâu?
Vietnam Airlines	Hãng hàng không Việt Nam
beach	bãi
bay	vịnh
ethnic minority	dân tộc ít người
festival	lễ hội
island	hòn đảo
lake	hồ
forest, jungle	rừng
mountain	núi
river	sông
temple	đền
museum	bảo tàng
pagoda	chùa
countryside	nông thôn
cave, grotto	hang

GETTING AROUND

train station	nhà ga
airport	sân bay
air ticket	vé máy bay
bus station	bến xe búyt
ticket	vé
one-way ticket	vé một lượt
return ticket	vé khứ hồi
taxi	tắc xi
car rental	thuê xe ô tô
car	xe ô tô
train	xe lửa
plane	máy bay
motorbike	xe máy

bicycle	xe đạp
cyclo	xích lô
How long does it take to get to...?	Đi .... mất bao lâu?
Do you know .... road?	Anh/chị có biết đường .... không?
Is it far?	Có xa không?
Go straight.	Đi thẳng.
turn	rẽ
left	trái
right	phải
passport	hộ chiếu
visa	thi thực
customs	hải quan

ACCOMMODATIONS

hotel	khách sạn
guesthouse	nhà khách
room (single, double)	phòng (đơn, đôi)
air conditioning	máy lạnh
passport number	số hộ chiếu

EATING OUT

I'd like to book a table for two.	Tôi muốn đặt trước một bàn cho hai người.
waiter	người phục vụ
May I see the menu?	Cho tôi xem thực đơn
Do you have any special dishes today?	Hôm nay có món gì đặc biệt không?
What would you like to order?	Anh/chị muốn gọi gì?
Can I have the bill, please?	Anh/chị cho hóa đơn
I am a vegetarian.	Tôi ăn chay.
tasty/delicious	ngon/ngon tuyệt
spicy (hot)	cay
sweet	ngọt
sour	chua
bitter	đắng
breakfast	bữa ăn sáng
chopsticks	đôi đũa
knife	dao
fork	nĩa
spoon	thìa
to drink	uống
to eat	ăn
hungry/thirsty	đói/khát
restaurant	hiệu ăn, nhà hàng
Western food	món ăn Âu
Vietnamese specialties	đặc sản Việt Nam

FOOD

apple	táo
banana	chuối
bamboo shoots	măng
bean sprouts	giá
beef	thịt bò
bread	bánh mì
butter	bơ
cake	bánh ngọt
chicken	(thịt) gà
coconut	dừa
crab	cua
dessert	(món) tráng miệng
duck	vịt
eel	lươn
egg	trứng
fish	cá
fish sauce	nước mắm
frog	ếch
fruit	hoa quả, trái cây
ginger	gừng
ice	đá
ice cream	kem
lemon	chanh
lemongrass	xả
lobster	tôm hùm
mandarin orange	quít
mango	xoài
menu	thực đơn
milk	sữa
mushrooms	nấm
meat (well done, medium, rare)	thịt (tái, vừa, chin)
noodles	mì, miến
noodle soup beef/ chicken	phở bò/gà
onion	hành
papaya	đu đủ
peach	đào
pepper	hạt tiêu
pork	thịt lợn, thịt heo
potato (sweet potato)	khoai tây (khoai)
prawn	tôm
rambutan	chôm chôm
rice	gạo
rice (cooked)	cơm
glutinous rice	gạo (cơm) nếp
non-glutinous rice	gạo (cơm) tẻ
salad	xà lách
salt	muối
snail	ốc
spring rolls	nem rán (chả giò)
starter	(món) khai vị
soup	xúp
soy sauce	tương
stir-fried beef with mushrooms	bò xào mấm
sugar	đường
vegetables	rau
Vietnamese noodle soup	phở

DRINKS

tea	trà, chè
coffee (white coffee)	cà phê (cà phê sữa)
water	nước
fruit juice	nước quả, nước trái cây
mineral water	nước khoáng
milk	sữa
soft drinks	nước ngọt
beer	bia
wine	rượu vang
glass	cốc
bottle	chai

HEALTH

What is the matter with you?	Anh/chị bị làm sao?
fever	sốt
accident (traffic)	tai nạn (giao thông)
acupuncture	châm cứu
allergy	dị ứng
ambulance	xe cấp cứu
antibiotics	thuốc kháng sinh
blood	máu
blood pressure (high/low)	huyết áp (cao/thấp)
cough	ho
diabetes	bệnh đái đường
diarrhea	đi ngoài
dizzy	chóng mặt, hoa mắt
doctor	bác sĩ
ear	tai
flu	cúm
food poisoning	ngộ độc thức ăn
headache	đau đầu
heart	tim
hospital	bệnh viện
hygiene	vệ sinh
insomnia	mất ngủ
illness	bệnh
injection	tiêm
malaria	bệnh sốt rét
medicine	thuốc

operate	mổ
pharmacy	cửa hàng thuốc
prescription	đơn thuốc
sore throat	viêm họng
temperature	sốt
tetanus injection	tiêm phòng uốn ván
tooth	răng
toothache	đau răng
Vietnamese traditional medicine	thuốc Nam

TIME AND SEASON

minute	phút
hour	giờ
day	ngày
week	tuần
month	tháng
year	năm
Monday	(ngày) thứ hai
Tuesday	(ngày) thứ ba
Wednesday	(ngày) thứ tư
Thursday	(ngày) thứ năm
Friday	(ngày) thứ sáu
Saturday	(ngày) thứ bảy
Sunday	Chủ nhật
season	mùa
spring	mùa xuân
summer	mùa hè/mùa hạ
fall	mùa thu
winter	mùa đông
dry season	mùa khô
rainy season	mùa mưa
rain (it is raining)	mưa (trời mưa)
wind	gió
sunny	nắng
weather	thời tiết
warm/cold	ấm/lạnh
lunar calendar	Âm lịch
solar calendar	Dương lịch
Vietnamese New Year	Tết Nguyên đán
What time is it?	Bây giờ là mấy giờ?
8:30	tám giờ rưỡi
8:45	tám giờ bốn mươi lăm phút/chín giờ kém mười lăm (phút)
10:15	mười giờ mười lăm phút
12:00	mười hai giờ
morning	buổi sang
midday	buổi trưa
afternoon	buổi chiều
evening	buổi tối
night	đêm

NUMBERS

1	một
2	hai
3	ba
4	bốn
5	năm
6	sáu
7	bảy
8	tám
9	chín
10	mười
11	mười một
12	mười hai
15	mười lăm
20	hai mươi
21	hai mươi mốt
24	hai mươi bốn/ hai mươi tư
25	hai mươi lăm
30	ba mươi
40	bốn mươi
50	năm mươi
100	một trăm
101	một trăm linh (lẻ) một
105	một trăm linh (lẻ) năm
200	hai trăm
300	ba trăm
1,000	một nghìn/ một ngàn
10,000	mười nghìn/ mười ngàn
1,000,000	một triệu

ACKNOWLEDGMENTS

The publisher would like to thank the following for their kind permission to reproduce their photographs:

Key: a-above; b-below/bottom; c-centre; f-far; l-left; r-right; t-top

123RF.com: amadeustx 4; Simon Dannhauer 24bl, 202tl; efired 116t; hanoiphotography 168cr; Thi Hong Hanh Mac 10ca; Melinda Nagy 172bl; Alexey Pelikh 236t; quangpraha 42br; Chan Richie 171tr; Surawut Sudha 212b; Rolf Svedjeholm 35cl; thaifairs 82bl; Minh Vũ 181crb.

4Corners: Stefano Coltelli 226-7t.

Alamy Stock Photo: Avanti 119crb; bamboofox 39cl; Judy Bellah 205crb; Oliver Benn 90cr; Pawel Bienkowski 107b; blickwinkel 199crb; Anders Blomqvist 125tr; Michael Brooks 78tl, 134t; Nacho Calonge 161t; Jordi Caml 76tc; Vicky Chan 197t; Felix Choo 99tr; Chronicle 220fbr; Piero Cruciatti 90t; Danita Delimont 96br, 106bc, 160bl; dleiva 34t; Godong 85br; Hemis 29tr, 33tr, 205b; Hemis.fr / Brusini Aurélien 29cra; Bob Henry 168bl; Cyril Hou 25br; imageBROKER 61br, 76br; Aztec Images 73tr; Design Pics Inc 183b; incamerastock 200cra; Intersection Photos 22-3ca; Jon Arnold Images Ltd 232cl; Johnny Jones 176bc, 189tl; Yann Jouanique 18cb, 164-5; Claudine Klodien 92-3t; Markus Kortlueke 108tr; Jason Langley 27cl, 153bl; Lazyllama 233cr; Leslie Garland Pictures 220bl; LOOK Die Bildagentur der Fotografen GmbH 173b; Loop Images Ltd 16, 54-5; M.Sobreira 229fbr; mauritius images GmbH 61cra, 155tr; MKilarski 43bl, 124tl; Gail Mooney-Kelly 66b; mvlampila 20crb; Duy Phuong Nguye 159clb; Quang Ngoc Nguyen 119br; B O'Kane 181cr; Dan Oldenburg 141bl; James packwood 158t; Efrain Padro 12clb, 180t; Thoai Pham 158-9b; Mark Phillips 145tr; Hanoi Photography 126bl, 127t; Tim Plowden 199t; Graham Prentice 74-5t; Prisma by Dukas Presseagentur GmbH 199c; Reciprocity Images 134bc; David Reed 173cl; Robertharding 61t, 104b, 119cr, 146bl, 211tc; Tony Roddam 149br; Yavuz Sariyildiz 152; David Saunders 40b; Leonid Serebrennikov 137r, 146t; Valerii Shanin 37br; Paul Springett 10 83tl; SPUTNIK 181bl; ClickAlps Srls 102t; Friedrich Stark 175bl; David Sutherland 215b; Bjorn Svensson 215cr; Beng Kwang Tan 11cr; Komal Thadani 222bl; Thanh Thu Thai 111bl; Universal Images Group North America LLC 58br; Lucas Vallecillos 93tr; Jelle Vanderwolf 35crb; Howard Walker 154-5b; Rob Whitworth 2012 25crb; Steve Whyte 232cr; Andrew Woodley 109cl; Robert Wyatt 22-3t, 187br; Ron Yue 233c; Ariadne Van Zandbergen 92-3ca, 230tl.

AWL Images: Jon Arnold 36l; Walter Bibikow 103bl; Jason Langley 228; Travel Pix Collection 230bl.

Bridgeman Images: Emperor Yang of Sui (569-618) from the 'Thirteen Emperors Scroll' painted by Tang Dynasty court painter Yan Liben (600-673) 45br; Tran Hung Dao, victor of the Second Battle of the Bach Dang River, commanding his forces (1287 CE) 46-7t; Musee National de Phnom Penh, Cambodia 229bl; Pictures from History 45bc, 46bc, 47cl, 48br, 48cr, 48-9t.

CPA Media: 44-5t, 46br, 47bc, 48tl, 50tl; Binh Giang 44bc; David Henley 44tl, 46tl.

Depositphotos Inc: ThaiThu 95cl; Winston 237br.

Dorling Kindersley: David Henley 173cr.

Dreamstime.com: Stig Alenäs 99br; Amadeustx 156-7b; Anandoart 28-9b; Alexander Arndt 236cla; Scott Biales 38b; Pipop Boosarakumwadi 141br; Panom Bounak 168t; Vladimir Cech 95crb;

Chrishowey 13tl; Chuotnhatdesigner 11br; Luke Derriman 220bc; Dinosmichail 26-7b, 41cl; Dndavis 40cra; Dragoncello 27br; Esmehelit 180cra; Feathercollector 80cla; Gopause 38tl; Franzisca Guedel 198tl; Hoxuanhuong 42cl, 71br, 116br; Ulf Huebner 27tr, 80-1l; Katoosha 72bl; Khellon 70ca; Olga Khoroshunova 98t; Yen Mai Kim 42cr, 62bl, 63t; Laraslk 124-5b; Quan Tran Minh 40tl; Minzpeter 149t; Anna Moskvina 38cra; Denis Moskvinov 70-1t; Hoang Bao Nguyen 45cra; Ongchangwei 26tl, 143tr; 150-1t; Outcast85 206bl; Phieulinh 196tl; Phoebe0317 189bl; Phuongphoto 78-9b, 110; Piccaya 58cl; Pradit Pinyopasakul 220cra; Pixattitude 230-1; Rodrigolab 58crb, 62cra; Luca Roggero 101tr; Chayuti Siritan 29cra; Softlightaa 13cr; Ngoc Tran Thanh 184-5; Huy Thoai 22clb, 68t, 142t; Ranulph Thorpe 215cl; Tienduong 211br; tktktk 178-9t; Tuayai 41crb; Viensaigon 123br, 186t; Richard Van Der Woude 96t; Oleg Zhukov 122-3bc.

Getty Images: AFP / Hoang Dinh Nam 42cra, 43tr, 43cr, 51bc, / Kao Nguyen 51br, / Linh Pham 8-9b, 157t, / Tang Chhin Sothy 50cr; Christophe Archambault 177t; Bettmann Archive 49br; Ho Ngoc Binh 8cl, 64-5t, 214t; Christophe Boisvieux 135bl; Nathalie Cuvelier 148bl; DEA / Biblioteca Ambrosiana 229br; Chau Doan 28tl; ExploringMekong.com 106tl; EyeEm / Karn Bulsuk 31cl, Philippe Capillon 174tl, / Minh Luan Dam 10bl, / Uta Gleiser 168cl; Godong 229cl; hadynyah 8clb; Hulton Archive / Liaison / Dirck Halstead 51tr; Jessica Page Photo 18tl, 128-9; Jethuynh 42cla; Wolfgang Kaehler 198cra; Reed Kaestner 19, 190-1; Domingo Leiva 207t; Lonely Planet Images / Anders Blomqvist 187tl; MeogiaPhoto 208-9t; Kevin Miller 84bl; NG Photography 17bl, 112-3; Quynh Anh Nguyen 20cr; Corbis / Tim Page 49bc; Pinnee 31bl; Andrea Pistolesi 204-5t; Phung Huynh Vu Qui 6-7, 42bl, 132-3t, 194t; Co Rentmeester 49br; Sino images 233tl; Inti St Clair 203; Andrew JK Tan 216-7; TASS / Nikolai Malyshev 50br; Jean-Philippe Tournut 196tr; Borja Sanchez Trillo 43cl; Pham Ty 52-3; Vu Pham Van 144t; Tran Tuan Viet 104-5, 162; nik wheeler 50-1t.

iStockphoto.com: 12ee12 10-1b; 1905HKN 220br; Alxpin 17t, 86-7, 94bl, 100b; Awesomeaki 208-9b; BirdHunter591 94tr; cristaltran 11t; CWLawrence 238-9; Degist 170bl; DeltaOFF 58tl; Matthew Digati 224-5t; ErmakovaElena 32-3b; galitskaya 122tl; Gargolas 47tr; hadynyah 90bl; HaiMinhDuong 33cl; holgs 47br; HuyThoai 92t, 119tl; Image Source 143bl; jejim 41t; joakimbkk 220crb; Kewadee 226br; Laughingmango 23tr, 36-7b, 75br; filipe_lopes 58cr; Lquang2410 24-5t; luctra_design 35tr; MasterLu 200t; mihtiander 39t; milos-todorovic 95tr; nicolasboivin 194clb; Nikada 13br, 22tl, 30tl, 171tl; ninelutsk 39crb; olyniteowl 37tr; OSTILL 232-3c; OwenPrice 196cr; piccaya 224br; PhongTranVN 136tl; Pradito 234clb; Quang_Vu 20t, 140t; RomanBabakin 45tr, 141tl; SamuelBrownNG 67tl; SanerG 229cra; Sergwsq 235t; Oleh_Slobodeniuk 223tr; Tazzy1 198bl; tbradford 20bl; tegmen 12-3b, 119cra; ThanhNgocTran 12t, 138-9; thesomegirl 30br; ThuTruong 31tl; TonyNg 51cra; Techa Tungateja 37cl; u3k 33br; VichienPetchmai 2-3; Vinhdav 178bl; VuCongDanh 85tr, 120t; xuanhuongho 43crb, 43br; yenwen 222tr; YinYang 171bl.

Lotte Coralis Vietnam Co., Ltd: 182-3t.
Picfair.com: Stig Alenäs 34bl; Dmitry Rukhlenko 221.

Rex by Shutterstock: imageBROKER / Gerhard Zwerger-Schoner 43tl.

Robert Harding Picture Library: Ryan Deboodt 163br; LOOK Bildagentur der Fotografen / Hauke Dressler 32tl; Alex Robinson 108-9b; G & M Therin-Weise 69b.

Stars & Stripes: 77cr.

Front flap:
Alamy Stock Photo: Michael Brooks t; Loop Images Ltd bl; **Getty Images:** Phung Huynh Vu cra; **iStockphoto.com:** cristaltran cb; MasterLu cla; tegmen br.

Cover images:
Front and spine: **Picfair.com:** Nguyen Quang Ngoc. *Back:* **Getty Images:** LINH PHAM tr; **iStockphoto. com:** Gargolas cla, hadynyah c; **Picfair.com:** Nguyen Quang Ngoc b.

Mapping:
Base mapping for Ho Chi Minh City and Hanoi derived from Netmaps.

Base mapping for Phu Quoc, Hoi An, Nha Trang and Halong Bay are derived from © www. openstreetmap.org contributors, licensed under CC-BY-SA.

For further information see: www.dkimages.com

Main Contributers Andrew Forbes, Richard Sterling, Charles Young, Peter Holmshaw

Senior Editor Alison McGill

Senior Designer Laura O'Brien

Project Editor Rada Radojicic

Project Art Editors Bess Daly, Hansa Babra, Stuti Tiwari Bhatia, Ankita Sharma

Factchecker Ron Emmons

Editor Scarlett O'Hara

Proofreader Debra Wolter

Indexer Hilary Bird

Senior Picture Researcher Ellen Root

Picture Research Marta Bescos, Vishal Ghavri, Sumita Khatwani

Illustrators Gary Cross, Surat Kumar Mantu, Arun Pottiyaril, Gautam Trivedi, Mark Warner

Senior Cartographic Editor Casper Morris

Cartography Uma Bhattacharya, Suresh Kumar, Reetu Pandey

Jacket Designers Maxine Pedliham, Bess Daly

Jacket Picture Research Susie Peachey

Senior DTP Designer Jason Little

DTP Coordinator George Nimmo

Producer Igrain Roberts

Managing Editor Rachel Fox

Art Director Maxine Pedliham

Publishing Director Georgina Dee

The information in this DK Eyewitness Travel Guide is checked regularly.
Every effort has been made to ensure that this book is as up-to-date as possible at the time of going to press. Some details, however, such as telephone numbers, opening hours, prices, gallery hanging arrangements and travel information, are liable to change. The publishers cannot accept responsibility for any consequences arising from the use of this book, nor for any material on third party websites, and cannot guarantee that any website address in this book will be a suitable source of travel information. We value the views and suggestions of our readers very highly. Please write to: Publisher, DK Eyewitness Travel Guides, Dorling Kindersley, 80 Strand, London, WC2R 0RL, UK, or email: travelguides@dk.com

First edition 2007

Published in Great Britain by Dorling Kindersley Limited, 80 Strand, London, WC2R 0RL

Published in the United States by DK Publishing, 345 Hudson Street, New York, New York 10014

A CIP catalog record for this book is available from the British Library.

A catalog record for this book is available from the Library of Congress.

ISSN: 1542 1554
ISBN: 978 0 2413 5828 3

Printed and bound in Malaysia.

www.dk.com